Cemetery Citizens

Cemetery Citizens

*Reclaiming the Past and Working for Justice
in American Burial Grounds*

ADAM ROSENBLATT

STANFORD UNIVERSITY PRESS
Stanford, California

Stanford University Press
Stanford, California

Printed in the United States of America on acid-free, archival-quality paper

Library of Congress Cataloging-in-Publication Data
Names: Rosenblatt, Adam (Adam Richard), author.
Title: Cemetery citizens : reclaiming the past and working for justice in American
    burial grounds / Adam Rosenblatt.
Description: Stanford, California : Stanford University Press, 2024. | Includes
    bibliographical references and index.
Identifiers: LCCN 2023058085 (print) | LCCN 2023058086 (ebook) |
    ISBN 9781503613973 (cloth) | ISBN 9781503639119 (paperback) |
    ISBN 9781503639126 (epub)
Subjects: LCSH: Cemeteries—Conservation and restoration—United States. |
    Volunteer workers in cemeteries—United States. | Cemeteries—Social aspects—
    United States. | Social justice—United States.
Classification: LCC GT3203 .R67 2024 (print) | LCC GT3203 (ebook) |
    DDC 363.7/50973—dc23/eng/20240131
LC record available at https://lccn.loc.gov/2023058085
LC ebook record available at https://lccn.loc.gov/2023058086

Cover design: Susan Zucker
Cover illustration: Drawings by Adam Rosenblatt and background art from
Shutterstock / Anastasiia Guseva

For Amanda, מײַן שבת-לאַמטערן

CONTENTS

LIST OF ILLUSTRATIONS

Beauty in Dirt

Some of you will have fine monuments by which the living may remember the evil done to you. Some of you will have only crude wooden crosses or painted rocks, while yet others of you must remain hidden in the shadows of history. You are in any case part of an ancient procession. . . .

KAZUO ISHIGURO, *The Buried Giant*, 267

. . . sharing what we love, what we find beautiful, which is an ethics.

ROSS GAY, *The Book of Delights*, 128

East End Cemetery is one of the most beautiful places I've ever seen. Not spectacle-beautiful like the Atacama Desert or the Northern California coastline. It's beautiful for the many kinds of green that pile up over one another and climb up the trees, as if they're all racing to be highest; beautiful for the slightly irregular rectangles of sunken soil—sometimes all that's left to mark a grave.[1]

It's beautiful for the moments when someone, usually Erin, finds a grave marker hidden under a layer of dirt. We dig the stone out from the ground, place it upright, and wash it until we see the person's name emerge. The names themselves can be strikingly beautiful: Zephaninah Cooper, Luvenia Lewis. Like someone was trying to find new, better words for what we mean when we say "dignity."

As soon as a name becomes visible, we say it aloud, each to ourselves. It's like we're passing along a secret or a song.

East End is beautiful for tossing balls to Teacake the dog or eating pizza out of a box on a car's hood in the evening. It was beautiful on that Saturday in spring when we were hard at work and thirty-odd motorcycles came squalling through the cemetery. We all stopped what we were doing. I was frightened, and then angry. When they left, droning into the distance, East End was beautiful again. It endured motorcycle noise and dust as it has endured dumped tires, vandals, trash, all the seasons and all the kinds of violence.

The buggy and bedraggled cemeteries I write about in this book—East End, Geer, and Mount Moriah—are beautiful. It's the hardest part to explain in words, even in photos or drawings. I'll tell you about how these cemeteries were founded, and how they gradually became the kinds of places where someone pulls up in a truck and drops their trash right on a person's grave. I'll tell you about how they came to be called "abandoned" even when people are still visiting, still caring about them. I'll tell you about the volunteers who pull vines, gather fallen branches, sweat, joke, snack, and sigh in all these cemeteries.

These cemetery citizens are reclaiming burial grounds while also trying to figure out what it really means to do so, what a reclaimed cemetery looks like and how it should be used. Sometimes they agree with one another about the answers, and often they don't. Many of them have become my friends. I can't tell you enough about the beauty of the places where they're weeding and cleaning headstones. You might have to go there yourself. Remember them so you can.

FIGURE FM.1. Black-and-white sketch of a tall, thin man from the Groove Phi Groove social fraternity raking during a workday at Geer Cemetery in Durham, North Carolina, October 31, 2020. He wears black pants, a long-sleeved shirt, a face mask, and a ball cap. There is a rake in his hands, pointed outward toward his left-hand side. Drawing by the author, November 2022.

Cemetery Citizens

Introduction

The Dead and Their Emergencies

The first time I went to East End Cemetery, in Richmond, Virginia, I rode in the back of Erin Hollaway Palmer and Brian Palmer's hatchback, next to Teacake, their ball-obsessed black dog. I wasn't prepared for the size of the place; I had only seen photographs. Walking into Evergreen, the cemetery adjacent to East End—also overgrown, also the final home of thousands of African Americans from Richmond and beyond—I was struck by one man's grave. It was almost in the bushes, at the edge of the cemetery. The headstone was shaped like a heart, and carved into it on each side were hands clasped together in prayer. It belonged to a man who died in 1984, at age thirty.

Erin, who does much of the research for the Friends of East End, said the man had died by suicide. Later, his death certificate told me he was found in his apartment, early in the morning, with a gunshot wound in his chest. His high school yearbook, which I found afterward—discovering pieces of his life in reverse chronology—showed him young, in a bow tie, looking sideways at something that was making him grin. He was a member of the Library Club and Student Council, and very handsome. He played on the basketball team. I thought of his parents picking out the heart headstone (he never married, so I assume it was them), wanting him to be buried beneath something whose very shape was a symbol of their love.

The first time I went to Mount Moriah, I was with students from a seminar I was teaching, called "Human Rights and the Dead." On a beautiful day, we toured the vast cemetery with a member of the Friends of Mount Moriah. He shepherded us past graves that sparked our curiosity: fancy family tombs, the graves of small children, and Mount Moriah's Muslim sections, their headstones carved with crescents and stars.[1] We spent most of our time at the various plots where soldiers and sailors were buried. The guide complained bitterly to my students about what he saw as the comparative neglect of Confederate graves in this northern cemetery. It was hot, and uncomfortable. The students and I left with the sense that there were many more stories to tell about this urban wilderness of graves.

The first time I visited Geer Cemetery, I was in Durham, North Carolina, for a job interview at Duke. I had read a bit about the cemetery before coming and told the department administrator that I hoped to get there during my visit. Robin Kirk, the codirector of the Duke Human Rights Center, picked me up at my hotel right when I arrived and brought me to the cemetery. Geer was smaller than East End or Evergreen, and closer to the heart of the city. Yet it was also quieter, showing fewer signs of activity.

The research you do beforehand prepares you only so much for what you'll see. When you set foot in these burial grounds, they become real, specific, beautiful, fragile, enraging. Your body reacts to all these things at once: a confusion of feelings. Sometimes there's an awkwardness or even fear that the dead are watching you, and that you can't find the right way to move, to act respectfully. That your presence might be another form of intrusion, a violence.

"Hidden histories,"[2] neglected graves, places of the dead: they might make you think this is a book about the past, about endings. It is not. It is a book about revisions. Revising is a way of relating to the past. You revise an earlier draft, tell an old story in a new way. But revision is ultimately oriented toward the future. We revise our writing so that the revised manuscript, the new story, can go out and have its own relationship with the world—impossible to arrive at without its previous versions, but also meeting them on its own terms. Cemetery citizens are people who found themselves in a place where the dead seemed abandoned— maybe not by the people who loved them, but by the surrounding world. They asked questions and got curious. They got angry. That's a beginning too.

Soon their questions became projects. Every grave a cemetery citizen finds in the weeds, or uncovers beneath the soil, leads to another story. Every new section of a cemetery they clear makes new demands on them: to keep at this work, tell more of the stories, craft more kinds of memory.

To walk, weed, and work with these people is to see our cities and neighborhoods in a new light. To think and talk about justice differently. To let the dead back in.

Cemetery Citizens is a book about these people and their work. It is not a history of cemeteries, though I do offer some historical background to show what drives and shapes the activities taking place at Geer, East End, and Mount Moriah today. Nor is this a manual on how to protect and preserve cemeteries. Rather, it is an exploration of why people are working in these burial grounds, what they think the work means, and where it is headed. It is a book about the *now* in these cemeteries, the things that are still beginning—the questions that are more alive than ever in these places of the dead.

Revising Cemeteries

A marginalized cemetery is never really an accident of fate. Rather, it is a document of structural violence written onto the landscape.[3] Structural violence is any constraint on people's opportunities, well-being, and sense of dignity that works through multiple institutions and channels. It may appear that no one is responsible for the violence, that it just "happens"; yet it always happens in patterned ways.[4] Marginalized burial grounds are places of structural violence and systemic vandalism, impacting both the dead and the living communities connected with them.

What looks like overgrowth and slow decay in historic Black cemeteries would in most cases be better understood as evidence of theft.[5] The theft started with the dispossession of land that African Americans owned or labored on, whether they were enslaved or free. It continued from there, with grave robbers targeting African American graves to provide bodies for medical schools in the late nineteenth and early twentieth centuries. The "urban renewal" that destroyed many Black neighborhoods in the 1950s through the 1970s, emptying out the communities that once cared for their local cemeteries, was a theft of wealth, space, social ties, and sense of belonging.[6]

Analysis of structural violence strives to be "historically deep and geographically broad."[7] It can help us make connections between seemingly disparate things, such as histories of enslavement and segregation, environmental racism, and graffiti painted on headstones. These things actually work in tandem, affecting the same communities across generations and producing cemeteries that people call "overgrown" or "abandoned."

It's fair to worry that when we link so many forms of violence together, we make it harder to be specific about any one of them—and to assign responsibility clearly.[8] In many cases, part of the labor cemetery citizens do is to document damage and demand action from those who are at least partially responsible for it.[9] In this book, I try to gather and amplify those voices.

Volunteers arrive in cemeteries with different ways of understanding what they see and thinking about why they are doing this work. Among the possibilities are reasserting the dignity of mourners and descendants, rebuilding a sense of the sacred in desecrated places, and revising the memory landscapes of our towns and cities to address legacies of violence and erasure.[10] In many cases, these cemetery citizens also revise their own relationships with living communities and the dead, crafting new ideas about belonging and kinship. Finally, they revise the ways that cemeteries serve as public space. An overgrown cemetery filled with the bustle of volunteers feels more vibrant and more meaningfully public than the well-maintained but sterile acres of lawn where many Americans are buried.[11]

The work cemetery citizens are doing in Geer, East End, Mount Moriah, and other marginalized cemeteries is often described as preservation, restoration, or reclamation. Reclamation might be the best of these terms. While many things can be preserved (homes, textiles, foods, human remains), people only seek to reclaim what has been stolen or silenced—or both. The cemeteries described in this book can be thought of as places of stolen dignity and silenced histories, which are now being reclaimed.

The notions of preservation, restoration, and reclamation all look backward, toward the past, asking what can be rescued.[12] That question can lead to constructive, if painful, conversations about the impossibility of fully preserving, restoring, or reclaiming anything. At every cemetery, even those that are well maintained, erasure and loss are central features of the landscape. They may even be part of how the memory landscape can and must function over time. Generations pass, along with their memories of the dead. Younger people might show dutiful respect and care without the same intimacy. Or they might move away, eventually losing track of which relatives are buried where. The inscriptions on older headstones slowly fade.

Progress in reclamation efforts at one cemetery can make you more aware of the many lost or precarious burial grounds all around it. I've spent the past few years working alongside friends at Geer Cemetery, celebrating the transformation of the space, while also learning about the city's other African American burial grounds, some of which are impossible to reclaim.[13]

Cemetery citizens grapple with these and many other limitations of their work. But their goals also go beyond reassembling fragments of the past. Caring for a cemetery is a beginning, a place where relationships start and where people are asking new questions.

Preservation, restoration, and reclamation are all noble ideas. If I had to pull together the various ways they are invoked on behalf of marginalized cemeteries, it would look something like this:

Preserving history is important because knowledge of the past enriches all of us and helps us understand our present. Reclaiming the past that has been erased and/or defaced is also about justice for living communities, especially those who still experience structural violence and marginalization in the present moment. We also restore burial grounds to recover the dignity of the dead—for their sake and for their descendants.

I believe these statements. They fuel me in the work I do at Geer Cemetery and elsewhere; and I know they do the same for many others who have been involved for much longer. But sometimes nobleness can fill up your field of vision; there is no room for other things you should be seeing. Noble statements like the one above don't do justice to how difficult the work will be, how human. They don't help us anticipate the struggles ahead: over how the stories of a cemetery should be told, who should tell them, who should steer a cemetery's transformation or get the funding to do it.

For this reason and others, I think of these projects in cemeteries as forms of *revision*. The term may seem more appropriate for my office hours with students than a workday pulling vines off of headstones. But not all revisions happen with pen and paper or on a computer screen.

Philosopher Jill Stauffer uses the term "revisionary practices" to describe courtrooms, truth commissions, and other collective efforts bound together by "the hope of opening up a future not fully determined by past harms."[14] Envisioning a future "not fully determined by past harms" is very different from forgetting, putting the past behind us, and moving on. It is about possibility—starting something new *without* forgetting. Revisionary practices are not the same thing as what we call revisionist history; they don't attempt to replace one grand narrative with another, competing one. But neither do they treat the past, or the dead, as static: as resources to be utilized, or lost property to reclaim.

Revision carries with it a sense of messiness. For the writer, revision can look like crumpled pieces of paper, pencil marks in the margins, words that must be rewritten or retyped so that they're legible. Even when using digital writing tools that leave fewer material traces of revision, you delete something, write a new version, then write it again—or realize you should go back a few steps to something you deleted too quickly. Work in cemeteries is more like this—messy, iterative, frustrating, and sometimes momentarily miraculous—than words like "preservation," "reclamation," or "restoration" capture.

Overgrowth or perpetual care, desecration or sacredness are not the only possibilities for marginalized cemeteries. These spaces can also become investments, sources of potential capital, for people seeking relevance, a moral high ground, a stage to stand upon. Big, noble ideas—like honoring the dead, preserving heritage, or educating the public—are not going to help you much at a meeting where everyone already believes in those things, and yet everyone is angry at each other.

If you have ever sat down with a piece of your own writing, intent on revising it, you know how daunting it is. You know that the word "revision" implies difficulty, but also seemingly endless possibilities. Revision is never complete; it just reaches a point where you have taken it as far as you can go. It is a process that combines humility about outcomes—an acceptance of the imperfectability of the world, perhaps even its fundamental brokenness—with tremendous creative power. This combination of brokenness and creativity, above all, is what makes grassroots work in marginalized cemeteries a project of revision.[15]

Cemetery citizens are concerned with righting wrongs that impact both the living and the dead, with restoring places and dignity. But they also make the dead matter in new ways. They offer new, challenging ideas about the lineages and linkages between the living and the marginalized dead, and they are fashioning marginalized burial grounds into new forms of public space. They are creators, and collaborators with the dead.

Citizen, Descendant, Researcher, Tourist

Revisionary practices such as cleaning up a cemetery and putting flowers on graves "open up a future not fully determined by past harms," as Stauffer says, but not cleansed of them either. It is a future given richness and power through connections to the dead and the harms they suffered.

While I was writing this book, I was also delving into my own family's Holocaust history. I came to see this, too, as a kind of revision. The more I confronted the impossibility of rescuing all the names, dates, and details about my ancestors, the more I realized that wasn't what it was about. I have been trying to know my grandparents in a way I didn't while they were alive, to "open up a future" where I could ask them the things I didn't.[16] Though they are dead, I am still revising my relationship with them. I'm also trying to understand *their* revisionary practices: how they moved on after the destruction of their families, the degradations of the camps, the hunger (which dominates my grandmother's published recollections from less than a year after she was liberated from Ravensbrück concentration camp, far more than firing squads or gas chambers).[17] Were their dead present at the long tables crowded with food where we celebrated Passover, in the basement where I made boats and swords out of wood with my grandfather? If so, how?

People can be connected to a cemetery in many ways. But in recent decades activists and their allies have argued that descendants—"folks with people in the ground," as Brian Palmer describes them—have unique moral authority over the places where their ancestors are buried, and should be granted corresponding control over any research, interpretation, or revisions there.[18] Researching grassroots work in cemeteries and my own family history in parallel, I've thought about who I am as a descendant. In Łódź, Radom, Auschwitz, Ravensbrück, Malchow, Sachsenhausen, and Ebensee, my grandparents were confined in ghettos, beaten, forced to work while starving and terrified. They lost spouses, parents, and siblings. My grandfather's nine-year-old daughter, Mira, was taken from him and killed—I don't know where or how.[19] Some of these places now have museums and memorials where I might learn about and even mourn what happened to my family. But I have no place—not a mass grave, not a cemetery—to associate with my forever-missing, graveless ancestors. As Menachem Kaiser, a fellow grandchild of Holocaust survivors, puts it, "You do all this memory-work, and you hunger for the unabstract, for place person object noun."[20]

The degradation and vandalism inflicted on the cemeteries in this book have outraged me, overwhelmed me, gotten under my skin. But sometimes I feel something bordering on envy when I gather with groups of volunteers in a real place where you can work for a few hours, in good company, and feel like you've done something for the dead.

This book also has been a chance for me to revise my ways of being a scholar and a citizen. I don't mean "citizen" in the legal sense. The word originally meant the inhabitant of a city, a city dweller. For the first ten years of my academic career, while I was moving my family from place to place and seeking secure employment, I pursued projects that I could do from anywhere, so long as I had access to a library and could travel occasionally. I was not doing much dwelling. Now I am doing research that changes how I move through the world. In Durham, cemetery work makes me feel more like I really live *here*, and not just amid a pile of books, clothes, and coffee gadgets that follow me around. I track the changes in cemeteries with my eyes, my camera, my sketchbook, and with successive groups of students that accompany me. Cemetery work has introduced me to Durham neighbors, and to Durham's dead.

In marginalized cemeteries I am a researcher, activist, professor, and sometimes a tourist. It has taken me years to admit that last one. But I always look up local cemeteries before I travel, visiting them even on trips where I don't see the other, better-known historical attractions. I usually skip the well-maintained cemeteries in the heart of town. I look for the overgrown cemeteries, the ones tucked away near hospitals or unmarked sites of enslavement, the ones that aren't listed on web pages with titles like "Ten Things to Do in . . ." I traverse these out-of-the-way places in my White and male-presenting body, with the confidence and sense of safety it provides—the luxury of knowing that anyone I encounter will likely take me for an eccentric tourist or history buff, not a trespasser or threat. When I do visit cemeteries that are well marked and maintained, I move toward the edges, to the less tended places. Though I sometimes criticize the "dark tourists" who document and share their forays into shuttered asylums and other sites of pain and ruin, I wonder how different I really am.

While working on this book, I was organizing events and exhibits, getting to know cemeteries and the species of plants that grow in them, finding out who was buried where. I was learning many of their stories from public historians, genealogists, and descendants. Then I forgot many of these stories again, as they multiplied beyond the capacities of my memory. The words in here are mostly mine, but the world of the book is a shared one: shared with living friends and collaborators, some of whom you will meet in these pages. And shared with the dead. You will meet some of them too.

What a Cemetery Does

Cemeteries then

Cemetery citizens try to make headstones visible again after they have sunk into the soil or been covered by weeds. They research the individual stories of the dead, sharing what they can of lives that were often recorded only in fragments. The idea that this is how we dignify the dead—by carving names in stone and recounting details of an individual biography—is itself a relatively recent invention in human history, and one that does not have equal prominence in all cultures.[21] Nevertheless, in most towns and cities today, "it is no longer easy to separate an attempt to understand the past and its meaning from agonizing about which bits of it to protect and keep . . ."—including cemeteries.[22]

If burial customs change, and ideas about dignity after death along with them, then describing a particular cemetery as "in decline" or "degraded" is also contingent. Old cemeteries have markers with inscriptions that fade to illegibility, that fall from their bases or go missing. Not all of these are places of marginalization; not all of them were *made to disappear.*[23]

Every summer I take walks in the Lanes Cove Cemetery (also called Cove Hill Cemetery) near my parents' house in Gloucester, Massachusetts. The tiny seaside burial ground was created in the early 1700s by White settlers who founded the hamlet of Lanesville.[24] A place of slow, profound erasure, its headstones sink a little bit deeper each year, the lichen making them illegible, though ever more picturesque. There is preservation work to be done there, undoubtedly.[25] Conditions in Lanes Cove Cemetery feel like a reminder of the brevity of our lives and the scale of history, as well as how nonhuman forces, whether in the form of powerful storms or slow-growing lichen, overtake our efforts to establish permanent signs of our presence. But they don't feel like acts of violence—at least, not in the same way that toppled headstones, piles of trash, and tangles of vines do in a place such as Geer, East End, or Mount Moriah.

An underlying assumption of this book is that cemeteries are degraded when people care that they are, when it causes them pain. This pain is particularly acute among people who already experience the public space of our cities, and the ways we talk about history, as forms of erasure, indignities against their ancestors, and attacks on their own living bodies.

When people were marginalized in life, their cemeteries sometimes offered them one last chance to write their visions of justice into the landscape. Cemeteries can embody ideas about eternal dignity and redemption, but they can also serve a more practical purpose: they can make an argument about the status of the dead who are buried there, their fundamental equality with people who held more power in life and whose cemeteries were more lavish.[26] Today's cemetery citizens extend that argument into the present by pouring their labor into burial grounds that public institutions have ignored or abandoned.

In asserting their equality with contemporaries, the people who founded these cemeteries were keenly attuned to national (and sometimes international) burial trends. Mount Moriah was created near the height of the rural cemetery movement in the United States, marketed to a more middle-class customer than its predecessors such as Mount Auburn Cemetery in Cambridge, Massachusetts (the first American rural cemetery), and nearby Laurel Hill in Philadelphia. Rural cemeteries embodied nineteenth-century ideas about communing with the dead in green, wooded landscapes and learning virtue from their "exemplary lives."[27] They also answered the practical problem of the increasing value, and scarcity, of land in growing cities; Mount Moriah is home to graves that were removed from churchyards in Philadelphia to its quieter (at the time) and more idyllic location.[28] Last but not least, an often overlooked impetus behind the rural cemeteries, with their gates and gatekeepers, was that grave-robbing was common in the nineteenth century. While marginalized and institutionalized people were often the targets of this hunger for corpses to dissect in medical schools, the upper and middle classes were not immune.[29]

In the United States, rural cemeteries were designed to be "leafier, wilder, and more untamed" than their European counterparts.[30] Architecture historian Keith Eggener writes:

Cemeteries we built for ourselves, increasingly after 1830, were places with winding roads and picturesque vistas. The idea being that you leave behind the mercantile world outside the gates and enter into the space where you can meditate, where you can come into contact with spirituality and concentrate. They were quite important spaces for recreation as well. Keep in mind, the great rural cemeteries were built at a time when there weren't public parks, or art museums, or botanical gardens in American cities. You suddenly had large pieces of ground, filled with beautiful sculptures and horticultural art. People flocked to cemeteries for picnics, for hunting and shooting and carriage racing.[31]

Cemeteries were "America's first public art museums and parks."[32] They inspired the great public parks developed afterward; in fact, the country's most famous public park, New York's Central Park, is built atop graves that were never moved.[33] Ultimately, parks largely replaced cemeteries as places where families sought to gather outside in their leisure time—laying the groundwork for the contemporary notion that cemeteries are spaces only for grief and remembrance.[34]

Wealthy White Americans were generally the only people in the nineteenth-century United States who had access to "large pieces of ground," groundskeepers to care for their horticultural art, or carriages to race. Yet the paradigm of the rural cemetery—the wish to bury one's dead in a place that was a peaceful respite from the dust, noise, and smells of the city—also influenced African Americans, Jews, and other marginalized groups. While Jim Crow and other logics of segregation were often forced on them in both life and death, these people also sought to create cemeteries where they could be buried among other members of their communities, and where their monuments and markers could reflect unique cultural aesthetics.

These differences aside, they designed their cemeteries to match the dignity, and status, of the rural cemeteries where White Protestants were increasingly burying their dead—even when they had to do so on less desirable land and with far less support or capital.[35] This included the pastoral, Romantic naming conventions of rural cemeteries, which partly explains why many post-Emancipation African American cemeteries have names like Woodland and Evergreen in Richmond, or Beechwood in Durham.[36] Others are named after African American churches, or have more intimate origins. Violet Park, an African American cemetery in Durham, was named after the mother of one of its founders, the entrepreneur John Merrick (both were enslaved in Clinton, North Carolina, at the time of his birth). Later, when a man took up residence in the cemetery with a pack of dogs, it was nicknamed Wolf Den. The names tell a story about the changing status of the cemetery, whose graves—many of them, at least—were eventually exhumed and relocated so that a parking lot could be put in their place.[37]

The rural cemeteries of the nineteenth century eventually gave way to more uniform, suburban lawn cemeteries. On the winding paths of rural cemeteries, graves were grouped together by family or congregation, and monuments differed wildly in size and style—often competing with one another to demonstrate the status of the dead and provide edifying lessons to the living. The newer cemeteries emphasized a collective national identity and central planning. Often featuring grave markers that lie flat on the ground, mapped out in orderly grids, they are also much easier to mow and maintain than their predecessors.[38] Though cemeteries in the United States number in the hundreds of thousands, more plentiful than McDonald's and Starbucks restaurants, many of us avoid them, only setting foot inside when we've lost someone close to us.[39] Or not even then, since cremation and other non-burial practices have steadily been overtaking the traditional funeral and burial plot.[40]

But the story of a lost connection between Americans and their cemeteries also reflects a mostly White, upper- and middle-class American experience.[41] African American homegoings are joyful celebrations of the dead, rooted in some enslaved Africans' belief that death would bring them home to the African continent, to freedom.[42] These are still major communal events in many African American communities, as is gathering around loved ones' graves to sing and celebrate.[43]

Some of the most lovingly tended graves I've ever seen, festooned with ribbons and plastic flowers, were in the majority Spanish-speaking southern borderlands of the United States. While living in Rio Grande City, Texas, I often heard stories about how the local Burger King was haunted by children buried in the cemetery across the street. These stories were not told in front of a campfire to scare people. They were delivered as a matter of fact, like someone was giving you directions to their friend's ranch. And they certainly didn't stop anyone from eating at Burger King, in the company of the dead.

Cemeteries now

A quiet, aloof respect mingles with a sense of creepiness, of intruding in a place where we're not supposed to be—and maybe exposing ourselves to some danger or contamination we can't quite articulate. My students cringe when they step into a depression in the soil, knowing that there is a body somewhere underneath. Have we disturbed the peace of the dead? A boundary has been crossed, and we're not sure what it means. When my friend Jenn O'Donnell takes my students and me on a tour of Mount Moriah, I ask if it's OK to share the cookies I have brought for everyone. Lying dormant in some corner of my mind is the idea that it's not appropriate to eat in cemeteries, to sustain our lives in the presence of the dead.[44] Through whatever mysterious process of transmission brought my kids the same knock-knock jokes and hand-clapping games that I remember from my own childhood, they, too, hold their breath when we pass a cemetery in the car (though I regularly drag them on foot through cemeteries where we stay far too long to avoid breathing).

Visiting Woodlawn, an overgrown African American cemetery in Washington, DC, writer and environmental scientist Lauret Savoy wonders, "At what point does a burial ground lose its sanctity?"[45] It's a question that has no single answer. To some, there is nothing sacred about soil where lifeless bodies lie, and nothing to lose but superstition. To others, a burial ground is always sacred, regardless of its condition.

I'm somewhere in between. Savoy's question makes me think about what degrades a cemetery. There are things anyone might guess if you asked them, like trash on the graves or graffiti on the headstones. But there are other degradations whose impact you only absorb when you've spent a lot of time in places of the marginalized dead. Cars and trucks, rushing by with speed and wailing noise—noise that has been planned, mapped out, authorized to be near some people's dead and not others. A speed that is its own form of forgetting. Even when the boundaries of a cemetery itself are well drawn and protected, a nearby road or highway overpass can make a mockery of the idea of preservation. Weeds and cracked headstones cause anguish; they remind us of the work that must be done, of inscriptions and signs of care that are lost, possibly forever. But to me, nothing degrades or desecrates like a busy road running alongside or even right through a cemetery.[46]

Cemeteries record flashes of hatred and slow, entrenched inequities

Cemeteries are bordered, bounded, crafted as the ultimate "space apart," time-less and sacred.[47] They also register changes in their surroundings in nuanced and surprisingly rapid ways. Right after Donald Trump's election in 2016, Jewish cemeteries that had been sleepy places for decades were suddenly noticed again—first by people who came out to tip tombstones and paint swastikas, and then by a wider public that reacted in horror. At family gatherings, we talked about paying more frequent visits to the graves of my Holocaust survivor grand-parents: not because we were newly embracing Jewish customs or a call to com-mune with ancestors, but to check for vandalism.[48]

Cemeteries bear signs of hate, economic decline, displacement, and gentri-fication. They show the small victories that keep some spaces of the dead from being paved over or overgrown entirely, even as they may remain "shoehorned between a Home Depot and a Target"[49]—nominally "preserved" but, as places meant to be dignified and sacred, undone.

Marginalized cemeteries are places of slow-motion structural violence. Their decline happens at a pace and in settings that allow it to seem natural.[50] The trash that people dump at East End Cemetery in Richmond is a direct prod-uct of over a century of racialized exclusion of the African American living and dead; and yet it bears no obvious symbol, like the swastikas painted on Jewish graves, to trigger reports of a hate crime.[51] I have stood in the Springfield/Hayti Cemetery in Marple Township, Pennsylvania, where Black soldiers who fought to end slavery are buried on an overgrown hillside. Their disappearing graves, and those of other congregants of an African American church that stood on the site until the early 1900s, are squeezed between a concrete supply facil-ity and a cacophonous highway overpass. When I visited, only a poster board hand-drawn in colored marker identified the place as a cemetery. Rain had penetrated the plastic wrapped over the sign, and the letters were starting to drip. What one experiences at a place like this is not the dramatic horror of the massacre site or mass grave. It is the quiet, grinding indignity of the marginal-ized dead. (In February 2023, my former colleague Eric Hartman texted me a picture of the cemetery with a bright, freshly installed marker explaining its history. A new wooden staircase led up the hillside, and rows of flags marked the graves.)

Cemeteries tell us about continuity between generations, the connections between a place and its history: whose histories are carved into stone, kept clear of overgrowth, protected from trash and vandalism, and whose aren't. Knowing that one's family members and ancestors are buried with dignity—knowing deep down without having to think about it, without the question even coming to mind—is one of the least discussed forms of privilege: death privilege. "[T]he extent to which relatives, friends or colleagues can impose their own perception of a particular corpse on a wider circle of society is in itself a measure of social power," writes Vanessa Harding.[52]

Cemeteries are governed, or ungoverned by design
Dead bodies left out in the open, dead bodies that are buried. Buried under clean rows of markers, buried in fields full of weeds. The bodies, and the places where they wind up, tell us about our systems of governance, and about our human rights.[53] A person buried in a cemetery with perpetual care funds, maybe even maintained by the public purse, is someone able to make claims of citizenship, to extract resources from the collective, even after death. A person whose body is left in the desert to be torn at by vultures (as Antigone's brother Polyneices was in Sophocles' tragedy *Antigone*, and as migrants in the Sonoran Desert are at this moment) has been denied access to all those things: the claims and obligations, the visibility, the belonging. As the anthropologist Jason De León argues, this "necroviolence" can be made to look like an unfortunate accident, or an act of nature. But it never occurs without a careful architecture of violence that was put in place to make the "accidental" happen.[54]

A cemetery can serve as one final place where a society takes internally inconsistent, morally repugnant ideologies and writes them onto bodies, into the landscape.[55] Fences, walls, and highways have long been used to separate the White and Black dead, resulting in what Jill Lepore calls "an apartheid of the departed."[56] In his historical study of cemeteries in Richmond, Virginia, Ryan K. Smith says, "While customs surrounding death, burial, and memorialization have changed dramatically . . . one element has remained stubbornly the same: the color line."[57]

The mechanisms driving this racial necroviolence have not disappeared, but they have become more complex. Journalist Seth Freed Wessler reports that, in 2014, archaeologists colluded with Microsoft, the Army Corps of Engineers, and county authorities to keep an African American cemetery in Mecklenburg

County, Virginia, from being listed on the National Register of Historic Places. Eventually, under the noses of local descendants who were kept in the dark, the archaeologists dug up the burial ground for the expansion of a Microsoft data center. "[I]n Virginia, as in most of the country, the power over what ultimately happens to these sites often belongs to whoever owns the land. And the labor of investigating what could make the site historic is often outsourced to for-profit archaeological firms working for property owners who have a financial stake in finding as little as possible," Wessler writes.[58]

Cemeteries are archives of love
Debra Taylor Gonzalez-Garcia is the president of the Friends of Geer Cemetery, the organization working to reclaim and revise one of Durham's historic African American burial grounds. On October 10, 2022, she put a "Day of Honor" post on the organization's website, commemorating the birthday of Annice Glenn. She wrote:

> Today, we celebrate the birthday of Annice Lunsford Glenn. She was born 201 years ago, and so much has changed. . . . Some portions of her life are difficult to piece together and some we will probably never know. Most likely, Annice spent the first forty plus years enslaved. . . .
>
> By 1880, she was living in Durham with sons Floyd (19, spelled as Floid in earlier census), Crockett (14), and daughters Aggie (25), Indiana (23). She would live in Durham the rest of her life. She made her living as a sack stringer. Women were often employed in making these tobacco bags. . . .
>
> Her daughter, Catherine "Katie" Louise married Riley Gilmore, who was one of the caretakers of Geer Cemetery. They all lived on Glenn Street, and Annice at different times in her life shared a home with them.
>
> Annice died on Christmas Eve 1904. She was buried in Geer Cemetery next to what would become her daughter, Katie Gilmer's final resting place years later.[59]

I visit Ms. Glenn's headstone every time I'm at Geer. Its inscription reads, "Her life was beauty, truth, goodness and love." As if inspired by the headstone to keep adding more beauty to the area around her grave, some friends of the cemetery held a small ceremony for her exactly two hundred years after her birth; a burst of color from plastic flowers sticks out in the green, brown, and gray of the cemetery.

Following Jewish tradition, I am named after dead relatives. My middle name, Richard, comes from my maternal grandfather's little brother who died in 1932 of scarlet fever. I've never felt particularly attached to the name. I probably noticed it most during the early years of adolescence when friends thought making "dick" jokes about it was funny.

While I was working on this book, my mother and I found a photograph of Richard's headstone in Mount Hebron Cemetery, in Queens, New York. Accordinging to her, the headstone was placed there by my grandfather's other brother, Milton Regenbogen. My great-grandfather and great-grandmother never purchased one, perhaps because my great-grandfather Saul, who worked as a window-washer, could not afford anything he felt would be adequate. The headstone reads:

RICHARD

FREDERICK

REGENBOGEN

MAY 22, 1930

APRIL 18, 1932

"DITTIE DOLL"

"Dittie Doll." Carved on a headstone I have not yet seen in person, photographed by a stranger who walked through the cemetery and posted the picture on the Find a Grave website. After forty-five years, I am no longer indifferent to my middle name, and have begun to use it again wherever I can. Cemeteries are archives of love.

At the Margins, at the Brink

I have struggled with what terminology to use in describing these cemeteries. Some cemetery citizens have heated feelings about this issue themselves. Here's a weedy glossary of terms I've encountered, what they clear up for us, and what they leave obscured from view.

Abandoned cemeteries: Jarene Fleming, whose ancestors are buried at East End and Evergreen in Richmond, told me:

> I really resent the narrative of these "abandoned cemeteries," because the families have always, at least in my short lifetime, been involved, you know, paid people every year to keep the graves cleared. But with migration, with families dying out, with people not being able to get to their plots, I can see how quickly things can get lost.[60]

Stay for a while at any of these cemeteries: you'll see walkers, cyclists, someone visiting a relative's grave, rabbits, deer. And of course, depending on the day, you might see cemetery citizens at work. So "abandoned" is both misleading and imprecise. It's misleading because it sounds like "empty," and that's not true. It's imprecise, as Jarene makes clear, because it suggests so little about who it was that abandoned these cemeteries.

Overgrown cemeteries: "Overgrown" is a slightly more ambivalent term than "abandoned." It can encompass the heartbreak of cemeteries so covered by weeds that they are impassible, swallowing even tall grave markers and preventing generations of descendants from finding their dead—sometimes even keeping passersby from recognizing there's a cemetery there at all. It also has room for some of the unexpected beauty and even awe one can find among the carpets of weeds and twisting vines. Yet "overgrown" tells us even less than "abandoned" about the story behind the story, how this growth came to exceed what had once been envisioned by the people who crafted a cemetery and buried their dead in its soil.

Neglected cemeteries: "Neglected" is at least slightly more accurate than "abandoned." Defined as treated with "disrespect or without proper attention or care," neglect implies a responsibility that someone did not fulfill.[61] But Jarene's objection still holds. It's far too easy to turn the knife of "neglect" around and cut the very people who fought the decline of these cemeteries—"the aunts, uncles, brothers, sisters, pastors, elders, who have been stewarding these spaces for generations."[62] At a minimum, the term should usually have a qualifier: "systemic neglect," used by city officials in Washington, DC, helps to clarify what kind of neglect we're talking about.[63]

Unmaintained cemeteries: When cemeteries are maintained, there is some institution or mechanism taking responsibility for upkeep out of the hands of descendants, mourners, neighbors, or volunteers. In fact, the key difference between maintenance, care, and revision is sometimes more a *who* than a *what*, since all three of these things may involve the same tasks. Cemetery maintenance is generally performed by paid staff. "Perpetual care funds"—the fees people pay into a fund for cemetery upkeep—are, in a way, a misnomer. They generally cover regular mowing, debris removal, fixing roads and clearing pathways, and other things we should refer to as "maintenance."[64] Depending on the cemetery, this may or may not include responsibility for the appearance and upkeep of individual graves.[65] Care is something more intimate.[66] It's the kinds of things family members and mourners do at and around the graves of their ancestors or other people they knew and loved.

Leaving a keepsake at a loved one's grave is one form of care. Offerings of various kinds—glass bottles, dishes, shells, figurines, and more—are common finds at historic African American cemeteries.[67] This tradition continues, with adaptations. At Geer we have found a Hallmark card wrapped in a plastic bag, a bar of soap, beer and liquor bottles of many shapes and sizes. At Beechwood, another African American cemetery in Durham, I once caught sight of someone placing a balloon at a grave, kneeling over it and weeping.

Care might also involve tasks that seem impersonal, but which become intimate when family members and friends take them on. At East End, I once saw someone pull up in their car and remove an old lawn mower from the trunk. They began to mow the area around a few graves while their passenger looked on from the car. We call this "tending" a grave, a word that shares its root with tenderness.[68]

The work of cemetery citizens, which I'm calling revision, occupies an interesting place between maintenance and care. Cemetery citizens are not paid maintenance staff. But they do often clear, mow, weed, and tend the graves of people they never knew, and with whom they may have no connection. The work can be very intimate; cemetery citizens sometimes come to feel deep connections to the people they research, or whose graves they worked beside. But when there are years of damage to undo, acres and acres of cemetery to clear, the work can also be less intimate in the scale of its concerns, and perhaps less tender.

Degraded cemeteries: I owe this term to a conversation with Lisa Y. Henderson, founder of the Lane Street Project, who is leading the revisions in three historic Black cemeteries in Wilson, North Carolina. Lisa described these places as "degraded landscapes."[69]

One definition of degraded is "deprived of dignity."[70] I think this is the simplest, most accurate description of what's been done to these burial grounds. It feels even more fitting once you have gotten to know post-Emancipation Black cemeteries as places that were exquisitely crafted to enshrine and project dignity.

The concept of degradation also helps explain why revising these places requires more than simply mowing and clearing. Reestablishing dignity takes physical labor, but also research, storytelling, gathering people to listen and to care.

Marginalized cemeteries *or* **places of the marginalized dead:** The word "marginalized" makes clear it's no accident that African American cemeteries, cemeteries of people housed in institutions, and burial grounds of poor and Indigenous people wind up abandoned, neglected, overgrown. It implies *doing*, action—people and institutions pushing the dead out to the "edge, brink, border, margin."[71]

Pushing them from where? For someone to be marginalized implies that their starting point, their rightful position, was always in the center too: that they are as much at the core of a place and its history as anyone else. To be marginalized—as a person, or as a cemetery—means to be at the *brink*: excluded, pushed to the edges, but also *about to happen*. Places of the marginalized dead, places of revision, stand at the brink of something new.

Landscapes of Memory and Forgetting

Racism, both openly expressed and quietly institutionalized, has often driven African American graves out of sight and official memory, more likely to be degraded or destroyed by public institutions than to benefit from their investments. Geer and East End are both artifacts of segregation: all-Black cemeteries carved out of their cities by people without access to nearby Whites-only burial grounds.

Mount Moriah is different. After Margaret Jones, a Black woman, successfully fought attempts to institutionalize segregation there, it came to be heralded as a space inclusive of all races and creeds.[72] But the current conditions at Mount Moriah, and the story of reclamation efforts there, are inextricably bound up with race and racism. The cemetery, once a rural retreat, is now situated in a mostly Black, low-income part of Southwest Philadelphia. Its degraded conditions reflect a larger pattern of deep inequities in this city where de facto segregation is the norm.[73]

The more stories I heard of people buried in the predominantly Muslim sections of Mount Moriah Cemetery, the more it became clear that race was also part of the story of their deaths and the politics around their burial sites. Anyone reading inscriptions in the Springfield Avenue section can see that it is home to a disproportionate number of dead young Black men. This is the legacy of racialized patterns in gun deaths, fueled by decades of housing discrimination, high rates of incarceration, and police violence (I researched the history of one young man buried in this section who died in police custody).[74] Some of these men's families, and the families of other Muslims buried in Mount Moriah, have come to feel that no one outside of their community is really concerned for their loved ones' graves. This story is not about race alone; but race is always present in it.

Intertwined with race, other forms of social exclusion influence the physical and social landscapes of the cemeteries in this book. Gender, class, mental illness, disability, religious affiliation, and ethnicity all leave their distinct imprints. People who fought for dignified burial grounds did not necessarily distribute that dignity equally within them. All three cemeteries are full of women whose lives were barely recorded, their ideas and accomplishments forgotten. Some headstones leave out their first names, subordinating these women to the men they married by recording them only as "wife of . . ." Sometimes, their inscriptions extol their roles as mothers and nothing else.

While researching these three cemeteries, I was also learning about the anonymous burials of people labeled mentally ill and disabled, and confined to institutions, in the United States from the nineteenth century onward.[75] I did additional fieldwork at MetFern Cemetery in Waltham, Massachusetts, near my childhood home.[76] The name MetFern refers to two institutions: Metropolitan State Hospital and the Walter E. Fernald State School. "Met State" was part of a massive infrastructure of state hospitals built in the nineteenth century, where people labeled mentally ill often lived in horrific conditions of overcrowding and abuse. The Fernald School, a residential facility for young people with social and intellectual disabilities, has a complex history of care, neglect, and violence experienced by those who lived on-site.[77] From 1947 to 1979, two hundred ninety-eight people were buried in a clearing in the woods, under small stone markers bearing only a number and a "C" or a "P," indicating if the person was Catholic or Protestant (though some were neither; their markers obscure not only their names but also their religious and cultural backgrounds).[78] This cemetery, like many others at state institutions, perpetuates stigma around mental illness and disability, as well as the removal and erasure of people from their families, neighborhoods, and the broader social world.[79]

MetFern, like other cemeteries around state hospitals, has been the site of important efforts to honor the dead and rethink the histories of psychiatry, mental illness, disability, and American eugenics.[80] The contributions of these cemetery citizens deserve wider and more sustained attention than I can offer here.

When the COVID-19 pandemic began in 2020, the virus tore through nursing homes and congregate living facilities for disabled people. Once vaccines were developed, many states deprioritized at-risk disabled people; or they focused on older Americans in nursing homes while remaining reluctant to address the vulnerable people in psychiatric care facilities and group homes.[81] Though the casualties of this indifference were not buried in a field of numbered graves, our society still puts real work into making the deaths of disabled people invisible and anonymous.

Here in the South, I visited the cemeteries and open fields used for

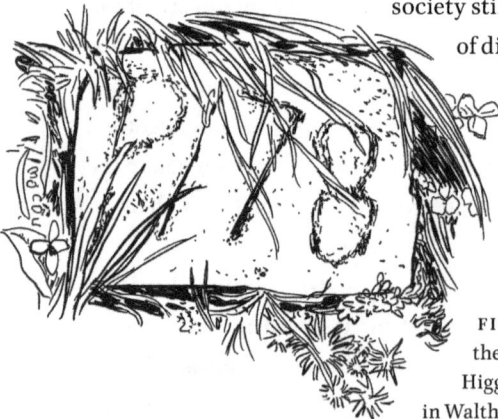

FIGURE INTRO.1. Black-and-white sketch of the small stone grave marker for Effie Bernice Higgins (1890–1970) at MetFern Cemetery in Waltham, Massachusetts, where two hundred ninety-eight inmates from the Metropolitan State Hospital and the Fernald School were buried from 1947 to 1979. The marker reads P-178, the "P" short for Protestant. It is partially covered by grass, with clover and small flowers growing around it. Drawing by the author, November 2022.

burying people who died at Central State Hospital in Petersburg, Virginia, and Cherry Hospital in Goldsboro, North Carolina (originally named simply the "Asylum for Colored Insane"). Both institutions had only Black inmates from their openings in the late 1800s until the Civil Rights Act of 1964 outlawed segregation in health care facilities.[82] Nineteenth-century racial pseudoscience claimed that Black people were suited for hard labor and subservience, not for freedom; these state institutions, their design and function closely intertwined with prisons, helped separate out individuals whose labor could still be exploited from those deemed too ill or dependent to be of use.[83] Sometimes people simply had no other place to go than the institutions—no land, no job, no place safe from racialized violence.[84]

Conditions at state hospitals for African Americans were significantly worse than at counterpart hospitals for Whites, as bad as those often were. From the late nineteenth century onward, eugenicists promoted the idea that public policy should protect the gene pool from "deviant" tendencies; these ideas quickly "melded with Jim Crow norms."[85] Blackness and disability, separately and together, fed into ideas of predatory, "animalistic" threats to society. Both Central State and the Goldsboro hospital carried out forced sterilizations on their inmates.[86]

Individual and family histories connect different anonymous and degraded burial grounds, reflecting the complex systems and institutions that incarcerated, exploited, and surveilled people in life. The headstone for Jeff Bass (1905–1923), with a lamb carved into it, is still visible at Geer Cemetery. He died at the hospital in Goldsboro; then his body was brought to Geer. His younger sister, Henrietta, died at the same hospital in 1927. She was buried in the cemetery there and left nameless. One of their other siblings, Harold Bass, is described on his death certificate as "born an imbecile." When he died at age twenty-one, of heart failure, he was buried at Violet Park, the Durham cemetery that became a parking lot.[87] These three Bass siblings traversed a landscape of race, illness, and disability, and ultimately of precarious burial grounds.

There are many other places where the dead are subject to the violence of abandonment, overgrowth, and erasure. Among the best known is Hart Island, on the Long Island Sound in the northeast Bronx, New York.[88] Originally inhabited by the Indigenous Siwanoy, it subsequently housed a training camp for United States Colored Troops, a psychiatric institution, a tuberculosis sanitorium, and a prison. Since 1869, the island has also served as a "potter's field" for the city's unclaimed and indigent dead. It is home to over a million burials, many of them infants and stillborn babies. Until 2020, incarcerated people from nearby Riker's Island carried out the duties of digging graves and stacking coffins in them.[89] In the 1980s and 1990s, thousands of people who died of AIDS were buried on Hart Island. The first seventeen victims were buried in a separate section by corrections officers wearing special protective jumpsuits due to a misplaced fear of contagion.[90] In spring 2020, New York morgues became overwhelmed with the number of people dying of COVID-19, and burials spiked at Hart Island. The island served as a temporary home for some of the pandemic dead, who would later be moved to a more permanent resting place, and as a final destination for unclaimed bodies.[91]

After decades of efforts by the Hart Island Project and other activists to gain access to the site and tell its stories, the New York Department of Corrections—which managed the site at the time—began allowing the general public to visit a small gazebo area on the island on a monthly basis. In November 2019, again thanks to sustained activism, the New York City Council passed legislation transferring jurisdiction of Hart Island from Corrections to Parks and Recreation. The new legislation was intended to "end . . . 150 years of penal control over city burials" and "create a public park where citizens can freely visit graves," though burials would continue at the site.[92] The parks department is still working out how to balance respect for Hart Island's history, and its dead, with visions of it as a scenic public space.[93]

Hart Island is an important reminder that mass burials of various kinds continue today as a common practice. In November 2022, I visited three historic psychiatric hospital cemeteries in New Castle, Delaware. At the "Spiral Cemetery" near the old hospital building, local activists Faith Kuehn and Kathy Dettwyler showed me newly dug graves and numbered markers for people whose bodies were unclaimed or who had no resources for burial elsewhere. In North Carolina, where I live, unclaimed remains are cremated after ten days, and stored for three more years awaiting someone to come looking for them. If this doesn't happen, they are "scattered at sea."[94]

The burial grounds of Indigenous peoples throughout the United States are still under threat, despite the landmark Native American Graves Protection and Repatriation Act of 1990. As anthropologist Chip Colwell writes, when archaeological reviews are conducted before the construction of pipelines or other projects, Indigenous voices and knowledge are often excluded from the process: "Archaeologists serve an important role in documenting historic properties. But they tend to view the world through the lens of science and history. They search out buried villages, pottery shards, bones, broken stone tools. Yet in my experience, they rarely have the expertise and knowledge to identify traditional cultural properties, which are grounded in identity, culture, spirituality and the land's living memory."[95]

Recent investigations in Canada have uncovered the remains of thousands of Indigenous children who were forced into the country's system of residential schools. They were abused, neglected, systematically stripped of their language and culture, and then buried in unmarked graves. In June 2021, Secretary of the Interior Deb Haaland announced that the United States would begin similar investigations into its own federal boarding schools for Native American children, which was likely to uncover burial grounds and lead to new repatriation projects.[96] At the time of this writing, the Department of the Interior had documented marked or unmarked burials at fifty-three different residential school sites.[97]

These schools should be seen as part of a broader project of pulling Indigenous families apart and placing their members in custodial institutions such as the Canton Asylum for Insane Indians, a federal facility in South Dakota.[98] One hundred twenty-one people are known to be buried in the cemetery there, though it is suspected there are more beneath the ground. Families often had multiple loved ones taken from their homes; some were shuttled between one type of institution and another. Susan Burch describes these processes as "sustained containment, surveillance, and slow erasure."[99] The Lakota journalist Harold Iron Shield, a survivor of federal boarding schools, organized ceremonies at the Canton Asylum cemetery from 1987 until 2007, making him a pioneer in the work that would continue at state hospital cemeteries a decade later.[100]

While researching this book, I also traveled to the Sonoran Desert, where I hiked with the artist Alvaro Enciso and other members of the Tucson Samaritans. As part of a project he calls "Donde mueren los sueños," or "Where Dreams Die," Alvaro makes wooden crosses, then paints them in vibrant colors and marks them with red dots resembling points on the maps of migrant deaths created by the organization Humane Borders. Alvaro and his companions place these crosses in the precise locations where bodies have been found, memorial-izing the individual dead and serving as a form of witness to the "killing field" that U.S. immigration policy has crafted at our southern border.[101] I also traveled from Tucson west through the Tohono O'odham Nation to Ajo, Arizona, where I joined a group of activists and college students, inspired by Alvaro, who were placing commemorative crosses in the desert. I witnessed how these people, many of them brought together by their Christian faith, were working to make lonely places of dying into sacred sites—a kind of substitute cemetery (I also visited the portion of Tucson's Evergreen Cemetery—not to be confused with Richmond's Evergreen Cemetery—where some unidentified migrants are in-terred). These places were stunningly beautiful when I visited in the daytime, with a group of hikers around me and plenty of water in my backpack. Yet it was easy to see how quickly they could become disorienting in the dark, or if you were hungry, thirsty, and overheated. How you could die wondering if anyone would ever find you there.

My analysis can't possibly encompass, or do justice to, all of these places—places of the marginalized dead, and of projects to mark, honor, and remember them.[102] The cemeteries I focus on in this book are just a few of many that have cemetery citizens actively working in and around them. In both my research and teaching, I kept to cemeteries I had been invited into, and where I could contribute in some way to the ongoing work. I didn't want to be an intruder. But sometimes figuring out where to draw that line wasn't simple, since at each burial ground there were multiple groups who might have something to say on the question. With students, I have puzzled through whether stepping into people's graves—a nearly unavoidable experience in cemeteries carpeted with weeds—was justified by the fact that our intentions were respectful. When we took photographs, we wondered which ones to share: Do images of disrepair and broken headstones contribute to people seeing the cemeteries only as injured, abject places?[103] Should we show the names written on damaged headstones, or is this another indignity visited upon the dead?

Over the course of my research, tremendous momentum and energy was building up around African American cemeteries.[104] Their physical state often remained precarious, and they continued to be subject to outrages and en-croachment; people across the country were still fighting plans that would put pavement or buildings over burial grounds.[105] But other signs pointed toward a major shift. Some of this new energy was likely fueled by the reaction to Donald Trump's election to the U.S. presidency, and his embrace of racist and xenophobic rhetoric and policies. Then came the murder of George Floyd in Minneapolis on May 25, 2020, and ensuing global protests for racial justice. While demanding that towns and cities throughout the South take down Confederate flags, monuments, and homages to enslavers, more people began to ask not only what needed to be removed, but what should be saved. Fragile African American heritage sites, including cemeteries, were increasingly in the public eye.[106]

Angela Thorpe is the executive director of the Pauli Murray Center for History and Social Justice in Durham and former director of the North Carolina African American Heritage Commission. Her family has a historic cemetery in Tarboro, North Carolina, that her aunt still cleans up with "a mop and bucket."[107] In an interview, she reflected on the developments of the past few years:

> There was a lot of energy around calling out harm that had been done to Black people and Black communities. . . . I think there's an opposite side of that coin, though, and that looks like: rather than calling out harm, how do we preserve and keep places? Black spaces . . . that are important touchpoints to our history, that are critical touchpoints to our culture, that are not necessarily spaces of violence and terror? How do we do repair work? . . . Rather than lifting up and leveraging harm, how do we move in spaces of repair?[108]

In 2022, the U.S. Congress passed the African American Burial Grounds Preservation Act, creating a $3 million grant program for preservation and research in African American burial grounds. At the time of this writing, however, the funds for the program had not yet been appropriated.[109]

As the bill was working its way through Congress, cemetery citizens such as Brian Palmer, Peighton Young, and Adrienne Fikes raised alarms about its language, which requires consent from property owners for a group to receive funds for cemetery work. In the case of African American cemeteries, these landowners are often people or entities with little concern for the dignity of the dead. The legislation also allows groups to receive funding without demonstrating connections to descendants or the local community—in fact, the word "descendants" does not appear in its text.[110]

After years of fielding inquiries about African American cemeteries "with zero dollars to support grassroots folks," Thorpe supported the bill and testified on its behalf before Congress. She called it a "starting point" that establishes at least some federal support for these sites. "A piece of legislation cannot do it all," she said, but she also warned:

> [I]t is going to be critical that folks are thoughtful about how and where funds are disbursed, and how and where, and with whom, technical assistance programs are established. . . . There are multiple, state-based African American heritage commissions that are working hand in hand with grassroots practitioners [and] that have the capacity to move programs and funds forward in a different way. I think this is an opportunity to create new models and new infrastructures, particularly for Black-led organizations . . . [where] there's built-in knowledge, there's built-in expertise, and, though it might look and feel different, there's built-in infrastructure. . . . Our folks know what they're doing.

Anthropologists Justin Dunnavant, Delande Justinvil, and Chip Colwell called for expanding the legislation into an African American Graves Protection and Repatriation Act, modeled after the Native American Graves Protection and Repatriation Act. They wanted this broader framework to address not only cemeteries but also the remains of African American people that are held in museum and university collections, as well as African Americans' genetic material.[111] As I was writing this book, activists and their allies were forming new interstate support networks for people working in African American cemeteries, including the Black Cemetery Network based at the University of South Florida and the African American Cemetery Coalition.

Still, the most common format for local and national news stories was to focus on one cemetery, one volunteer project at a time. Few people were tracking how the cemetery citizens behind these projects were watching and influencing one another: how revisions at African American cemeteries and other sites— state hospital cemeteries, Hart Island, residential schools and other Indigenous burial grounds, and more—formed an emerging national dialogue about our landscapes of memory, our places of the marginalized dead.[112]

The Whole City

According to political theorist Benjamin Barber, "Public space is not merely the passive residue of a decision to ban cars or a tacit invitation to the public to step into the street. It must be actively created and self-consciously sustained against the grain of an architecture built as much for machines as people, more for commercial than common use."[113] Cemetery citizens are doing this work. They are seeking to create meaning and invite people into spaces that don't have obvious commercial uses—spaces vulnerable to development, or treated as dumps precisely because they couldn't be developed for commercial use.

I have always been drawn to public spaces, and yet uncomfortable in crowds. So for me cemeteries are the ideal public space. Generally easy to access, they have a beauty and wildness unseen by passersby who think of them only as places for grieving and ghosts. Cemeteries allow you to engage with history in its broad sweep—to see the wars that have been fought, the uptick in deaths during a pandemic, how the demographics in a city changed as new immigrants came. Yet the history is also intimate, spoken in snippets via individual birth and death dates, and the few phrases that a family chose to inscribe on their loved one's headstone—windows into the particularity of each life that was lived, or the ideals that mattered most to the person's community.

Unlike most museum exhibits or monuments, a cemetery has no linear paths or explanatory captions telling you where to go next, or how to interpret what you see. You read one headstone, walk past another. You wander, you linger. To me, that rich mix of information and beauty—and that freedom from "scriptedness"—is magical, even in a space marked by loss.[114] We can never recapture the whole of a person's life from their headstone—or from the archives where cemetery citizens do their research. This loss is echoed in the way I move through cemeteries, pausing at some grave markers while passing over others, unable to take in the whole space at once. Every cemetery, whether it is well cared for or not, is a landscape of memory and forgetting—and anyone who steps into it becomes a participant in both of these things.

In this book, you'll meet some people who keep very, very busy in cemeteries. But cemeteries can also be great places to do nothing.[115]

As the COVID-19 pandemic unfolded, public space underwent a crisis; death, and the fear of death, entered every space where people gathered. A hush sank over the world: at first gradually, and then like bricks. Duke's East Campus, near my home, emptied of students during a spring break that stretched into months of lockdown. A few students without a place to go, or a way to get there safely, stuck around. They played frisbee on the quad and ate outside in small groups. Then they got moved to West Campus, two miles away. East Campus was close to empty much of the time. Kids appeared on bikes as the day wore on, families picnicked on the grass. One day someone was wearing headphones and practicing what looked to me like Irish step dance. There were more dogs than before, fewer people. We spread apart to avoid contagion, creating big pockets of silence. It became a place where anyone could be present, but no one assembled, a place where crowds were impossible. The quad, the whole city, like a cemetery.

Doubts and Emergencies

People will inevitably question the justification for work that involves pouring money, time, and expertise into dead bodies and their burial grounds. The famous forensic anthropologist Clyde Snow once told me he questioned the resources spent exhuming mass graves after genocides and other atrocities—a field of human rights science that he pioneered—in places where people desperately needed food, schools for their kids, and other basic things.[116] The cities surrounding every cemetery in this book are places of urgent needs and stark injustices. Are these projects in cemeteries claiming scarce resources from people and causes that need it more? Would the volunteer hours be better spent somewhere else, like tutoring kids, or advocating for more affordable housing?

Jarene Fleming described her own struggles to juggle her responsibilities as a descendant, cemetery volunteer, and busy professional:

> Even though this [work in cemeteries] is really important to me, sometimes I feel like I spend too much time on it because the living really need some attention. And, you know, I work in maternal-child health, right? So I'm like: *every minute that I'm not—that I'm using to try and preserve this legacy in these cemeteries, I'm not trying to save a baby's life, you know?* Sometimes I really get exasperated myself, like: *Am I too, you know . . . do I spend too much energy into this?* I'm so passionate about it, but even I get like: *I only have X number of hours a day, a week, a year.*[117]

Katrina Spade is the founder of Recompose, a public benefit corporation developing ecological alternatives to traditional burial and cremation. She repeats a phrase that hospice workers use: "Death is not an emergency."[118] It's meant as a reminder to mourners that a loved one's death can be an occasion for slow and reflective action, rather than panicked attempts to "solve" the problem of our mortality or our discomfort with the bodies of the dead and dying. If death isn't an emergency, then the dead aren't either. But the indignities of the dead cause real pain, even in cemeteries where the burials stopped long ago. Despite her struggles over how to budget her time, Jarene is among the people who first showed me how much a cemetery can mean to descendants, and how much its degradation and misuse can hurt.

Feminist scholar Carol J. Adams points out that often we "separate caring into deserving/undeserving or now/later or first those like us/then those unlike us." All these boundaries, she says, promote "a conservative economy of compassion": a scarcity mentality about the consideration we can offer others and the availability of our care.[119] I wrote this book at a time when talk of crisis was everywhere, in the form of our unfolding global climate emergency, police violence, a pandemic, and explicit attempts to undermine the democratic process. Every few months an article would appear analyzing the efficiency of protests, or what it takes for a "moment to become a movement." My students always wanted to know, by the end of the semester, how we could fix the problems we studied.

The more these conversations repeated themselves, the more I felt pulled to places where care and activism seemed stubbornly inefficient. Cemeteries are not places for "effective altruism," for measuring the good produced by every action we take and figuring out how to maximize it. The weeds keep growing back, the graves remain where they are. And as if care existed in endless supply—far more than one lifetime's worth, at least—cemetery citizens lavish it on people who are already dead.

But not only the dead. The person you worked alongside on a Saturday at the cemetery, unearthing a grave marker hidden in the soil, might become over many such Saturdays the person who brings you homemade soup when you are recovering from surgery, or the person who texts you the meeting time and place for the protest downtown. Care begets care. More community creates more opportunities to act on the world in thoughtful and concerted ways.

In fact, maybe there is something special about caring for things when we're *not* certain what they mean, not sure about their urgency. Caring for them, despite the doubts, is the only way to keep the question of value open. Revisions are sometimes about discovering new value in something that was right in front of you all along, hidden in plain sight. Something like a cemetery.

Cemetery Citizens

The people buried in marginalized cemeteries suffered overlapping forms of oppression in life. The conditions of their burials extend that violence further. Yet, in some way, they make a claim on the land that their graves occupy. Through labor and learning, volunteers work to reinforce this claim and make these people grievable again.[120] They reimagine the dead as full citizens.

I use the term "cemetery citizens" to describe the living volunteers working in cemeteries.[121] Their work is often mundane: searching public records, organizing workdays, raising funds, entering information into databases. But it is also an imaginative political act, widening our circles of belonging and altering our stories. In creating the term, I was influenced by families of the missing and disappeared, and the scholars who write about them. In places where disappearances are common, authorities cannot be trusted as partners in the search for missing people; they may even be complicit in massacres and cover-ups. In response, grieving loved ones establish networks of mutual support and their own forensic procedures. Scholars such as Arely Cruz-Santiago and Robin Reineke refer to these efforts as "citizen-led forensics" or "forensic citizenship."[122]

While a clandestine mass grave is different from a cemetery, and produces different kinds of desperation, cemetery citizens resemble forensic citizens in their insistence on attending to the dead whom society has abandoned. They insist on keeping the dead public through political speech and acts of care. Both groups also wind up acquiring many forms of expertise, some of it quite technical, with little outside support.

The word "citizens" is one I use cautiously. The people buried in marginalized cemeteries may not have been granted legal citizenship; some may have been citizens in the formal sense while in practice they were denied many of the rights and privileges accorded to other citizens.[123] Measuring civic engagement or pride by the attachment local people feel to their cemeteries can reinforce a dangerous sense that there are "real" locals, rooted in a place for generations, and that migration and multiculturalism dilute these sorts of ties. Poet Jean Sprackland writes, "What does it mean, anyway, to belong somewhere? During the Industrial Revolution, in that period of mass migration from countryside to town, it was sometimes said that the new immigrants did not belong because they had no dead in the churchyard. The right of belonging in a place could only be earned by dying there."[124] Stories of displacement and migration are part of the history of every cemetery I describe in this book. Sometimes even the dead themselves have migrated. Mount Moriah is home to dead people who were exhumed from little church graveyards as Philadelphia expanded; some families moved their dead out of both Geer and East End as they became overgrown.

Cemetery Citizens is not driven by nostalgia for a world where people all tend to the graves of their own ancestors, where there are no migrations, where "rootedness" is considered a good in and of itself, or where professional cemetery management gives way entirely to some idealized model of community care.[125] People should be free to choose *not* to spend their time or labor in cemeteries. I don't often visit the graves of my own grandparents, in their sprawling and tidy lawn cemeteries in New Jersey.

As I listened to my interlocutors and became involved in this work myself, I realized that the people I admired most, and learned the most from, shared some approaches in common. The term "cemetery citizens" started as a descriptor and slowly became an ideal—even more so as a crisis in Richmond's cemeteries deepened. The story of East End, Evergreen, and the Enrichmond Foundation showed me that it is possible for people to claim responsibility for a marginalized cemetery without embracing the core practices of cemetery citizens, or asking enough of the hard questions they ask.

Cemetery citizens practice arts of noticing in cemeteries, looking not merely for master plans or best practices but for direct responses to the cemetery's landscape. They are conscious of the many kinds of life within it, its history, its dead, and the context in which it is situated. They don't merely maintain a cemetery, mowing and weeding. They also offer it things that go beyond simple maintenance: getting a duplicate grave marker made after one was stolen, helping family members locate the graves of their ancestors and connect with their dead, leaving origami cranes on an altar. I have begun to think of these acts as "scrappy care": low-budget, improvised ways of relating to the cemetery, and to the dead.

More like tending a garden than historic preservation as most people would understand that term. Sometimes, scrappy care involves cemetery citizens plumbing the depths of their own grief, which they brought along with them when they started volunteer work.

I found people who embody this rich model of cemetery citizenship in Geer, East End, Mount Moriah, and many cemeteries beyond these main research sites. Cemetery citizens such as Alex Green, Lisa Y. Henderson, and Yamona Pierce spoke so beautifully about the possibilities and challenges of cemetery revisions that I include them in this book, even as their work takes place in cemeteries that are not its focus.

Many of the people I interviewed, and worked alongside, as I researched this book have no familial relation to those whose graves they tend. They have fashioned their own links to a particular cemetery, and to the dead, through shared identities, political commitments, or the wish to carve out new forms of belonging in a place where they are still relative newcomers. They are teachers, genealogists, students, journalists, history and archaeology enthusiasts, and weekend volunteers. They are making new kinds of kinship with the dead, based not on biological ties but on understanding local history, addressing an overlooked injustice, and embracing a call to care.

These people never asked to be the subjects of a book. They are hard at work telling the stories of the people buried in the cemeteries, and the communities to which they remain connected. When cemetery citizens bring too much attention to themselves, or too much ego into the cemetery, it makes the work harder. It risks becoming a new form of exploitation, another way of degrading these places. That risk is present in these pages. But focusing on these volunteers—not in a newspaper profile about cemetery "heroes," but with patience, honesty, and nuance—allows us to see the full complexity of cemetery revisions, especially when they involve caring for "other people's" dead.

Writing about cemetery citizens, and not simply about cemeteries, allowed me to ask why people do this work. How does this seemingly strange pastime, pulling up weeds and cleaning headstones in an overgrown burial ground, move into the center of someone's life? Underneath that question is a universal one: how do we come to care about specific places, to invest part of our lives in them?

So much of the loss in these cemeteries is permanent: grave markers are gone, records are lost, the archives are fragmentary. Cemetery citizens are experts in "broken world thinking," innovators in finding meaningful forms of partial repair, and of honoring that which can't be repaired.[126] In their research, they often highlight the histories of forgotten "ordinary" people, who have always interested me more than the relatively few well-known, celebrated figures buried at these cemeteries. During our Friends of Geer Cemetery meetings, we sometimes talk about descendants who contact us, or visit our website, looking for information about an ancestor's grave. What kind of experience should they have when the answer is that we know that the person is buried in Geer (usually based on a death certificate), but also that the grave is either unmarked or buried beneath the soil? This is a question about web design and communication, but also a question of ethics. How do you give someone a gift that is also a broken thing?

Most of the time, we think of cemeteries as places to mark the end of a life, or of lives in the aggregate. In telling the stories of people who come together in cemeteries, this book is less about grief or the past than it is about the "attentive practices of thought, love, rage, and care" happening right now in places of the marginalized dead.[127]

Words and Pictures

Part I of this book, "The Fields Full of Weeds," gives an overview of each of the three cemeteries where I did most of the research for this book. The order of the chapters evokes the route I often took between the three burial grounds: starting at my home in Durham, near Geer Cemetery, and driving north through Richmond to visit East End. Then on to Philadelphia, and Mount Moriah. These introductory chapters begin with a found poem or life history about the dead and their graves—an intimate view of the burial ground I'm describing. I then move on to the cemetery's history. In nearly every case I am drawing from published histories that are more detailed than I can be here. Instead, I have sought to combine important elements of each cemetery's past with stories of the work happening there now—the real focus of *Cemetery Citizens*.

Each chapter follows a similar timeline. It starts with a cemetery's founding and early burials, then moves through a long period when conditions deteriorated. Eventually, efforts to preserve and reclaim the cemetery begin. But the details of this timeline differ immensely, starting with why these cemeteries were founded—in response to what needs, or what lack of other burial places—and what drove them into decline.

The chapters in Part II, "Revisions ('It Will Never End, That Work')," weave together scenes and issues from across the cemeteries, rather than following the cemetery-by-cemetery approach of the book's first half. Cemetery citizens, more than the cemeteries they work in, move into focus. What brings these people to put their time and labor into places of the dead? What identities and purposes do they share, and where do some of them—such as descendants of the people buried in the cemetery—have a different kind of relationship, a different kind of moral authority?

Volunteers arrive at a cemetery with different skills and motivations, but also with different ways of knowing the cemetery itself. In Part II, I examine these differences, and how they create tensions over what it really means "to have the work done right," as cemetery citizen Melissa Pocock puts it. There are best practices for *preserving* a cemetery, and right ways and wrong ways to do something like repair a broken headstone; but *revising* a cemetery is a different thing. It is political, even spiritual, work with soil and stories amid irreparable loss. Places of the dead—which are also, in the case of these cemeteries, wild and green plots of land surrounded by growing, gentrifying cities—can serve as public spaces where mourning, reckoning, enjoyment, and learning are all possible. But finding the balance between these different things is painfully difficult.

Throughout the book, I use line breaks and careful edits to make some portions of my interviews with cemetery citizens into poems. Working with my interview transcripts in this way, spending meditative time with the profound words of my interlocutors, was my favorite part of writing this book. The technique I used is sometimes called "found poetry"; and using poems to identify and emphasize themes in academic research, as I do here, is a form of "poetic inquiry."[128] I shared each poem with the person whose interview transcript I was working with, inviting them to comment and suggest edits, or to express their preference for a more traditional prose quotation.

People use poetic inquiry for many reasons. I like how sharing my interviews in this way slows everything down, asking both writer and reader to pay more attention to the particular words people are using. In a book where I have the privilege of deciding whose voice goes where, in what frame of analysis—a book where my own voice occupies many more pages of the text than my interviews—

poetic inquiry does something subtle but important with my interlocutors' voices. Visually, it gives them space on the page. Their words stand out, demanding a different kind of attention. Things that may appear, in prose, like odd grammar or verbal tics—such as the way we circle back on ourselves when speaking, or repeat phrases—instead become moments of added meaning. Why did the person stop at that particular point, leaving the rest of the sentence unfinished? How did they wind up somewhere so distant from where their sentence seemed to be headed? Why did they reach out to the listener at just this moment ("you know?"), or feel the need to repeat this particular word so many times? The more I worked with the voices of cemetery citizens on the page, the more I appreciated how poetic inquiry allowed the looping, mid-sentence revisions of their speech to come forward.

Some of the poems open doorways to issues I barely analyze at all, such as Jenn O'Donnell's references to burnout in cemetery reclamation work (appearing in the poem "I Don't Know If There Is a Fix"). The book provides space for the experiences cemetery citizens wanted to talk about, and issues they raised, without accompanying commentary on each of them.[129] Though I chose which interview excerpts would be featured in the book, and how to reshape them into poems, I didn't want to loom over everything my interlocutors said, connecting and interpreting. Often their words are enough.

After learning about poetic inquiry from writing studies scholar Collie Fulford, I unexpectedly found myself writing poems of my own, which had no direct relation to other sources. I have included a few here. To me, these are the real "found poems" (the ones I constructed from interview transcripts seem more like "heard poems"). Poet Marilyn Nelson says, "Poetry consists of words and phrases and sentences that emerge like something coming out of water. They emerge before us, and they call up something in us. But then they turn us back into our own silence."[130]

It's common to think of poetry as more complex than prose, or at least requiring more interpretation to find the hidden threads of meaning in metaphors, line breaks, and other techniques. Writing this book, I experienced poetry as the opposite. My poems often came out of moments when I was stuck, and in them I have expressed my thoughts in as direct and unfiltered a way as I could.[131] All the footnotes, the qualifiers, and the work of separating different kinds of truth—especially the scholarly and the personal—fell away.

Cemetery Citizens also includes drawings. When I first started this project, I thought I'd take my sketchpad along on cemetery workdays and draw the things I was seeing there. I wanted a way to capture not just the grave markers and landscapes, but also the activity of volunteers: the way people crouch when they are digging at the roots of a vine; how they gather around a marker they've just discovered underneath the dirt, watching with quiet reverence as someone washes it with water.

A few of those drawings are in my sketchbooks. But for the most part I haven't made them. Usually, I am just too busy at the cemeteries. When I go to workdays, I'm not comfortable sitting and sketching while other people work. I join in the weeding and brush-clearing, trying to be of use while occasionally scribbling some notes. Anthropologist Andrew Causey describes this dilemma well: "How can one, after all, join in on the dynamism of life while also being in the state of reserve required of careful watching?"[132] I often felt overwhelmed by all the things that might be in my compositions: the plants, graves, people, dogs, and more.

When I do draw in cemeteries, I am usually alone. At Geer Cemetery, in the early days of the pandemic, I found myself drawing the cemetery when it felt empty, lonely, unnoticed: the opposite of the workdays where I had struggled to step out of the action and make a sketch. Suddenly I was writing a book about cemeteries as vibrant places of public life and political dialogue, while drawing a reality that contradicted it.

Eventually, I found a compromise: snapping photos on busy workdays and then sketching them, or parts of them,

FIGURE INTRO.2.   Black-and-white sketch of two volunteers bending toward the ground, from a March 2023 workday at Geer Cemetery. One volunteer is facing the viewer, with bangs, glasses, a ponytail, and gardening gloves. She crouches low with one arm resting on a knee and the other reaching down. The other volunteer has short hair and glasses; she faces away from the viewer, reaching with two gloved hands toward weeds on the ground. Drawing by the author, March 2023.

afterward. The drawings wind up somewhere in the gray zone between documentary and a more imaginative response. They are less complete and less
detailed than photographs. They emphasize the movement that I saw, the interactions between living bodies and spaces of the dead. How "we move in spaces of
repair," as Angela Thorpe put it.

Cemetery citizens teach themselves new skills, operating forever at the edge
of their own expertise. My drawings—done in the hand of a lifelong doodler
under no illusions about his formal skills—are similar. They are my own form of
scrappy care: full of imperfection and effort, in excess of any obvious need. The
time and effort I've spent drawing, like the poems, is a way to bear witness, to
love these places and these people beyond the limits of academic prose. A drawing, "good" or not, is a way of caressing things with lines.

Part I

THE FIELDS FULL OF WEEDS

There are times—and finding Zora Hurston's grave was one of them—when normal responses of grief, horror and so on do not make sense because they bear no real relation to the depth of emotion one feels. It was impossible for me to cry when I saw the field full of weeds where Zora is.

ALICE WALKER, "Looking for Zora"

There are no unsacred places;
there are only sacred places
and desecrated places.

WENDELL BERRY, "How to be a Poet"

ONE

"When Summer Comes Again, the Cemetery Disappears"

Geer

I WATCHED THE CHANGING OF THE SEASONS AT GEER CEMETERY
(Found poem using text from Jessica Thompson Eustice's
"The Geer Cemetery," June 8, 2002)[1]

In the summer the cemetery becomes
completely overgrown
with brush and vines. One cannot see
grave markers from the road
at all. When the fall comes,
and the leaves start to die down,
the markers start to appear.

By late winter Reverend Joyner's headstone,
in the shape of a lily, is clearly visible
from the road. Then in spring,
the trees are draped in blooming wisteria
and daffodils spring up.
When summer comes again,
the cemetery disappears.

African American Burial Grounds in Southern Memory Landscapes

East End and Geer Cemetery are post-Emancipation burial grounds created by
and for African Americans at a time when White cemeteries would not admit
them. They are both verdant places with a wide variety of grave markers, from
humble stones to ornate obelisks. In their materials, sizes, and inscriptions, the
markers reflect differences in wealth and status. They also feature declarations

of religious faith and affiliations with businesses, churches, and mutual aid societies that helped pay for burials.

Both cemeteries are situated in southern cities with a deep sense of history. They both had thriving business districts once referred to as "Black Wall Street": Durham's Hayti neighborhood and Richmond's Jackson Ward (Jackson Ward was also sometimes called "the Harlem of the South"). In both cities, these hubs of Black wealth and civic life were destroyed by highway construction, housing discrimination, and other "urban renewal" policies.[2] (Another neighborhood referred to as "Black Wall Street," the Greenwood District of Tulsa, Oklahoma, was burned by White rioters in the Tulsa race massacre of 1921.)

Over the past few years, Geer has transformed dramatically. In many ways, it is a model of what can go right when a community organizes around a marginalized cemetery. For decades, local community leaders and activists tended to the cemetery itself while building public support for its reclamation. Despite eras of waning activity, one way or another someone has always stepped in again. Sharing this history of Geer Cemetery and the Friends of Geer, I offer an affirming but realistic portrait of the years and dedication it takes to revise a marginalized cemetery, making it once again a valued public space for descendants and many others.

The successes at Geer, however, are taking place in a memory landscape full of other, even more precarious African American burial grounds. Through work with the Durham Black Burial Grounds Collaboratory, a university-cemetery partnership that I cofounded in 2021, I have learned about Little River, Snowhill, Holman Cemetery, and other burial grounds sandwiched between corporate offices, new subdivisions, and abandoned railway tracks. Geer is closer to downtown, accessible from residential streets. Burials there also span a unique period in the history of Durham and the nation: beginning just over a decade after Emancipation, continuing through the rise of Jim Crow segregation laws in North Carolina, and ending just before what is traditionally considered the dawn of the civil rights movement in the 1950s. Geer's landscape marks this transitional era in many ways. Its visible headstones (a small minority of the burials in the cemetery) are not the plain fieldstones or simple, hand-carved markers one sees in many burial grounds of enslaved people in the area. But neither does it have the wide pathways and clear grids of the public cemetery opened for African Americans in the mid-1920s, Beechwood.[3] Geer speaks to

FIGURE 1.1. A plot at Geer Cemetery with stone posts and a bent wrought iron gate at its front. One of the posts has a large heart motif, with the initials "R. D." at its center. In the background, tall, vine-covered trees are visible, and some headstones. Photograph by the author, October 12, 2020.

what Black Durham aspired to be when slavery ended, and its conditions—now and during its period of burial activity—reflect the entrenchment of Jim Crow and the broken promises of Reconstruction.[4]

The energy around Geer Cemetery has helped mobilize people against development that threatened other local cemeteries; but it also creates a stark contrast with the continued systemic neglect and precariousness of these other sites. Descendants of the Fitzgerald and Henderson families have expressed outrage at the historical distortions, encroachment, and degradation of the two historic African American burial grounds bearing their names.[5] Both cemeteries border Maplewood, the city's most famous cemetery, which is home to the pristine tombs of many prominent White families, including a mausoleum for the Dukes and the grave of the prominent White supremacist Julian Carr.

In contrast, Robert and Richard Fitzgerald, buried in their family cemetery just down a slope from some of Maplewood's most lavish tombs, still await the recognition due to them and their graves. The Fitzgeralds were brothers who grew up as free Blacks in the mid-Atlantic. Both served the Union in different capacities in the Civil War and then made the uncommon choice to move South after the war ended. Robert became an educator, and Richard a highly successful brickmaker and bank president who helped build Durham's Black Wall Street and its key institutions. Robert's granddaughter Pauli Murray, the famed civil rights activist, feminist, priest, and poet, chronicles her upbringing in the family home next to Maplewood in her book *Proud Shoes: The Story of an American Family*. Murray describes the Whites-only cemetery as "a powerful enemy advancing relentlessly upon us," whose twentieth-century expansion gradually flooded the family land and rotted the house. Yet she also spent her childhood playing and wandering throughout the cemetery: "Strange, now that I think of it, but I was on better speaking terms with and knew more about the dead white people of Durham than I did about the living ones," she writes. Murray fought, unsuccessfully, to have the city take responsibility for the Fitzgerald cemetery. This was finally accomplished by other advocates in 1993, eight years after her death, and thus far has not led to the kind of care she would have wanted for this burial ground, which has no city marker and is often strewn with litter.[6] Every step forward we take at Geer becomes a lens for seeing the failures that still surround us.[7]

Geer and East End show how differently cemetery revisions can unfold— how the deep history of a place, and the local politics of preservation, can change the story. The two cemeteries are situated in very different memory landscapes. Richmond is the former capital of the Confederacy. The city's Hollywood Cemetery is a kind of living memorial to Confederate narratives, home to the grave of the Confederacy's president, Jefferson Davis, twenty-eight Confederate generals, a towering pyramid-shaped memorial for dead Confederate soldiers, and a Jewish Confederate Memorial (the day after my first visit to East End Cemetery, I went there and confronted how little I knew about Jews who fought for the enslavement of other people).[8] These features helped make Richmond one of the most contested and creative sites where Black Lives Matter activists and their allies reshaped public space after the murders of George Floyd and other victims of police violence in 2020.[9]

Meanwhile, as human rights advocate Robin Kirk explains:

> Durham is distinct from many southern cities that host universities and have Confederate statues: neither the city nor the county existed during the Civil War. Durham took shape after the war, fed by tobacco and the railroad. To get prized bright-leaf tobacco to northern markets, merchants such as Washington Duke and Julian S. Carr needed warehouse workers to grade and pack leaf, to weave tobacco bags, and later to run newfangled cigarette-making machines. Formerly enslaved people flocked here for work. . . . Although Durham enforced the same violent segregation as other places, the African-American community found ways to prosper.[10]

A limited "spirit of biracial cooperation" offered Black entrepreneurs opportunities to succeed and shape Durham's future, even as the city remained structured with "a vast disparity in wealth" between its Black and White populations—and a heavily exploited population of female tobacco workers (the famed Black Wall Street entrepreneurs were all men; women, while providing much of the labor in the tobacco factories, were rarely able to build businesses).[11]

After a visit to Durham in 1912, the pioneering African American sociologist W. E. B. Du Bois wrote that in Durham,

> a black man may get up in the morning from a mattress made by black men, in a house which a black man built out of lumber which black men cut and planed; he may put on a suit which he bought at a colored haberdashery and socks knit at a colored mill; he may cook victuals from a colored grocery on a stove which black men fashioned; he may earn his living working for colored men, be sick in a colored hospital, and buried from a colored church; and the Negro insurance society will pay his widow enough to keep his children in a colored school. This is surely progress.[12]

In 1925, another sociologist, E. Franklin Frazier, called Durham the "capital of the Black middle class" in the United States.[13]

The "Negro insurance society" Du Bois mentions is North Carolina Mutual and Provident Association. Founded in 1898 by seven prominent African American businessmen, the company became a major engine for building Black wealth in Durham and the largest Black-owned insurance company in the United States (defrauded by a New York investor, the ailing company folded in 2022).[14] In *Black Businesses in the New South*, historian Walter B. Weare writes that it was among "the most conspicuous institutional legac[ies] of the ideas of racial self-help and economic solidarity" at the turn of the twentieth century.[15] North Carolina Mutual's first specialty was burial insurance. The company collected a small weekly fee so that insured clients would have access to a dignified funeral and burial.[16] Durham's great Black business was also a bridge directly to its Black burial grounds.

"Entitled to the Respect of Decent People"

Geer Cemetery's history begins before the founding of North Carolina Mutual, on land that was not yet part of Durham.[17] In 1877, a White farming couple in Orange County sold two acres of land to three African American men: Willis (Willie) Moore, John O'Daniel, and Nelson Mitchell. The deed specifies a cost of fifty dollars, with the land to be used "as a cemetary for the colored people."[18] The couple, Jesse and Polly Geer, along with their son Frederick C. Geer, owned hundreds of acres of land and had enslaved dozens of people.[19]

Why the Geers chose to sell this plot of land for a cemetery is unclear. According to a 1992 interview with Willis G. Carpenter, a White man who grew up near the cemetery, the first person buried there was an eleven-year-old boy who had been dragged to his death by a mule on Jesse Geer's farm. After that, Jesse Geer offered up the spot as a burial ground—so, according to one interpretation, the 1877 deed was formalizing or expanding upon an earlier understanding.[20] A monument marking the entrance to the cemetery now tells the story of the boy killed by a mule, though no documentation has been found to verify it, and it originates outside the community that buried their dead in Geer for generations. It is possible that, as is the case with many African American cemeteries founded after Emancipation, the site had long been used to bury enslaved people.[21]

The founders worked to expand the cemetery as burials began to fill it up. Geer's trustees, who now numbered seven, purchased just short of another full acre in 1887.[22] Another one-acre purchase was completed in 1905.[23] Art and visual culture historian Kaylee Alexander led a major effort to compile and analyze data about burials at Geer in preparation for *In Plain Sight*, an outdoor exhibit mounted at the cemetery in 2021 (and again at Duke two years later by my students). The team's work resulted in a searchable database with information on over seventeen hundred people buried at Geer. Only about two hundred of them have visible markers.[24] Alexander estimates that as many as two thousand people were buried at Geer Cemetery; the number remains indeterminate because no death certificates are available before September 1909, meaning that many of the burials for the first few decades of the cemetery's existence are unrecorded.

Many notable Durham pioneers are buried at Geer. Margaret Ruffin Faucette was born enslaved and is thought to have taught herself to read using a Bible. After Emancipation, she held prayer circles in a rented room, laying the foundation for what would become White Rock Baptist Church, an important Black congregation in Durham.[25] In February 1960, just after the start of the famous civil rights sit-ins at a Woolworth in nearby Greensboro, Martin Luther King Jr. delivered his speech "A Creative Protest" at White Rock. In it, he declared, "You students of North Carolina . . . have taken the undying and passionate yearning for freedom and filtered it in your own soul and fashioned it into a creative protest that is destined to be one of the glowing epics of our time."[26] Augustus Shepard, the founder of an orphanage and a pastor at White Rock, was also buried at Geer. His body was removed in 1935 and brought to Beechwood, Durham's city-owned Black cemetery, founded half a century after Geer.[27] There he joined his wife, Hattie, a graduate of Hampton Institute and an educator, and their son James Shepard. James was the founder of the religious training school that has since evolved into North Carolina Central University.[28]

Another set of church founders, Edian Markham and Mollie (or Millie) Markham, are also buried at Geer. Their church, St. Joseph AME, still has an active congregation and is now home to the Hayti Heritage Center, which commemorates the neighborhood dismantled by city planners and fosters arts and cultural programming in Durham.

The cemetery has gone by many names: City Cemetery, City Colored Cemetery, and Geer Cemetery among them. As historian and Friends of Geer board member Nicholas Levy points out, the "City Cemetery" and "City Colored Cemetery" monikers are misleading: this cemetery was, in his words, "a private response to a lack of public responsibility."[29] The people who buried their dead at Geer were, in a sense, double-charged for burial; they "paid taxes to support the maintenance of a cemetery—Maplewood—that they could not use, while maintaining a large, community, nondenominational cemetery—Geer—at their own expense."[30]

Persistent references to Jesse Geer's having "donated" the land seem strange to me.[31] The fifty dollars paid by Moore, O'Daniel, and Mitchell was no small sum at the time.

Students often ask me why we still use the name Geer Cemetery, since it commemorates the enslavers who once owned the land. But the memories, histories, and lines of descent that travel through the name Geer are not so simple. Priscilla, a woman enslaved in the Geer household, had four children fathered by Frederick Geer. One of Priscilla's sons, John Wesley Geer, is buried at Geer Cemetery. Priscilla is believed to be in the cemetery too. Neither has a visible marker, and we do not know the exact location of their graves.[32] John Wesley Geer's great-granddaughter, Deidre "DD" Barnes, has been among the most engaged members of the Friends of Geer Cemetery since its first incarnation in the early 2000s, and now serves as the organization's vice president. She has family members on both her mother's and father's side buried in the cemetery. Her father, Ernie Barnes, left a career in professional football to become a celebrated painter.

I asked DD what she thought about when she referred to the cemetery by the name "Geer." She paused for a moment, then replied, "I think of John [Wesley Geer]. Yeah, that's who I think of. . . . I think about John and wonder, you know, what type of person was he? Then I think about Fred too, what type of person was he?"[33] The name Geer Cemetery commemorates both Frederick and John Wesley, father and son: a White farmer who enslaved people; and a Black man born into slavery, who appears in a portrait with a long nose, bow tie, and handlebar mustache, and whose death notice describes him as "an old citizen of Durham and well respected in the community in which he lived by both white and colored citizens."[34] Both of those types of person.

According to neighbor Willis Carpenter, Geer was once a grand place: "It had a fence going around it. It had a big gate with an arch on it. . . . It was a nice place out there. Folks would drive buggies out there and work on the graveyard."[35] By 1900, though, reports of Geer's declining conditions appeared in the *Durham Sun*:

The colored burying grounds, or cemetery, just beyond Mr. F. C. Geer's, out on the Roxboro road, is in rather bad shape. Numbers of the graves have sunken in, and in some instances not a thing can be seen to even indicate exactly where some of the graves are located. There are traces of where fire has recently burned the grass and straw over a portion of the burying ground, and several of the pine boards at the head and foot of the graves were burned, destroying all mark to show where the graves were.

A gentleman tells us that not very long ago, on one of the head boards he noticed that some vandal had written some very unbecoming words. As soon as the gentleman saw it, he very properly set about to erase them and succeeded in doing so. A person, be he white or colored, that would stoop to such a despicable act, is mean enough to do anything and is not entitled to the respect of decent people.[36]

African American citizens of Durham tried their best to get the city to do something about the situation. The minutes of a Board of Aldermen (later renamed City Council) meeting from 1904 records a petition for the city to purchase land "for the burial of colored persons." It continues: "The City is asked to buy a lot and let it remain in charge of the City with regulations similar to those that obtained in the case of the Cemetery for white people."[37] These requests would remain unheard for over twenty years, during which time the most the city would do for Geer was to enclose it with a modest fence.[38]

A panel from the *In Plain Sight* exhibit describes how the cemetery's surroundings were changing even as it was kept in a relatively consistent state of neglect. As the city grew, development expanded into the farmland around the cemetery. Levy says, "By the mid 1920s, Geer Cemetery had become an uncomfortable outpost of African American bodies amidst a segregated, White neighborhood."[39]

African American citizens once again came before the City Council, in 1926, asking for it to purchase the land just to the east of the cemetery for more burials. The White neighbors petitioned against it, and they won. That land has been occupied for over forty years by a parking lot for telephone company trucks, which are always in view from the otherwise secluded, woodsy east side of the cemetery. It is a different kind of vandalism than graffiti or trash, but it radically alters and degrades the conditions at Geer.[40]

In the mid-1920s, African Americans seeking a dignified place to bury their dead could celebrate an overdue victory: the opening of Beechwood Cemetery, the first city-funded burial ground for Black people in Durham. Some families who could afford it had their deceased loved ones moved to Beechwood from the overgrown, underfunded burial grounds where they had been interred. These included Geer, the Fitzgerald family cemetery, Hickstown Church Cemetery, and Violet Park. As poet and scholar Alexis Pauline Gumbs writes, "In addition to being a contemporary burial site, Beechwood is where Black people go when they are evicted from what would have been their final homes."[41] The Black dead were on the move, toward a place where their loved ones hoped they could receive perpetual care. John Merrick, the influential Durham entrepreneur who had named Violet Park after his mother, was buried in that cemetery in 1919. But he was moved to Beechwood along with most of the people buried there, before it was paved over and turned into a church parking lot.[42]

By the mid-1940s, the Board of Health closed Geer Cemetery, declaring it full. By this time, it appears, people were already being buried on top of one another.[43] A 1942 letter from Caleb W. Morgan, who calls himself the "custodian" of Geer Cemetery, pleads for help from the city "to have this cemetery cleaned up and the trash and filth removed therefrom." The city tersely denied the request.[44]

A sequence of aerial photographs used in the *In Plain Sight* exhibit, from 1940, 1955, and 1972, shows the open land around Geer gradually filling in with buildings. As the spaces around it grow less green, the cemetery itself becomes a forest. In a video made for the exhibit, DD Barnes recalls:

> The first time I actually saw the cemetery was when I was a young girl riding with my grandfather. We didn't even know it was a cemetery because it was overgrown; there were so many leaves and trees, poison ivy, vines. You couldn't see the markers, the grave markers. And he just told us, "You have cousins up in there." And we thought, "Oh my gosh, we have cousins that are living in the woods over there!" I found out later that no, there was a cemetery there.[45]

A path of dirt and gravel, referred to as the carriage road, loops through the middle of Geer Cemetery. After years of clearing, on a five-minute walk around this road, you can now see most of the cemetery. Some of the grave markers, such as George W. Pearson's (1821–1902; "Death Is Eternal Life, Why Should We Weep") are in pristine shape. In some places you can see what's left of rows of stones, which once likely supported metal fences and railings that distinguished one family's plot from another's. Along the path, granite markers divide the cemetery into loose, boundary-less sections named after prominent people who were buried in the cemetery: Margaret Faucette, Edian Markham, Augustus Shepard. These were installed in the early 2000s by one of the earliest groups of volunteers seeking to reclaim the cemetery.

Many of the grave markers have not fared so well. There are cracked headstones, and precariously balanced headstones that were subjected to well-intentioned but hasty repairs (not conducted by the Friends of Geer Cemetery). The headstone of Mary Sparkman (birth date unknown; died 1915), who worked in the Duke household and was laid to rest under a headstone proclaiming that family's beneficence ("Erected to the memory of Mary Sparkman by Mr. & Mrs. B.N. Duke whom she served faithfully"), is in a wooded section at the edge of the cemetery. It was upright when I started visiting Geer; now it is flat on the ground about six feet from its base. Amid humble cement markers, many likely purchased from a mail-order catalogue, are striking signs of ingenuity. The headstone of Reverend Abraham (or Abram) Joyner, who worked as a doorman at one of Durham's tobacco factories and preached the gospel outside of work hours, resembles a flower with five petals.[46] The ornate headstone was designed as an architectural element for a building façade but seems to have been repurposed for use in the cemetery. A simplified version of it now serves as the logo for the Friends of Geer Cemetery.

The inscriptions on Geer's headstones often reflect the religious faith of the people buried there. "Budded on earth to bloom in heaven" (Charles T. Evans, 1910–1913). Others praise virtue amid hardship: "He was true to his friends, devoted to his church, loyal to his state, and made the best of his opportunities" (George W. Macklin, 1847–1907); "As a wife, devoted; As a mother, affectionate; As a friend, ever kind and true" (Susan Richardson, 1867–1919). One humble marker declares, "She hath done what she could" (Julia Newby, abt. 1853–1912).

When I first set foot in Geer, in 2018, roughly half of the cemetery had been cleared enough for the graves to be visible from the path. You could explore further if you were willing to walk over vines, into and out of the depressions in the earth that were often the only remaining sign of someone's burial location. The other half of the cemetery, on the east side of the carriage road, was a wall of ivy.

I usually go to Geer by bike. I travel from my neighborhood close to Duke's East Campus into the Duke Park neighborhood, which gets its name from a neighborhood park at its center. The park has colorful play structures, a small dog run, and a badly aged tennis court. I ride past a sign that reads, "Gentrifiers out of our neighborhood!"—the phrase repeated over and over, like a mantra.

In recent months, Carissa Trotta, the volunteer coordinator for the Friends of Geer (and an archaeologist), began scheduling Saturday workdays at the cemetery. The goal was to prepare for an upcoming archaeological survey, but it also wound up creating a tight community of "regulars" who showed up reliably, pouring hours into a site where work had previously been far more sporadic. Geer is no longer nearly as overgrown as it was when I arrived in Durham. As I write this, little flags dot its surface, marking depressions and objects that have been found in the cemetery—many of them likely grave goods, left intentionally in memory of the dead. Neon-colored flags may not be the best aesthetic choice over the long term, but for now they speak to the level of attention and care that Geer is receiving—which some Durham residents have been dreaming of, and fighting for, since the beginning of the twentieth century.

Reclaiming Yesterday and Today

In the mid-1980s, R. Kelly Bryant Jr. began organizing a chorus of voices to express their concern about Geer. Bryant was the great-grandson of Margaret Ruffin Faucette, the church pioneer buried in Geer; his grandfather, Robert Lee Poole, was also buried in the cemetery. Raised in Rocky Mount, North Carolina, Bryant moved to Durham after graduating from Hampton University. He then spent most of his career at North Carolina Mutual Life (the name, from 1919 onward, of the former North Carolina Mutual and Provident Association). He was a trustee at White Rock, scoutmaster, Freemason, NAACP member, and more. A beloved historian of Black Durham, he collected funeral programs and other archival materials that are now part of the Durham County Library's collections. Bryant seems to have turned his attention to Geer after receiving a request for help from Doris Tilley, a local archivist and historian who was conducting a survey of local cemeteries.[47]

As the *In Plain Sight* exhibit recounts, Bryant "unleashed a relentless stream of letters to libraries, archives, local historians, fellow descendants, and potential allies in the push to better document—and hopefully clean up—the over-grown burial ground."[48] Among his key partners were historians Jean Bradley Anderson (who had written a letter to a local newspaper advocating for the cemetery's preservation) and Alice Eley Jones, a professor at North Carolina Central University, as well as Frances Rollins, the president of the Historic Preservation Society of Durham. Their efforts resulted in the first city-sponsored cleanup efforts in the cemetery, approved in 1989.

In the early 1990s, a youth work-study program, the Durham Service Corps, won a grant to work in the cemetery and create a social studies program based on it. The curriculum, spearheaded by local educator Denise Rowson, begins with a series of thoughtful questions about the burial ground:

Who owns the cemetery

Who let it get so run down?

Why is the cemetery all Black?

What famous people, if any, are buried there?

Why isn't it a Durham landmark?[49]

Within a few years of the publication of the group's experiential-learning curriculum, "Reclaiming Yesterday," the Durham Service Corps folded due to lack of funding.[50] For nearly a decade, progress at the cemetery stalled.

In 2003, Bryant, who was in his mid-eighties at that point, sought to reinvigorate efforts to maintain the cemetery and form an organization dedicated to the space. Jessica Eustice, a former history teacher, joined him. She and her husband, David, had bought a house facing Geer in 1999; they were told it was an "abandoned lot" but soon discovered grave markers, sunken burial plots, and the humble sign Bryant had made to mark the cemetery.[51] Eustice made researching the cemetery her focus for a "Documenting Durham" class she took at Duke's Center for Documentary Studies, and left a copy of her paper in Bryant's mailbox. Soon the Friends of Geer Cemetery was born.[52]

This incarnation of the Friends met regularly for at least five years and made important progress. They raised funds to put an elegant granite marker at the entrance to the cemetery, telling a capsule version of its history and surrounded by plantings. Eustice, a White woman, is ambivalent about the marker now. She wanted something permanent that would speak to the group's capabilities and determination. But she worries that Bryant and the others were humoring her, going along out of politeness with her suggested location for the new marker, at the other end of the cemetery from Bryant's handmade sign—which would also have been an appropriate site for something more permanent.[53] (In January 2023, I snapped a photo of Bryant's handmade sign during a workday. It looked fragile but was still standing, a tribute to his efforts. When I returned in early April with Debra Taylor Gonzalez-Garcia, we found that the sign had split and fallen. Half of it was on the ground near the post, and the other half was nowhere

FIGURE 1.2. A rectangular metal sign midway down a metal post, reading "Geer Cemetery 1877–1944," installed by R. Kelly Bryant. The sign has a vertical crack running down the middle. It stands among fallen leaves, with trees and headstones behind it. Photograph by the author, November 12, 2022.

to be found. Near where the sign had stood, strangely, eggshells were scattered on the ground.)

Friends of Geer Cemetery member Carrie McNair led the group in analyzing city records to come up with biographical data on over fifteen hundred people buried at the cemetery. They pushed, unsuccessfully, for the city to take ownership of Geer.

In what would become a familiar cycle, the City of Durham promised the organization quarterly maintenance, contracting with a local nonprofit for the work, but didn't sustain the effort. The funding was meant to be temporary while the organization sought other sponsors.[54] Friends of Geer Cemetery minutes from 2005 show concern that "the weeds are growing up again."[55]

In 2012, David Eustice posted a video describing the cemetery as overgrown and asking for renewed attention to it.[56] The Friends organization, too, was entering cycles of dormancy and "reconstitution."[57] Kelly Bryant, after a long illness, died in December 2015 at age ninety-eight. Jessica Eustice and city councilman Eddie Davis were left trying to keep the cemetery in the public eye.

On February 16, 2019, I attended a meeting that Eustice convened at a local library branch in Durham. The small basement conference room was filled with people who had been working at the cemetery for years—Eustice, Eddie Davis, DD Barnes, and preservation advocate Tom Miller among them—as well as some local students and other newcomers. Eustice introduced everyone to Debra Taylor Gonzalez-Garcia, a genealogist who moved to North Carolina from Virginia to attend North Carolina Central University. Debra then stayed in Wake County, near Durham, to work at IBM. Her interest in the cemetery was sparked via her research on Millie/Mollie Markham, the St. Joseph AME Church pioneer. Markham was interviewed for a collection of narratives of formerly enslaved people, funded by the Works Progress Administration in the late 1930s.[58] Debra had read the interview and was trying to get a sense of what was going on with the cemetery where Markham was buried. Once she had learned about Geer, she volunteered to help with the flagging efforts there.

A month later, these conversations went from tentative to urgent. A neighbor who owned a house bordering the cemetery had hired a crew to cut down some trees, claiming they were in danger of falling on his house. (This same neighbor had, years earlier, constructed a shed on what was rather obviously part of the cemetery, not his land.) The crew felled a massive tree that slammed down into the cemetery, cracking headstones. Someone called the police, who said they could not do anything because the property lines were unclear. Tom Miller began to fear that the neighbor's real intent was to clear a lot for building, encroaching further on the cemetery and with yet more damage to come.

We had a meeting at Jessica and David Eustice's house, across the street from Geer. The long-term solution might be getting the city to take ownership of the cemetery—something we are still working on today. In the meantime, we agreed, the most we could do was keep up a steady presence there. We needed regular workdays, and more people with their eyes on the cemetery: signs of life and presence in this place of the dead. Over the next few months, a reinvigorated Friends of Geer Cemetery formed, with Debra Taylor Gonzalez-Garcia as the new president, and DD Barnes stepping into the role of vice president a few years later.

The newest incarnation of the Friends of Geer Cemetery is going full steam, with regular workdays and community events, a committee dedicated to locating and engaging descendants (led by descendants themselves), and a cadre of volunteers researching the people buried in the cemetery. "Day of Honor" posts on Facebook commemorate their birthdays and share details of their lives. Duke students, working with my colleagues Alicia Jiménez, Andrew Tharler, Ed Triplett, and me, have documented the locations of grave markers, created three-dimensional photogrammetric models of them, aided in historical research, and brought the *In Plain Sight* exhibit about the cemetery to Duke's campus.

As the organization continues our work, we will also face major decisions about what the cemetery should look like, where and how to share its stories. How "clear" should the cemetery be, and how much should we preserve it as a wooded space? How do you best acknowledge those interred at Geer who have no marker? Finding living descendants is a slow process, requiring research in incomplete archives, tracing complex family trees and people on the move. How much descendant input is enough to make consequential decisions about the cemetery's future? How do we get there without putting too much of a burden on the small group of descendants who regularly participate in the organization?

"The Graves Became Bigger"

Historian Thomas Laqueur writes, "As far back as people have discussed the subject, care of the dead has been regarded as foundational—of religion, of the polity, of the clan, of the tribe, of the capacity to mourn, of an understanding of the finitude of life, of civilization itself."[59] Attacks on this foundational institution, care of the dead, have been manifold and ever-present in American experience, beginning with "trampling over the bones of indigenous peoples" and robbing their graves.[60] During the Middle Passage, slave traders threw the bodies of the dead or ill overboard.[61] On North American soil, an untold number of enslaved people were buried with only trees or fieldstones to mark their resting place, if that. From the late 1870s through the mid-twentieth century, White mobs turned the extrajudicial murder of Black people into the public spectacle of lynching, often attended by White families with their children and captured in popular postcards.[62]

Black mourners and activists have long made funerals into sites of resistance. "Funerals may have been one of the few times that antebellum slave communities could assume control of the symbolism around them, and thus create the dignity at death that negated the 'social death' of their slave status," writes archaeologist Ross W. Jamieson.[63] An 1800 rebellion of enslaved people near Richmond, Virginia, led by a man named Gabriel, was thought to have been partly organized at an infant's funeral.[64] This tradition of pairing death rituals with acts of resistance continued into the mid-twentieth century in funerals, collective mourning, and artistic responses to the murders of Medgar Evers, Emmett Till, and the four young girls killed in a church bombing in Alabama: Cynthia Wesley, Addie Mae Collins, Carole Robertson, and Denise McNair. Karla FC Holloway observes, "Giving bodies back to grieving mothers, being taken to bodies by anxious grandparents, or anticipating the graphic photos of *Jet*, we inscribed these mourning stories into our national culture until they told us, surely and consistently, about the quality of our living and the quantities of our dying."[65] In the twenty-first century, as poet Claudia Rankine writes in the *New York Times*, "The Black Lives Matter movement can be read as an attempt to keep mourning an open dynamic in our culture because black lives exist in a state of precariousness. Mourning then bears both the vulnerability inherent in black lives and the instability regarding a future for those lives. Unlike earlier black-power movements that tried to fight or segregate for self-preservation, Black Lives Matter aligns with the dead, continues the mourning and refuses the forgetting in front of all of us."[66] That "alignment with the dead" is reflected in the new interest, nationwide, in the preservation of African American burial grounds.

During the period I was working on this book, George Floyd, Ahmaud Arbery, Breonna Taylor, Daunte Wright, Andrew Brown Jr., and many, many other African Americans were executed by police, or by White people who had invested themselves with the authority to patrol their homes and neighborhoods with murderous and unprovoked violence.[67] Family members of Emmett Till, Breonna Taylor, Philando Castile, and Oscar Grant all gathered at Daunte Wright's funeral in Minneapolis in April 2021.[68] Calling for justice and accountability, they formed a community of mourners.

The decline of a cemetery is not as violent a spectacle as lynching, mutilation, or other forms of necroviolence that a White supremacist nation has visited upon Black bodies.[69] But it, too, leaves its mark for generations, disrupting the care that binds the living to the dead.[70] Landscape architect Anjelyque Easley-DeLuca associates degraded African American burial grounds with the violation of three basic rights: the right to grieve, the right to land, and the right to history.[71]

Morgan Jerkins writes, "Black cemetery loss is a national crisis."[72] Around the United States, this crisis takes the shape of overgrowth and vandalism, climate change and increased flooding, cemeteries paved over for highways and parking lots, "cemeteries underwater, cemeteries hidden underneath sprawling golf courses, cemeteries inaccessible to those whose relatives are buried there because they are tucked within gated communities called plantations."[73] Describing Richmond's long history of disturbing and erasing Black graves, genealogist and cemetery citizen Lenora McQueen writes, "My ancestor's grave did not cease to exist because she may now be scattered across the landscape, or stuck under a road. Her grave just got bigger. Many of the graves became bigger. . . . It is all sacred ground."[74]

When it comes to assigning responsibility for the crisis, people tell different stories—stories that sometimes contradict each other. "The black cemeteries are being destroyed, accidentally or on purpose," says Judy Jennings, a longtime researcher and volunteer at Booker T. Washington Cemetery in Southern Illinois, in a story by journalist Jerrel Floyd. At the end of the article, Floyd writes, "After spending time in St. Clair County and talking with descendants of some of those buried at Booker T. Washington and St. George, as well as with researchers like Jennings, I concluded the abandonment of the cemeteries was mostly the result of a series of unfortunate circumstances, instead of deliberate neglect."[75] But "deliberate neglect" is a hard thing to pin down. Neglect does not generally announce itself as intended or deliberate; it works in more subtle ways.[76]

Historically, African Americans have sometimes offered a narrative of their own communities' responsibility for the decline of burial grounds. A 1941 article about Geer Cemetery in Durham's Black newspaper the *Carolina Times* says, "Not only is the manner in which the grounds are kept a reflection on the city, but the colored population, for whom the place was originally set apart, as well. . . . Because surviving Negro relatives have not enough respect for their dead to keep the place cleared or see to it that it is kept, those living in the vicinity, supported by the usual race prejudice, have no respect for it also, and contribute what they can to destroy the place and make it unsightly."[77] Decades later, in her book on Richmond's African American cemeteries, Veronica Davis takes a similar view, acknowledging the context of White supremacy while reserving her greatest frustration for Black Richmonders: "There are not one or two people responsible for the death of black cemeteries, but an entire race. Sure, we could spend years finger-pointing and looking the other way, or we could spend just as much time ourselves lifting a rake, water hose, repairing our cemeteries and keeping them memorable."[78]

This narrative is deeply frustrating to other advocates. In a *New York Times* column about Richmond's African American cemeteries, Brian Palmer writes, "People often ask me how these cemeteries got so bad. Why can't they be like the Confederate Section of Oakwood or Hollywood Cemetery, the immaculate burial ground of thousands of Confederate soldiers? The subtext is: Why can't black people take care of their own stuff?"[79] In this article and his subsequent reporting on how much federal and state funding still goes to monuments and sites of Confederate memory, Brian answers the question by tracing the public investment in White graves and divestment from Black ones.[80] Where both the *Carolina Times* and Veronica Davis lash out at Black communities, and Jerrel Floyd lands mealy-mouthed on the phrase "unfortunate circumstances," Brian follows the money and exposes the structures that undergird neglect.

Marginalized African American cemeteries ask us to think differently about accidents and purposes, and about whose "accidents" are treated as an emergency. While the passing of generations has led to decline in all of Richmond's cemeteries, Ryan K. Smith writes, "white leaders assembled systematic resources to take over care of those grounds' private plots. The city or state came to their assistance while private groups initiated successful fundraising drives among the wealthy. Black cemeteries could count on none of those resources, throwing the sites' destiny into the laps of individual black families trying to make their way."[81] In these families, as East End descendant Thomas A. Taylor recalls, "the people who used to come and take care of the plots"—and who once packed the cemetery so full that on Memorial Days it was hard to find parking—"started to die off."[82]

Segregation, Black disenfranchisement, and White control over resources are among the most obvious structural forces that have fueled overgrowth and degradation in African American cemeteries. But migration and the displacement of descendant communities are also key elements of their histories, and powerful factors in their fates. Greg Melville writes, "In rural areas, Black cemeteries are often the only remaining visible record of African American communities that vanished during the Great Migration, when more than six million people fled the South during the Jim Crow era."[83] As for more urban settings such as Richmond, according to Smith, "Given the push of Jim Crow and the pull of northern factory jobs during the Great Migration, Richmond's overall black population declined for a time in the 1890s and did so again in the 1920s. Many families stayed put, but the few surviving cemetery records also show descendants scattering to New Jersey, New York, and other distant locales."[84]

Durham's economy and infrastructure, physical and social, owe much to African Americans who migrated into the city as it grew in the late nineteenth and early twentieth century. Its population remained about a third African American through the first half of the 1900s. Two of Black Wall Street's most prominent figures, C. C. Spaulding and Aaron McDuffie Moore, petitioned the city's Chamber of Commerce for more investment in education for African Americans and a wage increase, partly to stem the outflow from the region during the Great Migration.[85] Durham has retained and even grown the share of its Black population over time, attracting students, young professionals, and retirees back from the Northeast and elsewhere.[86] But for the Friends of Geer Cemetery, outreach to descendants still involves tracing the migratory paths out from the region and far afield.

Displacement is not merely a matter of migration out of state. The destruction of Durham's Hayti neighborhood, Richmond's Jackson Ward, and ongoing gentrification have pushed people in these cities farther away from their historic neighborhoods, churches, and cemeteries. Seemingly isolated indignities at the cemeteries must be seen in the context of this loss and destruction: a loss of individual people and their stories, but also of neighborhoods, wealth, and networks of care.

The Friends of Geer Cemetery's activities are most obviously directed toward restoring a historic burial ground; but many other things spin out from there. The group hosts workdays with Black social fraternities such as Groove Phi Groove, and partners with Black businesses and organizations. My students Nyrobi Manuel, Kerry Rork, and Huiyin Zhou have mapped the relationships between Durham's "burial networks" of Black funeral homes, businesses, and cemeteries.[87] In a city where the "hurt is so deep," as DD Barnes says about the loss of Hayti, this work is a slow reassembly of the disassembled.[88]

I CAN REMEMBER
(Debra Taylor Gonzalez-Garcia, Friends of Geer Cemetery, March 5, 2021)

I can remember going with my grandmother
to the cemetery, the church cemetery
where her father and mother were buried
and some of her siblings, taking flowers out there.

Even when she wasn't driving, she'd get flowers together
and somebody would take them out. I don't see families
doing those kind of things. I know
in modern-day cemeteries it's kind of frowned upon.
They're like, *Yeah, you can put them out here,*
and a week later we're taking them all up.

I think some of it goes back to the Jim Crow era.
It may not have been welcoming to come out
to that side of town to visit [Geer] cemetery and so,
you know, eventually it did become lost. I think of it

in terms like what they called "sundown towns,"
where you wouldn't be caught after a certain time.

If people were not welcome, they still kind of feel
that way. I think the people who are instrumental
in this preservation don't look like them, didn't grow up
with them. We're outsiders.

                                    I'm an outsider

And I think that's something that the organization,
you know, we just need to be cognizant of.
I don't want it to dampen the spirit
or keep the work from being done. But I know
that there have been too many times
that the communities have been disappointed
or it has that patronizing kind of effect, you know:
Yeah, OK, here they are
coming to save us again.

"The Contrast in the Care and Keeping of Our Cemeteries"

East End

WHERE THE CEMETERY ENDS

Graves dressed up with plastic flowers
beer bottles
under the tree

The question is not where the cemetery ends
but what thin layers of separation
keep us thinking that it does

"The Loss of Stories Sharpens the Hunger"

According to his 1942 draft registration card, Pernett Anthony Jr. was five-foot-three and weighed one hundred twenty-five pounds at age nineteen. A small man. Aside from his height, weight, brown eyes, and dark brown skin, he is listed as having no "other obvious physical characteristics that will aid in identification." At the time, he worked at Richard E. Byrd Flying Field, called "Byrd Air Port" on the draft card. It would later be renamed Richmond International Airport.

We can be relatively certain that Pernett never got to fly in an airplane himself. But they were coming and going, around and over him, while he did his work.

Though young, he had already lived through some trouble. The 1940 U.S. Census found him in the Richmond City Jail. It lists him as eighteen years old, but according to the birth date on his draft card and other documents, he was only sixteen at the time (another kid imprisoned along with him, and listed on the same page of the census, was seventeen). I could find no record of the charges that put him in jail so young.

Four years later, in the October 3, 1944, *Richmond Times-Dispatch*, Pernett's name is listed along with those of four other men as having been indicted on a "housebreaking charge." In 1955, he's in there again, convicted of driving while intoxicated.

In 1946, Pernett married Magnolia Thompson, a twenty-two-year-old from Elizabethton, Tennessee, who lived in Richmond and did laundry work. Pernett's occupation is listed on the marriage certificate simply as "laborer"—a common, if vague, description. Maybe he was still at the airport. Maybe not.

Magnolia lived into her early thirties. As with her husband, the exact dates don't always correspond between documents. She was found unconscious on the corner of St. James and Leigh streets in Richmond, and died later that day, on September 2, 1956. The medical examiner recorded her cause of death as subdural hematoma: a head injury usually caused by trauma from a fall or an assault. She died at St. Philip Hospital, attached to the all-Black St. Philip School of Nursing, which was established to treat Black patients.

Magnolia's death certificate lists her, incorrectly, as "never married." Its terse lines read, "Manner and place of injury unknown." Initially, the police said they could not determine "whether she was struck or fell."[1] Later, detectives ruled it an accident because "they learned that . . . [she] had fallen and struck her head several days before her death."[2] No one who handled her body in her final days of life, or in death, knew much. The documents and newspaper clippings read like the paperwork version of a shrug.

Magnolia's body was taken from the hospital to the State Anatomical Division and cremated soon after. That agency lost most of its early records in flooding decades ago, so I could not get a definite answer as to the whereabouts of her cremains.

Pernett died of neck cancer on May 29, 1964, just nine days after the anniversary of his marriage. He was forty, based on the birthday listed on his draft card. He'd been treated at the Richmond Nursing Home (originally called the Almshouse, and later City Home), a facility serving the poor located just north of Richmond's downtown. His body went from there to Chiles' Funeral Home, a Black-owned family business that opened in 1933 and is still in operation today. It's the same place that had handled his father's body back in 1946.

He was buried at East End, a cemetery in the midst of a long decline. A place where you could be buried without a vault, returned directly to the earth.[3] As with many other people interred there, his grave was marked only with a metal "courtesy marker," a small square picture frame with a stem to poke into the ground, usually offered by funeral homes as a humble substitute for a headstone.[4] "Pernett Anthony, May 1964," it read.

And then it was swallowed up in the soil.

I was with a small group of Saturday volunteers at East End on March 30, 2019, when Erin Hollaway Palmer of the Friends of East End uncovered Pernett's marker a few inches below the soil. She used the occasion to teach a new volunteer how to brush it gently and make it legible.

Finding his grave led us to researching his life. Much of this happened at odd times of night. Erin and I used Ancestry.com and other websites to find documentation, texting each other when we came up with something new (with Erin, who is far more skilled at this type of research, usually taking the lead). Maybe we're the first strangers not employed by a school, prison, or hospital to try to make this sort of record of Pernett Anthony Jr. We gather in cemeteries, and we gather up stories of the dead. The encounters make a relationship of sorts, but not one that is always clear or comfortable.

In *These Silent Mansions*, the poet and essayist Jean Sprackland writes, "The small scrap of detail on a gravestone can make it possible to retrieve the individual. It can open up a story, spring a life into three dimensions. It can be the beginning of a long act of reconstruction, perhaps even of rescue."[5] But in a place like East End, nearly all of these "R" words ("retrieve," "reconstruct," "rescue") seem optimistic. "There are things that cannot be remembered without admitting that a knot of half-signs weaving a story and marking a limit is the story," Avery Gordon writes.[6]

Archival research, whenever its focus moves beyond a few notable, elite, and relatively well chronicled individuals, usually offers us only fragments from lives lived at the margins. They are recorded, if at all, casually and with an explicit lack of care. In Pernett Anthony's case, what little schooling he received (according to the 1940 census, it ended at fifth grade) gave way to time spent in other public institutions: the jail, the nursing home. Those are more or less the only institutions where his existence—and his death—were recorded. The archive for Pernett Anthony is, in the words of philosopher Michel Foucault, "little more than a register of [his] encounter with power."[7] Once Erin started researching others in his family, she found much more of the same: asylums, nursing homes, prisons.

Pernett had a short life, and seemingly not an easy one. Now we come along and start trying to put that story together from the fragments. While I must get permission from a university ethics review board to interview living people, no one (aside from friends I voluntarily consult) tells me what to do with a life like Pernett Anthony Jr.'s, or whether calling up his story only to splice together

FIGURE 2.1. A small metal marker at East End Cemetery, which was provided by Chiles' Funeral Home. It reads "Pernett Anthony, May 1964." The marker is legible but has some rust. The soil around it is moist and freshly dug. Photograph by the author, March 30, 2019.

depressing fragments might be, in Saidiya Hartman's words, "a second order of violence."[8]

Pernett was in jail at sixteen and then he got out. He married a woman with a lovely first name: Magnolia. The research on them forged a strange, one-sided sense of connection for me, a tug in my chest. It has led me many times to call up scenes between these two people whom I'll never know: to imagine haircuts, clothing, voices. You may have already started to do this yourself, trying to know Pernett and Magnolia by imagining them. As Hartman says, "The loss of stories sharpens the hunger for them. So it is tempting to fill in the gaps and to provide closure where there is none. To create a space for mourning where it is prohibited."[9]

Finding ways to reconstruct whatever is possible about a life based on archival research, all the while "amplify[ing] the impossibility of its telling," is a kind of ethics.[10] "Honor silence," Hartman suggests.[11] I include Pernett and Magnolia here because I think it's important to find the stories of the non-notables, the people not invoked in opinion pieces, press releases, or petitions arguing for the cemetery's status as historic, as worthy of preservation.

Well-intentioned people sometimes collapse all of these individual stories into a narrative of struggle, uplift, and overcoming odds. But the odds were against Pernett and Magnolia. Almost all that is left to reconstruct or "rescue" are stories of the way poverty, White supremacy, incarceration, and surveillance constrained their lives, scattered the traces they left in the archives after their early deaths, made them all but disappear.

Pernett's family, if he was still close to any of them, didn't have the money for a headstone when he died—not yet. And in the end, not ever. Magnolia's burial location, if it was ever recorded, is gone.

Dignity and Damage

Brian Palmer, Erin Hollaway Palmer, and their dog, Teacake, live in Church Hill, a rapidly gentrifying Richmond neighborhood. Brian is a tall Black man with glasses, a striking jaw, and bald head. He is a commanding speaker with a deep voice, often gesturing with his fingers outstretched as he talks. Brian grew up in New York, but his family has deep roots in Virginia. Erin is a White woman, also quite tall, with long brown hair, a warm and self-deprecating sense of humor, and an eagle eye for toads, snakes, insects, and headstones hidden among the weeds.

From Brian and Erin's two-story house, I can walk a few blocks in one direction to a dimly lit discount supermarket. A few blocks in the other direction, I can get designer coffee and hip pastries.

East End Cemetery anchors life for Brian, Erin, and Teacake. It's the place of their love and their anger, their passion and pain (Teacake's relationship with the cemetery may be less fraught: it's where she races around off-leash, chasing a ball, and finding the old balls she left on past visits). East End is an artistic muse, a never-ending project, a source of heartbreak, and many other things. But above all, it's *where they go.*

East End was founded in the same post-Emancipation era as Geer, by African Americans who had in many cases been born enslaved. They were building a new world, and that world needed a dignified place to bury their dead—a project they undertook, like so many others, amid the indifference or outright opposition of the White establishment. But East End inhabits a much different memory landscape than Geer, due in part to Richmond's status as the former Confederate capital, a place where contests over memory and public space are acute and closely watched. Work in the cemetery has been difficult due to its scale and the extent to which it was allowed to decline. These challenges are greatly magnified by the fact that East End is adjacent to the much larger Evergreen Cemetery, also a historic African American burial ground. The two cemeteries were in similar, degraded conditions for decades, and many Richmonders understand them as a single place.

I met Brian and Erin when my spouse mentioned Brian's essay in the *New York Times*, "For the Forgotten African-American Dead." She had seen Erin post it on social media; they were elementary school classmates in Denver. I invited Brian and Erin to speak to my class on "Human Rights and the Dead" at Haverford College; not long after, I traveled to Richmond and pulled up weeds at East End with them and other volunteers on a Saturday morning. That afternoon, we stripped to our underwear in their entryway and put our dirty, possibly poison ivy–contaminated clothes straight into their washing machine. I started to imagine this book.

Despite their proximity to each other, I decided to focus on East End rather than Evergreen, because the Friends of East End were my hosts, interlocutors, and my first teachers about how to make revisions in marginalized cemeteries. Their energies, as the name suggests, were directed principally toward East End, though they have also worked in Evergreen.

Something about the scale of East End, and its winding paths into the woods, has also stuck with me. Even with its vines, its broken markers, its many imprints of injustice, the cemetery's beauty sometimes makes me think I'd like to be buried in a place not so different. A place that reveals itself slowly.

East End's sixteen acres begin with a small, mostly flat section that has generally been kept the clearest. Like Geer, it is dense with the dead—graves crowded together, sometimes with vestiges of the dividers that marked off different plots.[12] There are flat grave markers, monuments, a seashell here and there left for the dead. If you walk through this main section, the cemetery rolls down into ravines and thick woods where many graves are hidden in the green.

My research spanned a tumultuous period, from the Enrichmond Foundation's acquisition of Evergreen Cemetery in May 2017 through the foundation's sudden collapse, in June 2022, just as I was finishing my manuscript. Throughout these years, the Friends of East End found themselves having to advocate for the cemetery in ways they had never imagined would be necessary. They wrote letters to politicians and the media, filed Freedom of Information Act requests to clarify how money and information were traveling between Enrichmond and the Virginia Outdoors Foundation, consulted lawyers about their rights to keep working at East End, brought in preservation experts to look at Enrichmond's master plan for Evergreen, testified in court about the ownership of East End, and more.

Even as Enrichmond espoused some of the ideas and discourses of cemetery citizens, it betrayed these things at nearly every turn. "They . . . disrupted a successful reclamation effort and then failed to create one of their own," as Erin puts it.[13] Enrichmond helps bring the values and core practices of cemetery citizens into focus by embodying, at defining moments for the African American cemeteries in Richmond, their exact opposite.

State agencies and individual politicians eagerly threw taxpayer money and support behind an organization with a spotty track record and no demonstrated prior interest in or knowledge about African American heritage sites or cemeteries. Opportunities for community members to follow this process, or voice their opinions, were nearly nonexistent. Seemingly paradoxically, East End and

Evergreen—and the descendant community around them—were being undervalued even as they seemed to be getting a long overdue burst of funding and attention.

The controversy over Enrichmond's control of the cemeteries pitted organizations against each other, dividing members of Richmond's African American establishment and descendants of people buried at the cemeteries, as well as other cemetery citizens. They argued over what counted as proper expertise to serve as stewards of East End and Evergreen, and who had the real backing of the descendant community—a community that is geographically dispersed and diverse in many ways, among them age, class, and politics.

The Friends of East End are the only grassroots cemetery group I know of that effectively went on strike: halting their work in the cemetery for which they are named while demanding accountability from Enrichmond. When they shared their story, I heard other cemetery citizens refer to it as a "cautionary tale." But we rarely elaborated on the cause for caution, or what lesson we ought to learn.

The "cautionary tale" label was sometimes substituted for a real analysis of what was happening in Richmond, and what it meant for anyone doing this work. That analysis is warranted. The situation in Richmond teaches us that new attention to a cemetery can do damage rather than foster revisions. It can damage the cemetery itself, the most important relationships around it, and a city's memory landscape. It can damage trust, the dignity of the dead, and that of living descendants. It can even damage any future attempts at revision.

Some descendants whose ancestors might have been friends or business partners, members of the same fraternal organization or mutual aid group, now think of each other as corrupt or duped. When terms such as "descendant input" and "community engagement" become contested, even weaponized, competing claims become extremely hard to judge. Whose relationships are more authentic? Who is granting more real power to descendants? Whose organization is Black enough, and whose is too White?

On the one hand, places of the dead are often granted less value—commercially, but also socially—than historic neighborhoods or homes, places with more obvious potential uses for the living. Yet large swaths of green space, in growing urban centers, still constitute an important resource.[14] The dead are stakeholders and silent witnesses to what happens at these burial grounds. It is far easier to invoke them in easy phrases about honor and legacy than to reconstitute the places and projects they left behind. Their "hopes, visions, and wisdom" are still written into individual headstones and the landscape writ large; but it takes both skill and care to read them.[15]

"Monuments Have Toppled"

East End is one of a number of cemeteries to the east of Brian and Erin's place, just past the boundaries of Church Hill.[16] To get to it, you head down Oakwood Avenue to East Richmond Road, passing Oakwood Cemetery. Oakwood is home to around seventeen thousand dead Confederates, many of them buried there after being treated at the nearby Chimborazo Hospital, established in 1861 to treat wounded soldiers. The section for Confederate burials runs right along the road, impossible to ignore as you pass by. Until recently, every grave had a small Confederate flag placed before it, with another full-size one on a flagpole waving above them. This display of Confederate memory was toned down only after the nationwide protests triggered by the murder of George Floyd. Before that, it stood arrayed before an apartment complex in a predominantly Black part of Richmond.

Traveling up Stony Run Parkway from Oakwood toward East End feels like entering the woods, except for all the trash on the side of the road: the remains of fast-food meals, torn mattresses. On the right, a sunken field of grass has a bronze sign marking this spot by its historic name, "The Burying Ground for Colored Paupers." This burial ground for poor and non-White people was once part of East End; it was sold back to the city amid early financial woes for use as a potter's field.[17] Once completely overgrown, it has been cleared and rebranded as "The Garden of Lilies": "For the delicate yet fragile children that are laid to rest here." It does not look much like a garden of lilies; it looks like a patch of grass.

If you take the route I have described from Church Hill to East End and Evergreen, one of the first things that may strike you is the contrast with Oakwood. Oakwood, once a segregated cemetery, is cut off from the two African American cemeteries by a creek and a roadway. Its well-manicured lawns are mowed regularly. It has a security booth next to its gate and paved roads running through it. Its headstones, though not all in perfect condition, are mostly clean, legible, and upright.

While East End is benefiting from vigorous, rejuvenated efforts by the

Friends of East End at the time of this writing, in its recent past vegetation covered hundreds of headstones. Some of them are broken, fallen, or with faded inscriptions. Some are under layers of dirt. Many of the metal courtesy markers have been mangled by careless mowing or scattered from their original places. Every time a marker is lost or destroyed, the connection between an individual's name and their burial location is lost.

Oakwood Cemetery has trash bins for visitors. At East End and Evergreen, over the years volunteers have had to remove thousands of old tires, mattresses, couches, construction debris, and, Erin tells me, the occasional dead dog.

On Google Maps, too, Richmond's African American burial grounds are subordinated. Zoomed out far enough to see nearly the entirety of Richmond, both Oakwood and Hollywood Cemetery, the tourist attraction where the Confederate president is buried, appear on the map with their names. From there, one must zoom in three more times to see Evergreen Cemetery noted as a place worthy of recognition. For East End, still one more click. Even Gillies Creek Industrial Recycling, the waste facility next to East End, is labeled before the two Black cemeteries.

Oakwood is significantly larger than Evergreen or East End; but anyone wanting to argue that this is a simple matter of acreage would have to explain why small recreational areas such as Powhatan Playground and Libby Hill Park are labeled when two large, historic cemeteries are not. A complex (and confidential) set of factors goes into determining what places get named, and when, on tools such as Google Maps. But new technologies often maintain rather than disrupt our unseen bordering and memory practices.[18] Only some places get to be recognized as places.

It remains a mystery how many people are buried at the two African American cemeteries, since burial records are neither continuous nor complete. Estimates range from as low as ten thousand to more than sixty thousand across the sixty acres of Evergreen, and upwards of fifteen thousand in East End's sixteen acres. By way of comparison, Oakwood sprawls across one hundred ninety-nine acres and contains roughly one hundred thousand interments; Hollywood totals one hundred thirty-five acres and has about eighty thousand burials. Even in overgrown sections of East End and Evergreen, it's safe to assume that wherever you step, there are graves.

Evergreen Cemetery was founded in 1891 with high hopes. Richmond's African Americans had been buried in a variety of conditions before that. The first place they could be interred was the city-designated "Burial Ground for Negroes" in Shockoe Bottom, now called the African Burial Ground—an acknowledgment that the preservation efforts of recent decades looked to the model of Manhattan's African Burial Ground, and the pioneering reclamation work there in the 1990s.[19] The neighborhood, now filled with bars and boutiques, was an epicenter of the trade in enslaved people—a history that is neatly sidestepped in at least one description from a local nonprofit, which calls Shockoe Bottom "[o]nce the commercial center of downtown given its proximity to the river and canals," without alluding to what kind of commerce was moving along these waterways.[20] This burial ground also incorporated the city gallows.

Portions of the African Burial Ground in Shockoe Bottom were destroyed over nearly a century of construction projects, culminating in the mid-1950s when I-95 was rammed through the heart of Richmond.[21] Only the fierce activism of a local group, the Virginia Defenders for Freedom, Justice & Equality (cofounded by public historian Ana Edwards and her husband, Phil Wilayto), and other advocates has saved it from further destruction and led to its inclusion on the Richmond Slave Trail.[22]

Efforts to find dignified burial space continued elsewhere, among them the cemeteries that are now known collectively as Barton Heights, founded by free Blacks in 1815. But these cemeteries came under attack as White "streetcar suburbs" surrounded them. The newly incorporated town of Barton Heights closed the cemeteries to further burials in 1904, citing their "objectional features"—meaning, above all, the Blackness of their dead.[23] Some of these bodies were stolen from their graves and used for dissection at the Medical College of Virginia, causing further outrage.[24] Evergreen offered a new beginning.[25] Though situated on less desirable land than Hollywood Cemetery or the great rural cemeteries in northern cities, it echoed those ideals in its name and professional landscape design.

East End was founded soon after, in 1897. Located near Evergreen and Oakwood, the new cemetery was carved out from land originally purchased by the Greenwood Memorial Association in Henrico County, bordering Richmond. Started by three prominent Richmond businessmen in 1891, the association had originally purchased thirty acres of rural land in northeast Richmond.[26] They had already sold sixteen sections and facilitated one person's burial when White landowners sued, claiming that having a cemetery adjacent to their land would destroy its value and spread disease.[27] The group looked for land elsewhere, but never really recovered. The Greenwood association evolved into the East End Memorial Burial Association, which ultimately settled for ownership of six acres of their earlier purchase near Oakwood and Evergreen Cemeteries, in Richmond's East End. In 1917, the cemetery expanded to sixteen acres, its current size.[28]

According to historian Selden Richardson, Evergreen "was one of many new institutions established by the Reconstruction-era blacks of Richmond to achieve parity with white society. Like Hollywood's dramatic setting on the bank of the James, so Evergreen would have once stood looking down Fulton Valley."[29]

East End, though smaller, was also a project that combined burying the dead with imagining a radically different future. In 1902, the *Richmond Planet* announced plots for sale in the cemetery. The *Planet* was the radical Black newspaper edited by businessman and anti-lynching crusader John Mitchell Jr. The advertisement proclaimed:

> The situation of this Cemetery is high, dry and rolling and accessible to the Richmond Traction Street Railway and Seven Pines Railway lines, adjoining Oakwood Cemetery.
>
> This Association has at a considerable expense divided this tract of land into sections, erected a fence around its boundaries which with the additional improvements contemplated, will be an inducement to those desiring or contemplating purchasing resting places for their deceased relatives and friends. The attention of the general public is solicited and advantageous inducements offered.[30]

Evergreen and East End became high-status places for Richmond's Black elite and their families to be buried. Some families moved deceased loved ones from older, deteriorating burial grounds to these two cemeteries. Along with John Mitchell Jr. (1863–1929), Evergreen is the final resting place of Maggie Walker (1864–1934), the first woman in America to charter a bank, and the physician Sarah Garland Boyd Jones (1866–1905), who with her husband founded a hospital to serve Richmond's African American community. East End is home to the graves of Rosa Dixon Bowser (1855–1931), who at age seventeen became the first Black teacher hired by the Richmond public schools, and Dr. Richard F. Tancil (ca. 1852–1928), who practiced medicine, founded banks, and along with

Maggie Walker and John Mitchell Jr. was a prominent participant in streetcar boycotts protesting segregated public transportation. Dr. Tancil's simple, flat grave marker reads:

IN MEMORY OF A DEAR FRIEND
DR. R. F. TANCIL
WELL DONE
WIDOW

The marker disappeared during the summer of 2015, likely stolen. The Friends of East End raised funds to create and install a replica.

Perpetual care funds were not legally mandated by the state of Virginia until after World War I. Before then, it was common in both White and Black cemeteries for families either to pay the cemetery owner for regular maintenance or to do it through their own efforts, gathering themselves to tend the plots or hiring a caretaker. For years, Thomas Miles—a "self-made man" who did odd jobs around the city—tended graves for many families. His light skin earned him the nickname "Whitefolks."[31]

Without perpetual care funds, East End and Evergreen relied on financial support from the Black community's extensive network of professional, religious, and philanthropic organizations. Records of these contributions are etched into headstones at both cemeteries. Institutions such as First African Baptist, Richmond's oldest Black church, and the National Ideal Benefit Society commissioned headstones for members, as did employees' groups such as the Porters of Byrd St. Station and Nurses Local Association 1. The Independent Order of St. Luke and other charitable groups, churches, mutual aid societies, and fraternal organizations often helped people pay expenses incurred when a relative died.[32] "Even beneath the poison oak and fallen leaves, these graves preserve a still-shimmering network of Black intentionality and mutual care," writes poet Kiki Petrosino.[33] When grassroots groups gather in these cemeteries to care for them, they do so in the tradition of these older networks.

In many cases, these burial societies purchased plots or entire sections of the cemetery in advance for their members. According to historian Kami Fletcher, "Predeath burial purchases helped guarantee black people security and dignity in death. With the guarantee of their burial space, black women and men knew that their loved ones and themselves would be protected from the nameless lots in potter's fields. Opting to participate in predeath burial purchase allowed the black community autonomy, fostered independence, and provided true eternal rest."[34]

These communal efforts inspire Ryan K. Smith to refer to cemeteries such as East End and Evergreen as "post-Emancipation uplift cemeteries."[35] Pastoral landscapes of the dead, founded and managed by Black entrepreneurs, given names like Evergreen and Woodland, were designed to project a politics of respectability to White and Black audiences alike. As in White cemeteries, they mapped out a social hierarchy through the sizes, styles, inscriptions, and positions of their monuments—answering racism with material achievement while also reinforcing internal class and gender hierarchies.[36] But the energy and capital that "freedom's first generation" poured into founding cemeteries often could not overcome the indifference or outright hostility of the White establishment, or the nation's sustained attacks on any and every kind of African American wealth-building.[37]

By the early 1900s, the patchwork of support had clearly begun to fray. Under the headline "Should Have Better Cemeteries," the July 10, 1915, edition of the *Planet* reports on a forum held at the Ebenezer Baptist Church in Richmond. The theme of the meeting was "The Negro and His Cemeteries"; over three hundred people attended. The assembled group approved a resolution that began:

> Whereas, the civilization of a people is generally measured by the manner in which they honor and care for their dead and control and keep their cemeteries,
>
> And whereas the contrast in the care and keeping of our cemeteries and those immediately surrounding us is so markedly apparent and to our chagrin, dishonor, distaste, and shame,
>
> And whereas general improvements in other cemeteries cost no more than we are charged and pay for graves and sections,
>
> And whereas our former cemeteries are closed against us on account of neglect and mismanagement, causing us much loss, inconvenience, and trouble . . .[38]

The resolution goes on to request improvements at the cemeteries, such as placing a protective fence around them to keep out "roving animals," grading the roads, and providing a water supply to families wishing to tend plots—an indication of the extent to which the care of the dead was still largely in the hands of families themselves.

The decline of the cemeteries continued throughout the twentieth century. Smith records a long history of "legal limbo" for East End, during which responsibility for the cemetery fell on one beleaguered member of the nonprofit East End Burial Association, Earl H. Gray.[39] The cemetery had gone from a burial ground for prominent families to a place of last resort.[40] In July 1981, the *Richmond Times-Dispatch* reported that at Evergreen, "Monuments have toppled over, or become hidden by thick weeds, undergrowth and trash. Some have virtually vanished from view, and all a passerby sees is an occasional piteous flash of color, from a plastic wreath wedged among the weeds."[41] The article tells a heartrending story: Jacqueline Hayden lost her seven-year-old daughter, Nytasha, to kidney disease. A funeral director told her that she could not afford a plot at Oakwood, and recommended burying her daughter at Evergreen, where no vault or grave liner (which incur significant expenses) were required. Hayden arrived with the funeral procession to find the area around the cemetery gate strewn with trash, and the cemetery itself covered in high, uncut grass. At the time of the interview, having already spent nearly thirteen hundred dollars, she was hoping to put together enough money someday to move her daughter somewhere else.

In the same article, Earl Gray describes East End as still offering a service to those "with no real financial means." He recounts staying there at night, waiting to see what construction company might be dumping "big slabs of concrete, everything imaginable."[42]

Vandalism at East End and Evergreen became not merely an occasional outrage; rather, in Smith's words, it was "a sustained campaign . . . [largely] carried out by outsiders hostile to black uplift and civil rights."[43] Many of these outrages occurred at the Braxton family mausoleum, which was repeatedly attacked, with bodies removed, mutilated, and set afire. The attacks prompted even more families to seek to move their loved ones' remains out of East End and Evergreen to a more secure resting place.[44]

The last burial at East End was in 2002, but regular burials had already stopped by the end of the 1970s. Evergreen has an accessible section near its gate where burials continued until 2016, though maintenance was irregular and much of the rest of the cemetery was engulfed in forest.

"A Form of Reparation"

Since the 1980s, people have gathered periodically to clear and maintain Evergreen, with efforts at East End coming decades later. But clearing must be sustained. A day spent weeding kudzu and other vines will produce gratifying images and a sense of accomplishment. But the plants will be back. To make any real progress on the cemeteries, you must continuously mobilize fresh volunteers even while you keep other groups coming back. Cemetery citizens must reproduce themselves.

An African American ranger with the National Park Service, James (Jim) Bell, ran a long-standing volunteer program in Evergreen from the late 1990s through the early 2000s. He earned the support of then–City Councilwoman Delores McQuinn, and librarian Veronica Davis, who in 2002 incorporated the efforts into a new nonprofit called Virginia Roots.[45]

In 2008, John Shuck, a retired bank analyst, began visiting Richmond's neglected and overgrown cemeteries to take photographs. Shuck is a tall, older White man with a combover of white hair and a long, ambling stride. Originally from the Midwest, he remembers the cemeteries back home being well maintained. He was stunned by the contrast at East End and Evergreen. An avid "FindAGraver" (that's his Twitter handle), he photographs headstones and adds them to the crowdsourced website. He has been taking photos of graves since digital cameras first came out.[46]

Shuck soon felt compelled not only to document individual graves, but also to do something about the cemeteries' neglected state, so he joined a volunteer cleanup effort at Evergreen through Davis's group. In 2013, amid ongoing disputes between volunteers and the cemetery's owners (and with Davis relocating to Hampton, Virginia), Shuck and other volunteers moved their project next door to East End.[47]

Shuck became the longtime site coordinator for the Friends of East End, until the organization stopped working at that cemetery in 2020. He also served as a member of the Executive Planning and Review Team (given the acronym ExPRT) for Evergreen Cemetery, advising the cemeteries' new owner, the Enrichmond Foundation. As the relationship between those two groups fell apart, he was a rare figure trying to straddle the divide.

Brian Palmer and Erin Hollaway Palmer started working at the cemetery in December 2014. Brian is a journalist and photographer. He has served as a bureau chief in Beijing and embedded with U.S. Marines in Iraq. Erin, formerly an editor in the New York publishing world, is now a magazine designer. They moved from Brooklyn, New York, to Hampton, Virginia, in 2013. Their plan was to devote themselves to a documentary they had begun the previous year, centered on a different African American cemetery, near Williamsburg, Virginia. Brian's great-grandparents, both born into slavery, are buried there. That site is difficult to access, hidden within the confines of Camp Peary, a top-secret military base and CIA training facility.

The couple soon wound up exploring other historic Black cemeteries on the Virginia Peninsula, saddened by the consistently poor conditions they saw. When friends in Richmond told them to visit Evergreen and East End, in spring 2014, they were stunned by the sheer size of the cemeteries and their state of degradation. In a blog entry later that year, Brian wrote, "At first glance, all you see is a sad little burial ground surrounded by woods—skewed, cracked, and upended headstones; plastic flowers ground into the dirt; a heap of old tires and a massive Dumpster smack in the middle." Even this "sad" scene, he noted, was a sign of transformation: "A little more than a year ago, East End Cemetery was all forest. You could drive past it down the dirt road that leads to another cemetery, Evergreen, and completely miss it."[48]

They became regular volunteers. On their blog, they made a record of themselves falling in love with East End, becoming cemetery citizens. Brian wrote:

> Four hours of ripping at vines, snipping branches, sawing limbs, and raking revealed the last corner of a burial plot belonging to the Dickerson family. I had been standing on Mr. James Dickerson's grave marker, which lay less than an inch below ground, without knowing it as I fought with an especially tenacious root system. Erin saw the stone, and another volunteer swept off the dirt with a broom. This was a small accomplishment, but it felt significant because we, strangers from different backgrounds, had done it together as part of a larger project to reclaim a monument to African Americans in a city and region that seem more invested in remembering dead Confederates and their mythic cause than the rest of us.[49]

Erin has sometimes alluded to the work in East End as "a form of reparation." The couple has brought unprecedented visibility to cemeteries that people have struggled to get the public to care about, even in Richmond. Accounts of their work at East End and Evergreen have appeared in the *Nation*, the *New York Times*, and elsewhere. At the same time, their continuing New York ties and itinerant histories make it possible to portray them as outsiders, careerists, people whose interests in the cemeteries stem from something other than "Virginia roots."

In 2017, Brian and Erin helped to establish the Friends of East End as a nonprofit. Their work is sustained by volunteer labor and small donations from private citizens, local companies, and organizations. After public workdays at East End, Henrico County authorities cart away brush removed by volunteers.

Other groups have been active at Evergreen, with its impressive monuments and more famous public figures. Marvin Harris, an alum of the Maggie Walker School, started the Evergreen Restoration Foundation in 2016. Later, Harris shifted his foundation's focus to Woodland, an African American cemetery in northeast Richmond founded by the *Planet* editor John Mitchell Jr.[50] Tennis star and humanitarian Arthur Ashe was buried at Woodland after his death in 1993—like Mitchell, he chose to be buried next to his mother, regardless of the cemetery's condition.[51] To some in the community, the Evergreen Restoration Foundation's purchase of Woodland in 2020 was an important counterbalance to Enrichmond's acquisition of Evergreen and East End. It put thirty acres of African American burial ground into the hands of a grassroots, African American–led nonprofit. One online commenter shared a much simpler wish: "Thank God, maybe I'll be able to find my parents."[52]

The Enrichmond Foundation grew out of the Richmond Recreation and Parks Foundation, created by the city in 1990. Its purpose was to support the Department of Parks, Recreation, and Community Facilities as a coordinator of volunteer activities and fiscal agent for various recreation, preservation, and open space–focused groups. The foundation acquired Evergreen Cemetery in 2017. In 2019, it became the owner of East End, announcing plans to acquire other African American burial grounds nearby.

In the early years I spent visiting East End Cemetery, the Friends of East End made extraordinary progress. They mobilized thousands of volunteers to clear acres of the cemetery. I witnessed the discovery of many lost graves and watched even more emerge in my Instagram feed.

During the summer of 2020, with Black Lives Matter protests erupting across the United States, Richmonders began covering the Confederate statues on Monument Avenue in anti-racist graffiti, eventually toppling the statue of Jefferson Davis.[53] People gathered day and night to transform this former shrine to the Confederacy into something different: a place to print posters and T-shirts, to picnic, plant gardens, ride bikes and skateboards. And to mourn the dead, especially Black and brown people killed by police, whose names appeared around the monuments in spray paint and on signs. In the context of all these contested histories and all these mourning rituals, Richmond's historic African American cemeteries began to seem like places where the dead and their burial sites really were an emergency.

Meanwhile, the Friends of East End were suspending their work at the cemetery. The grave markers I had watched emerge at East End were disappearing again, into the flourishing vines of a Virginia cemetery in summer.

Starting in 2017, the uneasy relationship between the Friends of East End and Enrichmond deteriorated rapidly. At times I felt torn between my friendship with them and the research opportunities that might be afforded to someone considered a neutral outsider.[54] For the first few years, I tended to be present as a witness without speaking up. But after Enrichmond acquired East End, I began to take part in the public debates about the fate of the two cemeteries.[55] I had already sought interviews with a number of prominent Enrichmond allies and received no answer, though eventually I was able to speak with John Sydnor, Enrichmond's executive director at the time, and with John Mitchell, the descendant and namesake of the famed *Richmond Planet* editor. Mitchell served on Enrichmond's board, and in 2021 became the organization's community ambassador for the cemeteries.

My account of the fight over the cemeteries in Richmond does not offer an evenly weighted balance between "both sides." Long before I knew how the story of Enrichmond's relationship with the cemeteries would end, I avoided this kind of framing because there were clearly more than two sides to the story. The two-sides narrative that often appeared in news coverage was a shallow one, and a missed opportunity for people to see how revisions in a marginalized cemetery—paths to deepening a community's connection to its history, its sense of pride and unity—can expose long-existing frictions and fractures, as well as making new ones.

"A Piece of Land"

For some, the Enrichmond Foundation's acquisition of Evergreen and East End cemeteries brought hope and relief. Veronica Davis, who had organized some volunteer efforts at Evergreen, told a journalist that when she heard the news, "I have to be honest with you, in that moment I started crying, because here is a dream that is being realized."[56] Davis hoped that a long history of systemic neglect was finally ending. John Mitchell had initial reservations about yet another African American heritage site in Virginia having "ownership with a White face"; but he saw Enrichmond as "bring[ing] the funds to get the job done."[57]

A fuller story of Enrichmond's yearslong entanglement with Richmond's African American cemeteries is chronicled in other places, by people who lived closer to the cemeteries and the conflicts.[58] Here, I focus on the politics of revision at these cemeteries, East End in particular.

Enrichmond's main function was to work with Richmond's Department of Parks, Recreation, and Community Facilities to help local volunteer organizations apply for grants and take in tax-free donations. In its move toward cemetery ownership, it relied on a $400,000 grant from the Virginia Outdoors Foundation, a "quasi-state agency formed to preserve open space and recreational lands in the state," for a conservation easement.[59] The easement would clear the way to ownership of a protected space, providing funds for things like legal fees, title search, and insurance. It also included money for "restoration and maintenance work" in the cemeteries themselves.[60]

Virginia Outdoors Foundation representatives had met with Brian Palmer and Marvin Harris to express their interest in supporting community work at the cemeteries. The foundation's original proposal for the $400,000 grant names Enrichmond, the Friends of East End, and multiple local universities and government agencies all as potential partners who might create a plan for the cemeteries and become their eventual owner. But that proposal, which seems to have been little more than a smokescreen, was soon scrapped in one of many "little handshake agreements," as one former Enrichmond staffer put it.[61]

The Virginia Outdoors Foundation's board soon approved making the grant to Enrichmond alone. Richmond-based archaeologist Ellen Chapman observed, "There was no visible public, competitive decision-making process to decide on

Enrichmond versus another non-profit—like for example Preservation Virginia, which already manages historic properties, or Groundwork RVA, which does community-based and inclusive work in Richmond."[62] A staff member at the Virginia Department of Historic Resources wrote a memo to the Virginia Outdoors Foundation recommending that the group "hold a few community conversations before making any final decisions, in order to understand how this might affect the descendant community"; but these did not occur prior to the acquisition of Evergreen.[63]

Enrichmond's press release in May 2017 called the purchase of Evergreen "our most significant and humbling endeavor to date."[64] Technically, the new owner was not Enrichmond but Parity LLC, a corporation established by Enrichmond whose sole member-manager was John Sydnor. Enrichmond also clearly signaled that Evergreen was just the beginning of the foundation's move into cemetery preservation: "Although this encompasses only our first step in the protection and preservation of the four cemeteries of Evergreen it signifies a new dawn for those interred, their families, and the rich African American history of Richmond and the Commonwealth of Virginia."[65] ("The four cemeteries of Evergreen," the name that appears in Enrichmond's statement, referred to East End, Evergreen, and the two nearby "Colored Paupers'" burial grounds, one of which is within the bounds of nearby Oakwood Cemetery.)[66] Over the next few years, the foundation took in over a million dollars of public funding.[67]

In May 2017, just before Enrichmond announced it had acquired Evergreen, Governor Terry McAuliffe signed House Bill 1547, Virginia's first piece of legislation providing public funds for African American burial grounds. The Friends of East End had pushed for this legislation; Brian's *New York Times* column supporting it, "For the Forgotten African-American Dead," was likely the most widely read article on the subject.[68]

Using a formula of five dollars "multiplied by the number of graves, monuments, and markers of African Americans who lived at any time between 1800 and 1900 and are interred in the cemetery," House Bill 1547 allots about $35,000 annually to Evergreen and East End.[69] The original bill's language said this funding would be available to any "qualified charitable organization," which would seem to include the Friends of East End and Marvin Harris's Evergreen Restoration Foundation. But House Bill 284, introduced by Enrichmond supporter

Delegate Delores McQuinn and passed in 2018, removed the word "charitable" and added that the state funds could also go to "any person or locality that *owns* a historical African American cemetery," regardless of charitable status.[70]

"[A]s the owners, it would not be very prudent of us to give up or reduce . . . the control of the property," Sydnor told reporter Michael Paul Williams in 2017.[71] With the support of allies in the legislature and state agencies, Enrichmond was soon well positioned not just to receive but to monopolize state funding for the cemeteries. In order for "third party" organizations to access the new state funds for African American cemeteries, the Virginia Department of Historic Resources required that they show evidence the property owner had approved a "proposed scope of work."[72] In May 2019, Enrichmond rejected the proposal the Friends of East End had submitted, saying they were still crafting a blanket agreement that would apply to all volunteers working in the cemetery.[73] The Friends of East End would still have minimal rights of "ingress and egress" based on state laws governing cemetery access, but the early talk of sharing resources and meaningful partnership seemed to have evaporated completely.[74]

Around this time, I showed up for a workday at East End to find separate signs along the road leading into the two cemeteries: one guiding Enrichmond volunteers over to a parking area at Evergreen, one directing Friends of East End to a table set up just off the road, on one of the pathways. The same kinds of tools and water coolers were available at each place, for each group of volunteers. On prior visits, the two cemeteries had bled together as I followed Brian, Erin, and Teacake from one into another in search of a grave someone had asked about, or one of Teacake's many lost balls. Now they were full of activity, but also starkly bordered.

Unlike Evergreen, East End was considered abandoned, so the state could convey the property to a new owner, Enrichmond, by placing it in receivership. On January 24, 2019, I attended the court hearing in downtown Richmond with Brian, Erin, and Mark Schmieder of the Friends of East End, along with a descendant, Brenda Williams Jones, and historian Ryan K. Smith (who later shared his thoughts on the hearing on his *Richmond Cemeteries* blog).[75]

Looking back at the chaos at East End and Evergreen over the past few years, it's hard to single out a specific moment as more worthy of focus than others. It felt momentous, though, to witness as legal ownership of East End was conveyed to an organization with no demonstrated experience preserving or managing cemeteries, and over protests from the cemetery's most constant caretakers and descendants whose ancestors were buried in its earth. I was used to seeing the future of a cemetery being shaped on-site, with clippers, rakes, and trash bags— not by people wearing suits, holding briefcases, watching the clock.

We waited in the lobby, Brian practicing his prepared remarks in a quiet part of the corridor, the rest of us making small talk. The Friends were not there to prevent Enrichmond from acquiring the cemetery: that outcome seemed a foregone conclusion. Nor was their organization interested in owning the cemetery themselves. Rather, they were hoping that the judge would add conditions to the transfer of ownership, enforcing greater transparency and engagement with the community and descendants.

In advance of the hearing, the Friends had submitted letters of support from allies and descendants. Ryan K. Smith's letter focused on Enrichmond's lack of transparency: Why, he asked, had the foundation not so much as mentioned its plans to the Friends of East End, the organization that for years had been East End's most active stewards? And why did it place its court-mandated announcement of the proceedings in *Style Weekly*, an alternative arts paper, rather than any of the news outlets favored by Richmond's African American community? One letter was from Adrienne Gray Rhone, who has multiple ancestors buried in the cemetery and is the daughter of Earl Gray, the last member of the East End Burial Association. She asked the court to require Enrichmond to give regular updates on its communication with partner organizations and families, and to commit to sharing state funds with the Friends of East End.[76]

As the hearing began, the older White judge talked about his upcoming retirement, then made a few jokes at the expense of his law clerk. Then he stated that he had "never been involved in anything about cemeteries." All the attorneys and speakers that day, aside from Brian and Williams Jones, were White. When it was her turn to speak, Williams Jones said she had asked Enrichmond to slow down, take more time reaching out to churches and engaging with the community—with seemingly no effect. "My grandmother left her children at home to work in White homes so people at the top of the hierarchy could do what they wanted," she said, asking that the same story not play out again. At one point the judge asked the two attorneys whether they had ever been to the cemeteries—not a legal question, but an interesting one. Both said no.

Enrichmond's cemetery caretaker at the time, Ted Maris-Wolf, spoke most openly about the conflicts over the cemetery. The scale of the project was new for Enrichmond, he said, and it takes a while to get to know the "rhythm of life" at the cemetery. The judge interrupted him at this phrase, asking with eyes wide what the "rhythm of life" could possibly mean in a burial ground. Maris-Wolf said he was referring to "who comes with a lawn mower in their trunk to mow a path to a family member's grave, who leaves balloons." Then he added, "East End needed a steward, and Enrichmond was interested in being that steward." It was a phrase that I knew could only rankle the Friends of East End seated around me, who had already cleared half of the acreage in the cemetery, found and cleaned hundreds of markers, researched the lives of the dead, and provided direct assistance to living descendants. What steward was East End needing, and how would this benefit the cemetery beyond what the Friends were already doing?

After a short recess, the judge returned and ruled in favor of Enrichmond's ownership of East End, without any qualifications or added demands. He said, "It's a piece of land; somebody needs to own it. Somebody needs to control it." The Friends of East End, he said, should have some input about the cemetery's future, but that was "organic" and not a legal matter, something a mediator should handle.

"It's a piece of land." That remark, more than the judge's decision, stuck with me. East End *is* a piece of land—land filled with thousands of the dead. Dead people whose graves were left to be covered over with weeds, broken or stolen, littered with trash. At cemetery workdays, it's easy to feel like the dead are present in some way—if not actively accompanying volunteers, at least witnessing the goings-on and even shaping their pace and tenor. You get distracted reading inscriptions on headstones, and you stumble into depressions in the soil, which have caved in over the bones of the cemetery's *real* owners. In this courtroom there was no physical sign, and barely a mention, of these people. Questions of ownership would be decided rationally, legalistically, without the dead really mattering. There would be no discussion of their presence, or what they would want. Thousands of witnesses could not take the stand.

The courtroom actually offered no framework for thinking about the *past*, let alone what might be required to "open up a future not fully determined by past harms."[77] The practicalities of land ownership were divorced from any discussion of history, of the dead, of what East End actually meant and who was present there. This de-centering of the dead, though painful to watch, would later help me see this same thread in nearly all of Enrichmond's cemetery work.

In summer 2020, with Enrichmond established as the owner of both cemeteries (through Parity LLC), a reporter asked Sydnor about the annual state funds allotted to East End and Evergreen, over which the organization then had exclusive control. "It is not fair. It is not fair, without a doubt, that a white-led organization receives the most money, mainly because we own 77 acres of historic African American sacred ground."[78] As if ownership was a thing that had simply happened to him.

Earlier that summer, Enrichmond had sent the Friends of East End a volunteer agreement, whose terms they found unacceptable.[79] When they refused to sign, Enrichmond's caretaker started confronting them at the cemetery, demanding they do so or leave. For a while, they began visiting at times when they believed Enrichmond employees would not be there, documenting deteriorating conditions at East End. They also sought out pro bono legal counsel to help negotiate an acceptable agreement with Enrichmond's lawyers. But by fall 2020, the relationship between the groups had become "basically irreparable," as Friends of East End president Mark Schmieder put it.[80] In November the Friends issued a statement announcing that they were suspending their physical reclamation work at East End. They promised to keep sharing stories, photographs, and oral histories. Meanwhile, they worked alongside volunteers at Woodland, the African American cemetery founded by John Mitchell Jr.

Degraded and Desired

Descendant Jarene Fleming was worried about the cemeteries falling into further neglect, because Enrichmond seemed to be making plans for everything but perpetual care. Brian Palmer accused Enrichmond of planning to make East End and Evergreen into a "recreation plantation" for gentrifiers on mountain bikes.[81] Some Enrichmond allies implied that their critics—especially Brian—were the ones with mixed motives, looking to sell photos and get bylines, to build careers based on the work in the cemetery and the attention that comes with stirring up controversy.[82] As an academic, I'm not immune from any of these questions about mixed motives. I earn professional rewards from doing scholarship in these spaces, praise and publicity as a teacher who's connecting my students with local history and community organizations.

People who care about the cemeteries are worried about them being abandoned, and about them being exploited. That might seem paradoxical, but the history of these places shows that abandonment and exploitation aren't contradictory: they flow together. The tide can shift in one direction or the other with unexpected speed; one process can accelerate the other. Revising a cemetery means taking a degraded landscape and reassigning value to it: making it accessible, exposing hidden grave markers, doing research, telling stories. A successful reclamation effort draws attention to a cemetery, makes it more visually attractive and more obviously a "resource"—a place of heritage, a place with stories people want to hear.[83] It can also constrain the meanings of the place, and the dignity people attach to it, in new ways.[84]

In some cases, the distinctions between insider and outsider, true believer and opportunist, are easy to recognize. Kaitlyn Greenidge writes in the *New York Times* about feeling a sense of loss when, in summer 2021, she saw a rack of T-shirts at Walmart commemorating Juneteenth. This longstanding African American celebration on June 19, the day that Emancipation was announced in Galveston, Texas (over two years after the Emancipation Proclamation came into effect), had just been made a federal holiday. Retail stores were quick to respond with clothing, decorations, and even Juneteenth ice cream.[85] Greenidge reflects, "I am sad because when a holiday becomes co-opted like this, those who can gain a sense of self and solidarity from celebrating it often lose it. The agency that comes from deciding your own traditions . . . becomes lost to a corporate calendar and a megastore selling you a Juneteenth cookout checklist. You can lose sight of the possibility that exists in marginalized histories, which is the space to imagine another, better world."[86]

East End and Evergreen are the final homes of people who, whether they were born enslaved or free, lived under regimes of debasement and exploitation. Once they died, their families struggled to dignify them in cemeteries where bodies might be stolen in the night to be cut apart at a medical school, in a city where some Black burial grounds would be paved over because the land had more lucrative uses. Enrichmond's staff and supporters often seemed inexcusably ignorant of the how these histories of exploitation are remembered and how they live on.

Historian Daina Raimey Berry uses the term "ghost capital" to illuminate the profitable trade in the remains of enslaved people after their deaths. It describes the final phase of an economy so efficient at exploiting Black people that it could extract value from them before they were born and after they were dead.[87] Along with grief and rage that cemeteries such as East End and Evergreen remain undervalued and forgotten comes the fear that they will be plundered again. Activist and cemetery historian Peighton Young, discussing Enrichmond's years of involvement with East End and Evergreen, put this anxiety in stark terms: "It's literally just, I don't know, some very weird space between slavery and . . . not quite free yet. It's something else. . . . It's like you're still exploiting the people and the places in death and you can't just let them be at peace and you can't let their families be at peace. . . . It's the same sentiments. It's the same impetus. It's the same process."[88]

Unearthing, Unhearing

In July 2020, an Enrichmond tree expert discovered human remains exposed at the edge of East End, where the earth slopes down toward the nearby "Colored Paupers" burial ground. Enrichmond called the police; but in the meantime, a news photographer who had come out to the cemetery that day photographed the exposed remains. Enrichmond soon issued a press release touting their collaboration with the Virginia Department of Historic Resources to remove the bones for further investigation. For days, the local news circulated the photographer's images, along with remarks from the employee who found the bones: "I don't want to say it was cool, you don't want to see someone's remains exposed but it's neat to kind of find a potential piece of history on a site that's been kind of lost and forgotten in time."[89]

To descendants and others concerned about the dignity of the people whose remains had been exposed, there was nothing neat or cool about the situation. And the references to East End as "lost" and "forgotten," from a staff member charged with the cemetery's care, ignored the communities—descendants, volunteers, and others—who have invested so much in keeping it found and remembered.

Enrichmond asked the local news to remove the images of remains only after community members expressed outrage, though in public statements executive director John Sydnor recast this as something done at their own initiative.[90] In fact, their first reaction was not only to repost the article with the offending images on their social media accounts, but also to include a link to the story in their Instagram profile. In other words, Enrichmond acted like the unearthed remains were great publicity, until they were told that they were not.

On October 23, 2020, the Virginia Department of Historic Resources organized an online public hearing, billed as a discussion about the discovery of remains at East End and Enrichmond's handling of the situation. Attendees of the hearing were required to register, and to indicate at that time if they wanted to give a public comment or not. At the hearing, no one who had not signed up to comment in advance would be allowed to speak.

This policy would perhaps have seemed more appropriate if the hearing had not begun with dramatic news. Archaeologist Joanna Wilson Greene explained that initial investigation of the remains—at least nine individuals total, male and female—showed signs that they had been subjected to medical dissection. The Medical College of Virginia, which would later merge with another school to become Virginia Commonwealth University, was infamous for using stolen bodies.[91] In the late nineteenth through early twentieth century, the school employed an African American "resurrectionist," or grave robber, Chris Baker, who lived on the campus. Baker was born to parents enslaved at the university.[92] The bodies that reemerged at East End had likely been exhumed from their original graves by Baker or another resurrectionist, used by medical students, and later hastily reburied in a common grave.

Descendants and relatives of those buried in the cemetery were reeling from this painful new information. The hearing proceeded quickly to the allotted time for comments. No one had received any information about the hearing after registering; no one had any idea in what order they would be called. Enrichmond's announcement before the event had said, "We do not know their families, and therefore, we ask you to serve as family. Please speak for those who can no longer speak for themselves."[93] But most attendees felt poorly prepared to speak extemporaneously for their "family" that had been dug out of their graves, cut up, and buried in a ravine.

Some of the attendees proceeded with the remarks they had prepared in advance. Some stammered, overwhelmed and unsure of what to say. Ana Edwards alluded to her work on this and other local sites, including the African Burial

Ground in Shockoe Bottom and the East Marshall Street Well, where bodies had been dumped after Medical College of Virginia dissections.[94] She found it shocking that the principles established in these major projects, including procedures for contacting descendants, had not been followed.[95]

Jarene Fleming called the media coverage of the found remains "exploitation" and shared her concern that, with a single owner, the cemetery's future was as "precarious" as ever. When she hit the three-minute mark, the moderator cut her off mid-sentence. Descendant Daniela Gladden-Green later gave up her own time so that Jarene could finish. "My tax dollars are now being funneled into an organization that has no oversight, no accountability, and truly it seems like they can do what they want with my ancestors' bones," Jarene said. "And that is upsetting, and that's what I wanted you to feel. I wanted you to feel how shook I am right now learning this news in a public venue about those bones. It just blows my mind."

Comments like this kept piling up, with no pause for anyone to answer them. The evening ended with a sort of chorus, from Sydnor and the Virginia Department of Historic Resources staff, saying:

> going to reach out
> > take these comments to heart
> feel the passion and the pain
> > the weight of responsibility
> share your sorrow
> > don't just need your help
> we welcome it

The hearing—which Ryan K. Smith called a "horror show" on his *Richmond Cemeteries* blog—galvanized many East End and Evergreen descendants.[96] Brian Palmer's suggestion to form an independent descendant organization, unaffiliated with Enrichmond or the Friends of East End, started gaining steam even during the public commenting period.

It was so much like that day in court back in 2019. When descendants spoke, they did so without their faces displayed onscreen, only their names listed along the side. Every face that was visible—those of the hosts, who were dispensing information and moderating the proceedings—was White. It was the job of Black people to receive information, to react, and then be mollified, whether their questions were answered or not. Evergreen descendant Daryl Thorne talked about descendants being "marginalized"; the WebEx platform and facilitation style made it literal.

Ownership, Stewardship, Care

While arguments about funding and descendant input swirled around the cemeteries, those spaces had their own things to say. I visited in June 2021, walking with Brian and Erin through parts of the cemeteries that had always been overgrown, but also areas the Friends of East End had cleared that were now being swallowed up again. Enrichmond contractors had left branches and grass clippings right on top of graves.

Enrichmond had just announced new preservation plans for East End and Evergreen, drafted by a reputable conservation firm. These plans were largely focused on preserving grave markers, rather than constituting an integrated approach to the cemeteries' history and landscape (which could follow models from many other historic burial grounds).[97] As an open letter from descendants and allies stated,

> There are thousands of grave markers at East End and Evergreen. Each exists not in a vacuum, but in an environment where forces and processes intersect, from erosion and unchecked overgrowth to vandalism and illegal dumping. The history of each site is given in a single sentence in each plan. Accordingly, the documents themselves offer essentially no direction on how the conservation of individual marker types fits within a broader approach to the preservation of the sites.[98]

In the meantime, while Enrichmond brought volunteers into Evergreen through the federal community service program AmeriCorps, the overall state of the cemeteries was not good—especially beyond the most accessible and visible areas, close to where people park. In an email shared with me, John Sydnor blamed the situation on labor shortages caused by the COVID-19 pandemic and the time it took to prioritize hiring Black-owned businesses. But Mark Schmieder and others pointed out the tremendous progress being made at Woodland

Cemetery, just down the road—the result of the type of community engagement that Enrichmond said was its specialty.

There are at least three kinds of relationships an organization or group of volunteers can have with a cemetery: ownership, stewardship, and care. These ideas overlap, and people in Richmond have invoked them all. But they also differ in important ways.

Ownership can be the legal possession of land, as in Enrichmond's formal acquisition of the cemeteries. But land is not the only part of a cemetery that becomes a commodity of sorts. So are research, knowledge, and even relationships with the cemetery and its descendants. Stewardship is a form of responsibility. It means responsibility to maintain the cemetery and be accountable to the various people and groups that feel a stake in it.

Stewardship also depends on claims of expertise. One of the key strategies of Enrichmond and its supporters was to portray other groups, especially the Friends of East End, as grassroots "partners" whose involvement was welcome but not sufficient for the task at hand—not rising to the level of what Sydnor referred to as a "present and engaged owner," especially one with greater fundraising capability.[99]

Sydnor told me the Friends of East End had essentially been "coming in and clearing the same space over and over again."[100] He commended them, but immediately pointed to the immense size of the two cemeteries put together (seventy-six acres) and the cost of creating a master plan. The implication was that reclaiming East End and Evergreen was simply a bigger game than the Friends of East End could play on their own. As urban planning scholars Meghan Z. Gough, Kathryn Howell, and Hannah Cameron put it, Enrichmond's strategy was often to present an "either-or scenario": the cemeteries could be under its chaotic and unaccountable brand of stewardship, or they could "deteriorate."[101]

What Sydnor didn't acknowledge was that Enrichmond itself had disrupted the Friends' ability to continue their work and keep it funded. To many observers, it seemed that the Friends had worked at a smaller scale but done their work extremely conscientiously—with research and storytelling projects growing directly out of it. They did spend some of their time "clearing the same space over and over again," because that's how cemetery maintenance *works*; the Friends, like all the other cemetery reclamation groups, sought a balance of clearing new spaces while maintaining the progress they had already made in other ones. Enrichmond, meanwhile, was playing a "bigger game" but poorly, with major, sometimes deeply offensive, missteps (which they were trying to manage with the help of "three marketing firms on monthly contract").[102]

To Brian, Erin, and allies such as Ryan K. Smith, the notion that Richmond's African American heritage needed an outside "steward," backed by the city's White-dominated political and nonprofit establishment, was itself an old, paternalistic pattern in Richmond's race relations.[103] If you see a marginalized cemetery as a space of universal heritage, which simply needs someone to take responsibility for it, then the best steward might be whoever can access the greatest resources and navigate the local power structures. But if it's a field of political struggle, then traditional dynamics of stewardship must be dismantled, transformed into something else.

What would it mean for the Friends of East End to work at a cemetery for years and not only reject claims of ownership, but also the paternalistic language of stewardship? What would be left to help us understand their hours of collective effort?

Care. What's left to them is caring for East End, its histories, and the community connected to it—embracing a vision of the cemetery as a "field of care," and their power to keep it that way.[104]

Care is intimately related with *noticing*. You must attend carefully to what you care for, whether it is a pet, a garden, or a manuscript; but attending to that person, animal, plant, place, or object also makes you notice new things about it—new needs or methods of care that you didn't perceive before.

The Friends of East End tend to measure their progress not just by how many sections they clear, but also how visible the graves are in each section. They talk about where there still might be graves to look for, how to clear around the flowers that have sprouted up around a plot. Brian and Erin are artists, chronicling small changes in the cemeteries through their images and words. Erin's introverted "art of noticing" focuses largely on the nonhuman drama, documenting the flowers peeking out from the ivy, the toads and caterpillars she sees while tending graves. Brian often finds moments of painterly drama in how people's bodies struggle against plants, and how they gather: parents and their kids, descendants and newcomers, college students at the precise moment when their shyness gives way to focus and determination, sometimes even joy.

When the Friends of East End stopped working in the cemetery, the issue was not only whether another adequate steward would keep up the work at the site. It was that a certain kind of noticing—of care—seemed to have left with them.[105] Members of the group became increasingly distraught not only about the sections of East End and Evergreen that hadn't been cleared, but also about the ones that Enrichmond was sporadically maintaining. In a text message, Erin wrote, "The 'care' they provide is the exact opposite of what we used to do. Instead of clearing first by hand to make sure no markers were hidden in the undergrowth, they plow right in with their mower."[106]

In 2019, Erin photographed a courtesy marker for Gayle Lucille Langhorne, who lived only seven months, from August 2, 1952, to March 13, 1953. It was rusty but intact. In October 2020, she and Brian found the same marker, uprooted and bent, cast off among the leaves.

In another plot, the metal letters from a courtesy marker lay exposed on the ground, scattered. Erin worked to gather the letters and used them to decipher a name she recognized because she had done some research on the plot's owner, Patrick Henry Allen. The marker belonged to his wife, Pearl Banks Allen—whose name and burial location might have been lost if someone like Erin didn't come along looking for traces.

In December 2020, Enrichmond insisted that the Friends of East End remove a hand-painted sign that had marked the entrance to the cemetery since 2015. The sign, which read "East End Cemetery, est. 1897," was painted by John Shuck's neighbor Ted Sanderson, who donated it to the cemetery. The Friends had surrounded it with a stone circle where they planted flowers, which Enrichmond also asked that they take away.

Enrichmond never replaced the sign. Rather, at a spot nearby, they installed a wooden kiosk—the kind you see at trailheads, where it usually holds a map and a reminder not to leave trash. The kiosk was, according to an Enrichmond email, a step toward fulfilling calls for unified "branding and signage" in the master plan that descendants had helped develop. But it seemed hard to believe that descendants had really intended for a hand-painted sign and flowers to wind up replaced by such a barren and impersonal new marker. Symbolically, the differences between these two ways of marking the cemetery and welcoming visitors—shown in the two photographs below—seem also to mark the boundary between formal stewardship and authentic care.[107]

FIGURE 2.2. The sign that used to mark the entrance to East End Cemetery, in Henrico County, Virginia. It is a wide rectangle, painted white, with an arch extending at the top and a simple rising sun design painted on it. The sign has cursive lettering that reads "East End Cemetery, Est. 1897" and small American flags attached to its sides. There is a plastic box for brochures on its left post; below the sign, inside a circle of stones, are yellow, purple, and orange mums. Photograph by Brian Palmer, October 15, 2015. Used with permission.

On one of my last visits to East End while writing this book, I asked Erin to tell me, honestly, how East End would look if the whole situation with Enrichmond had not gotten so bad, if the Friends of East End were still working in the cemetery on Saturdays. She freely admitted that they had always struggled, would inevitably struggle, to keep large portions of the cemetery clear.[108] But even in sections they couldn't clear, Erin said, volunteers with the Friends of East End had often pulled a few vines here and there, just to restore some visibility to graves that were being overgrown.

That evening, Erin said we were "just going for a short walk" into Evergreen to see if we could find a gravesite that Thomas Taylor, a local descendant, had mentioned to Erin: the place where his grandparents were buried. Erin had an idea where the graves should be based on her research, but still couldn't—still can't—find them. She soon disappeared into thickets of vines, hunting so hard she didn't notice how long we were staying, how late.

FIGURE 2.3. The kiosk placed at East End by the Enrichmond Foundation in 2021, a simple wooden structure with two unpainted sides and a slanted roof. It stands in front of a wooded area. A painted black wooden board is attached to the front of the structure, with a few signs and notices on its upper left side, one of which reads "Cemetery Property: No Trespassing, No Hunting, No Relic Hunting, No Dumping." Photograph by the author, June 6, 2021.

How late. What John Sydnor derided as "clearing the same space over and over again" is productive in ways that can't be measured in acreage. It generates knowledge of the plots—and the dead people—that cemetery citizens are visiting while they work. It produces a relationship between the two kinds of cemetery citizen, the dead and the living—exactly what was missing from that courtroom where Enrichmond's ownership of East End was formalized in 2019. As with so many other forms of care (such as putting a child to bed, or watering a garden), repetition is not inefficiency. It reaffirms commitments, provides new chances to notice. It deepens care.

Other mistakes can be forgiven, corrected; but a lack of care not so easily—not crushed metal markers, photos of human remains turned into publicity, trust and patience tested and lost. A lack of care is not a mere oversight to be corrected the next time, and then again the next time after that. It is a stage in the destruction of the cemeteries, and it poisons future opportunities to care.

I'm not saying that care solves everything. Nor do I think that being conscientious, effective caretakers of a cemetery gives anyone ultimate moral authority. As critic Maggie Nelson argues, "Care is not as simple a solution or a panacea as it can often be rendered. . . . [C]are edges up against a lot of difficult arenas. I mean, it edges up against paternalism. It edges up against presuming to know for others how they want to be cared for."[109] We have to be political about care: to pay attention to who does most of the caring, and who seems exempt from having to think about care at all.

Jill Lepore points out that the reclamation of African American cemeteries is led, in many places, by Black women "who have families to care for and work full-time jobs but volunteer countless hours and formidable organizing skills."[110] Cemeteries can become another site where Black people, especially Black women, are burdened with figuring out "who is harmed . . . and what you need to do to fix it for everyone," as Heather McGhee puts it.[111] The ethical dilemmas are magnified when care is directed at dead people, whose needs and interests can only come to us through complex practices of interpretation. Talking about care moves us beyond simple questions of duties and whether they are being performed. It makes us confront the intimacy, power, and messiness of some people's privilege to be caregivers, the decisions that must be made even when there is no good or right answer.

In May 2022, Enrichmond announced that John Sydnor was leaving his position as executive director.[112] A brief period of confusion followed, during which representatives of both Enrichmond and the Virginia Outdoors Foundation attended a meeting they cast as an attempt to build bridges, move on from the troubled past, and plan for the future of the cemeteries.

Just a month after that meeting, Jeremy Lazarus of the *Richmond Free Press* reported that Enrichmond's board had "resigned without notice or replacement and . . . the foundation's treasury may have been depleted."[113] No one interviewed for the story would make a substantive comment. The people who had argued for years that only Enrichmond could serve as the cemeteries' stewards went silent.

The organization's website disappeared: "Sorry, that page doesn't seem to exist." The fate of the cemeteries was unclear, as was that of the eighty-six organizations that depended on Enrichmond as their fiscal agent. Community gardens, neighborhood recreation associations, and other groups were all told there was no way to access the funds they had entrusted to Enrichmond, totaling at least $200,000 and possibly much more.[114] The Virginia Attorney General and the Federal Bureau of Investigation soon launched criminal probes; local politicians set aside new funds in the city budget to help these organizations.[115] Ryan K. Smith wrote, with earned skepticism, "There's little reason to believe that the powers that put the cemeteries into this scenario will find a better solution going forward. We turn yet again to the families and the volunteers for that hope."[116]

In the meantime, the owner of East End and Evergreen cemeteries is still Parity LLC, the corporation created so that Enrichmond could acquire the properties.[117] A biographical sketch of Sydnor, used by multiple organizations with which he is affiliated, describes him as transforming Enrichmond from "a one-person operation to the vibrant, multi-jurisdictional organization that serves as a steward for public spaces through conservation and programming." It's all in the present tense, as if Enrichmond still existed, and wasn't suspected of criminal behavior.[118] Enrichmond is being investigated for the funds that it seems to have made disappear. But Sydnor and other leaders of the organization should also be remembered for acting like they were the inevitable best stewards of the cemeteries, while in fact they profoundly disrupted care of these spaces—and then walked away.

Meanwhile, as my research was concluding, the Friends of East End began to return in force, and publicly, to the cemetery. Photos they posted on Instagram reflected a mix of feelings. They expressed heartbreak at the overgrowth covering grave markers they had once cleared and tended. But they started making fast and consistent progress, far beyond merely "clearing the same space over and over again." Erin wrote, "It has been kind of amazing to see how consistent care—even just a couple of hours a day, often by just one of us at a time—can tame the worst of the overgrowth and even keep much of the cemetery looking tidy."[119]

The Friends of East End once again started sharing photos of tiny toads, grave markers reemerging from the weeds, Teacake dashing around while the volunteers were hard at work: "[M]oments of beauty . . . despite the BS."[120]

THREE

"The Largest, Most Beautiful, and Popular of All Our Cemeteries"

Mount Moriah

MICHELLE & MARCEL
(Michelle Smallwood-Kassab, November 5, 2017 and July 19, 2021)

That the "pepper death" of a 21-month-old child
in Levittown on Jan. 9 was "accidental"
was the verdict rendered Thursday night
at an inquest held in the Falls Township Municipal Building
by Bucks County Coroner Dr. Wilmer S. Trinkle.[1]
I recently found out my departed brother Marcel Smallwood
who died in Jan 1960 (21 month old)
is buried Mt Moriah. I do not think he even had or has

a headstone

marker

anything.[2]

(brown-haired, brown-eyed Marcel Smallwood)[3]

Like all of us he was a foster child.
I want to make sure he is treated in death
better than he was treated in life.[4]

Hugh Trantum, director of the Child Care Society,
said that the Smallwood children had been placed
in foster homes because their mother had been ill
and their father worked out of the country.

Saturday evening Marcel had a temper tantrum
at the dinner table. He ran crying
into his bedroom. Mrs. Forsberg
followed the lad into the room

and placed pepper on his tongue
as punishment for his tantrum.
When she noticed that the child
was having difficulty breathing,
she gave him water, called a doctor
and started artificial respiration.

Mrs. Ralph Smith lives across the street.
Mrs. Smith said, "She's a wonderful person.
It's a shame such a thing could happen
to such a wonderful girl. Why did it have to happen
to such a devoted couple
                    and above average parents?[5]

All the family that I've found
I've spent forty years trying to find myself.
All of them didn't know I existed. Almost half
of my siblings have either died or committed suicide.
It was a bad legacy. I had to stop my research sometimes
because it got too heavy, too personal.

Ken Smith from the Mount Moriah volunteers
had to tell me that [Marcel] was in an angel grave
and I said *that's a politically correct term*
for a potter's grave, isn't it? And he said, *yeah.*
He said there's forty other unwanted people
from Philadelphia buried in [Marcel's] plot.
Forty people.[6]

The challenge we face is being able to work the plot
as it is not an area that we have gotten to yet.
The positive thing is that the area has many tall trees
with a canopy which keeps the area somewhat clear of brush. . . .

As I approached the plot this morning
I found three deer grazing.
So while it is not what you would envision
as a modern cemetery
with manicured grass
it's really quite peaceful.[7]
They said they were going to adopt him.

Well why'd they let him get buried
in a potter's grave with no marker, then?

It's like an empty lot. You can just feel the unwanted about it.
There's nothing having his name on it. Nothing at all.[8]

I have added a record for him on FindAGrave
so that he can be remembered forever.[9]

I wish there'd be a marker for all those unwanted people
that are buried in his plot, forty other people. That they
would be recognized as important as anybody else
in that cemetery. I just wish
they had like a little thing
where all their names were on it.

Because he was somebody.[10]

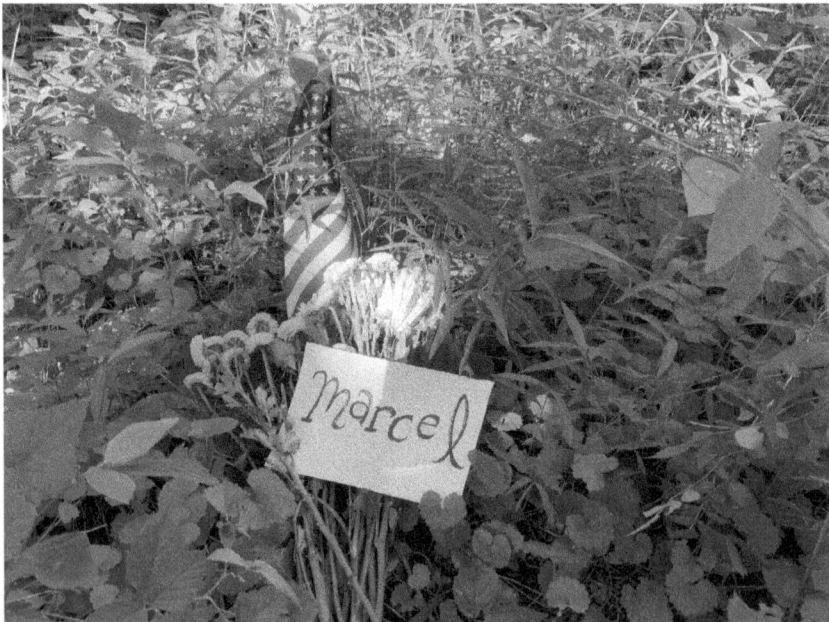

FIGURE 3.1. An overgrown patch of green at Philadelphia's Mount Moriah Cemetery: the unmarked spot where Marcel Smallwood and others are buried. An American flag, bouquet of flowers, and hand-painted sign reading "Marcel" have been placed amid the weeds. Ken Smith and Jenn O'Donnell helped me locate this grave on behalf of Marcel's sister, Michelle Smallwood-Kassab. Photograph by the author, July 25, 2021.

"To Define but Not Necessarily Tame the Landscape"

On a spring day in 2011, a caretaker closed the gates of Mount Moriah and locked them. Mourners and descendants came to visit the graves of family and friends and couldn't enter. People who had recently buried a loved one could not get authorization to place permanent markers at the grave. One woman, whose son was buried there just before the cemetery closed, recalls that if she hadn't put a rod with a reflector on the ground, she would have had no way to find his plot again once the cemetery opened back up to visitors.[11]

Mount Moriah currently spans well over one hundred acres, crossing from Lower Southwest Philadelphia into the borough of Yeadon, in Delaware County.[12] It is the vastest and wildest of the burial grounds I write about here—a place to see hawks, deer, and foxes. To feel lost, swallowed up, enchanted. Yet it is also the most urban of the cemeteries in this book, close to the center of a metropolis. Alongside its woods and wildlife, many of its features and surroundings are—to use a word Philadelphia has fully embraced—gritty.[13]

Mount Moriah didn't start out gritty, or even urban. Established in 1855 by the Pennsylvania legislature, it reflected a trend toward large, wooded cemeteries intended to allow for more development in city centers and provide people with an alternative to crowded church graveyards.[14] It was accessible by rail from both the center of Philadelphia and the suburbs to the west.[15] Sometimes called "Philadelphia's most democratic burial ground," Mount Moriah catered to the middle class rather than the city's elite, with an 1871 brochure touting it as "the largest, most beautiful, and popular of our cemeteries."[16]

Benjamin Gilbert Buckley describes what Mount Moriah was like when it opened: "The cemetery was located on a large tract of land on the west edge of Southwest Philadelphia that had only recently been incorporated in the city limits, and some of it still lay outside the now sprawling city. . . . The bucolic landscape contained clusters of old-growth trees, a meandering creek, and open meadows. The cemetery company went about creating a series of improvements to define but not necessarily tame the landscape. . . . Soon after its founding, the natural landscape developed a forest of marble and granite monuments that rose between the trees and shrubs and which varied greatly in height, shape, and style."[17] These monuments remain impressive, especially the thirty-five-foot column in an area called the Circle of St. John.

The enclosed ten-acre Naval Asylum plot on the Yeadon side, where 2,400 officers and sailors are buried, contains rows of identical headstones provided by the Department of Veterans Affairs. The agency maintains this plot and a smaller one on the Philadelphia side, separate from the sprawling wilderness of graves around them. Mount Moriah, unlike East End and Geer, also has buildings on-site: a small office building for cemetery caretakers (currently being restored by the Friends of Mount Moriah), and an arched brownstone gatehouse built in 1855. Only the façade and a few other portions of the gatehouse remain, currently supported by wooden beams to preserve it from further ruin.

An 1871 guidebook promised that Mount Moriah would be "forever secure against disturbance from opening of streets or the growth of the city."[18] Surrounded by row houses and bisected by a four-lane highway, the cemetery now sits amid dense, mostly low-income neighborhoods. Once predominantly Irish American, the population is now majority Black. African immigrants, many of them refugees, have settled in the area, opening restaurants, markets, and hair braiding salons.[19]

Mount Moriah's estimated two-hundred thousand or more graves are home to notable Philadelphians, veterans of the Revolutionary War, Civil War, and other conflicts, Freemasons, members of many church congregations, and the indigent dead in potter's fields.[20] "Masons, Methodists and a Philadelphia mayor are buried at Mount Moriah, as are widows and orphans, Presbyterians and Episcopalians, senators and inventors, Baptists, Jews, and Catholics. All races, religions, and classes are represented," writes journalist Pamela J. Forsythe.[21]

According to some people I interviewed, Mount Moriah was also the only Philadelphia-area cemetery offering traditional Muslim burials without a concrete vault. Imam Suetwedien A. Muhammad recalls having buried "thousands of Muslims" there over the years.[22] Philadelphia has a longstanding, diverse network of mosques, cultural centers, and other Muslim institutions.[23] Its Muslim population, according to the Council on American-Islamic Relations, is eighty percent Black; whereas Black Muslims make up only twenty percent of the Muslim population in the U.S. as a whole. The city's Black Muslim heritage includes enslaved people who brought their Islamic faith with them from West Africa in the seventeenth century, as well as many African Americans who converted in the mid-1950s when Malcolm X (who ministered at Nation of Islam

Temple 12 in Philadelphia) and other Muslim leaders were inspiring radical Black activism nationwide.[24]

Though cosmopolitan in some respects, Mount Moriah and other rural cemeteries map out social boundaries and hierarchies through the arrangement of plots, the size and type of monument, and other status symbols.[25] In 1875, the funeral procession of an African American caterer, Henry Jones, was turned away at Mount Moriah's gates. His wife, Margaret, wanted to bury him there due to the precarious conditions of the city's African American cemeteries, which she said were "about to be cut through by streets."[26] White plot owners at the cemetery objected to the burial on the basis of race; they claimed that it would probably lead to "acts of violence and breaches of the peace," as well as "large numbers of the dead interred there [being] removed."[27] (In fact, whether they knew it or not, the cemetery already had Black people buried in its soil, including Jones's sister-in-law Elizabeth.[28]) The petitioners threatened that the cemetery "would be financially ruined" and its burial association "forced to leave the thousands of existing graves to abandonment and neglect."[29] Financial ruin and neglect *are* the fates that would eventually come to Mount Moriah—over the course of more than a century to follow, and through no fault of Henry Jones.

In 1876, the Pennsylvania Supreme Court affirmed Margaret's right to bury him at Mount Moriah. "The fact that said Henry Jones was a colored person did not in law justify the respondent in refusing to permit the burial of the body in said lot of ground," the court found, effectively declaring the segregation of burial grounds unconstitutional.[30] By that time, Margaret had taken over her husband's catering business, and interred his body elsewhere.[31] The fight was no longer about his final resting place, which she judged would no longer be secure from protests or vandalism at Mount Moriah (the cemetery had subsequently also denied burial to her sister, Mary Cooper). It was about justice.[32]

The dead at Mount Moriah have become marginalized by the cemetery's long decline and sudden closure; but in life they occupied many different social positions. The cemetery's landscape is a complex mix of shared fates and stark differences—not only in the burials themselves but, more recently, in how people are making their revisions.

Race is among the most salient of these differences. The cemetery's degraded conditions are bound up with the disenfranchisement of the communities around it. As cemetery neighbor Tracy Gordon pointed out, many of Mount Moriah's current problems begin at Cobbs Creek Parkway, which roars through it, dividing the larger Philadelphia portion of the cemetery from the Yeadon side.[33]

The parkway is a poorly maintained, busy artery separating historically African American neighborhoods from the parklands on the other side of the road. It is known for traffic, drag racing, and violence; neighbors have been asking for safety measures there for over a decade.[34] Where the parkway meets the cemetery, it often floods. Its guardrails are bent or altogether collapsed. Gordon warned against treating the cemetery as exceptional or isolated, as the rhetoric of "sacred burial grounds" tends to do. She cast Mount Moriah as one piece of a larger tapestry of racial neglect in Philadelphia, an issue that remains a central challenge for the organization focused on the space within the cemetery gates.

Following a long period of decline, Mount Moriah became technically unowned once the last member of its cemetery association passed away in 2004. One employee seems to have remained for the next seven years, responsible for the upkeep of the whole expanse of woods and graves.[35] In April 2011, due to its condition and lack of ownership, the city issued a court order closing the cemetery.[36] It does not seem that anyone informed families they were about to lose access to the graves of their loved ones.

Since its abandonment, the Friends of Mount Moriah have undertaken herculean efforts to reclaim the vast, overgrown cemetery. The group's charismatic leader in the years after the cemetery closed was Paulette Rhone, an African American budget analyst who grew up near the cemetery and buried her husband there in 1993.[37] Paulette and another volunteer, Donna Morelli, started with nothing but a push mower. Since then, through the dogged efforts of Paulette and many others, the group has gained members, notoriety, and institutional clout. In recent years, the Friends won a series of major grants to salvage the cemetery's historic gatehouse and create a strategic plan for preservation. In fact, Paulette's successor as the Friends of Mount Moriah president (until 2023), Ken Smith, argues that the cemetery's closure was "the best thing that ever happened" to it. After decades of neglect, with the cemetery being used as a dump, "it effectively jump-started this grassroots effort."[38]

In February 2019, Paulette died suddenly. Her death was a major, tragic event in the life of the cemetery and its revision process. Though Mount Moriah is no longer operational, Philadelphia's Orphans' Court granted permission for Paulette to be buried there next to her husband on June 8, 2019. The corner of South 61st Street and Kingsessing Avenue, abutting the cemetery, now has a street sign bearing the name Paulette Rhone Place.

Smith's quick, sensitive response to Michelle Smallwood-Kassab's inquiry about her brother Marcel's grave, featured in the poem at the start of this chapter, is typical for this volunteer community. The Friends of Mount Moriah's Facebook site is the most active I've seen for a cemetery organization, with over seven thousand members. They receive frequent queries and requests, which are always answered, often with photographs and research; some of the volunteers even reset headstones that have fallen.

FIGURE 3.2. A view of Mount Moriah Cemetery with its hills, paths, stands of trees, and grave markers from multiple eras and in varying conditions (including stone mausoleums in the background). Photograph by the author, April 3, 2021.

"Once It's Started, They're Just Grieving People"

In 2017, I attended a meeting at a church a little over a mile from Mount Moriah. Naji Muhammad was an unforgettable presence there, with a tidy mustache, trim suit, and fedora. He filmed the proceedings via smartphone. A retired construction worker, Muhammad had buried his son, Hakim, in a section of the cemetery along Springfield Avenue not long before the cemetery was abandoned. Nearly all the visible grave markers in that section belong to Muslims, many of them men and boys who died young—in their teens, twenties, and thirties.

Muhammad was a proud member of the Nation of Islam. He "hosted, produced and funded" a radio show called the *Friends of Farrakhan*, which he broadcast via Facebook.[39] The show replayed speeches by Louis Farrakhan, the Nation of Islam's longtime leader, a conspiracy-spouting anti-Semite and virulent homophobe.[40] These were not issues Muhammad and I ever discussed. We did meet at Mount Moriah twice in the years after the public meeting to discuss the state of the cemetery. We also spoke by phone a few times.

Visiting the cemetery after the city closed it, Muhammad was horrified at how conditions had deteriorated. He began to tend his son's grave, along with the rest of the Springfield Avenue section. He placed a sign quoting the Quran facing the street. Paulette Rhone and some other members of the Friends of Mount Moriah objected (at least privately), saying that no religious texts or symbols should be used on public signs at a nondenominational cemetery.

The meeting I attended was organized by Rosalyn McPherson, a consultant hired to promote community input as part of the city-funded strategic plan for the cemetery. During the event, admirers praised Muhammad's efforts and insisted that their loved ones' graves were being neglected by the Friends group. Members of the Friends, who are mostly White, seemed caught off guard, as did McPherson. Some of the Friends explained that they had started their reclamation work in the most visible, accessible sections—partly to send a message to the community, especially potential vandals and trash-dumpers, that someone was watching over the place and taking care of it ("Dumping breeds dumping," said Ken Smith at a later meeting, stressing the need to get trash out of visible spaces quickly).[41] From there, the group was gradually moving outward to other sections, with neither race nor religion playing any role in their plans. According to Paulette, there were ten or more plots between the areas the Friends had already cleared and the Springfield Avenue section, "and those people matter too."[42] During her turn at the microphone, Paulette said that tensions with the Muslim community were "a longstanding thing." But, she emphasized, "Mount Moriah is one cemetery."[43]

The event was fast-paced and often tense, with McPherson struggling to re-focus the conversation. The topic jumped from cemetery preservation to gentri-fication and city politics, to the illegal burials allegedly still taking place at the cemetery. Dante Leonard, who grew up a ten-minute walk from the cemetery and worked at a nearby homeless youth center, said he had buried four friends in Mount Moriah—and helped to dig the graves. "I should be there myself," he said, referring to his own experiences with gun violence. Paulette said she had seen burial parties headed into the cemetery, but didn't intervene because "once it's started, they're just grieving people."[44]

The strategic plan for the cemetery was written up in 2018 by consultants from Fairmount Ventures, a firm that works with nonprofits and the public sector. It establishes a vision of the cemetery as both a nature sanctuary and a historic site, with a new owner who would be responsible for maintenance while the Friends focus on more "traditional" activities for a volunteer group, such as event planning and education. Regarding the tensions that were on display in the 2017 community meeting, the plan's Stakeholder Engagement Report—written by McPherson's company, the ROZ Group—establishes a goal of moving on from an "'us vs. them' mentality" to "a collaborative or cooperative spirit be-tween the Friends and the other deeply passionate groups of individuals who have family buried at the site."[45]

Though its overall tone is conciliatory, McPherson's report alludes to "mis-information & miscommunication" about the Friends and their work, especially regarding funding. Citing the community meeting and follow-up interviews, it says, "There is a misunderstanding that FOMMCI [the Friends of Mount Moriah Cemetery Incorporated] is unduly benefiting from the grant funds received for strategic planning. As a result, these same people do not understand the process of securing grant dollars and private funds, which is critical to Mount Moriah's long-term sustainability."[46] When I interviewed McPherson, she elaborated: "Sometimes the Muslim community was feeling that Paulette was selling out to the White people. And that's not what was going on, but . . . Look, she's the one that got the money, she knew how to pursue stuff, and she knew how to make the right friends to achieve her goals. And sometimes I had to explain to folks why you need to respect that as a skill and a talent."[47]

The report also suggests that critics of the Friends of Mount Moriah have unrealistic expectations: "Many believe that the City of Philadelphia has an obligation to fund Mount Moriah, at the level of maintenance of the Woodlands." The Woodlands (not to be confused with Woodland Cemetery in Richmond) is a National Historic Landmark District on the banks of the Schuylkill River in a busy, heavily gentrified part of Philadelphia. It is fifty-four acres, roughly a third of Mount Moriah's size, and features initiatives such as the Grave Gardeners, a program where people plant and maintain a small container garden at a gravesite they have "adopted."

Finally, the report seeks to defuse the narrative of a "Muslim section" that is being targeted for neglect. It's a term Naji Muhammad used frequently in our conversations, referring to the Springfield Avenue area that he maintained as the "Muslim section."[48] There are Muslims buried throughout the cemetery, in multiple sections—current Friends of Mount Moriah president Jenn O'Donnell counts at least four.[49] The report warns that the "leadership of Mount Moriah should not view 'the Muslim community' as a monolithic group."[50]

A Separate Effort

It was thirty degrees on a slate-colored day when I met Naji and Inez Muhammad in Mount Moriah's Springfield Avenue section, across from a few tight blocks of row houses. When they emerged from their car to greet me, Inez was bundled up with a gray scarf around her head, a fur-lined hood, and a long coat. Under his red baseball cap, which read "Embrace the Journey," Naji wore only a hooded sweatshirt and light Carhartt work jacket.

The couple's son, Hakim, was born in 1978 and died in August 2009, when he was 31. This means that he was buried about a year and a half before the gates to Mount Moriah were locked. His flat stone grave marker gives his name, birth, and death dates. Below that, it says simply, "HOLY QURAN CH 3. 154."

Standing next to Hakim's grave, I asked about the verse. Naji Muhammad said that it explains "every essence" of what happened to his son, so much that he almost cried when he read it. He did not say more.[51] In a follow-up email, I asked if he would be willing to share more about the inscription. He said he would call me to discuss, but never did. While I did learn more about Hakim's death via my own research, here I follow his father's lead: I focus on the place where Hakim was laid to rest rather than the story of his death.

At the cemetery, as my hands began to freeze, making my notebook and pen useless, Muhammad vividly described what it was like when he came to visit his son's grave and instead found grass growing "like maybe over four feet, five feet high." Most of the graves were invisible. "It was really terrible. I mean it was terrible. You wouldn't even recognize that it was a cemetery."

When he came out with a lawn mower to clear a path to Hakim's grave, he noticed other people doing the same. So he decided to get organized. He put out a call for help that got fifty or sixty people out to the cemetery. Over the years, he purchased lawn mowers and other equipment himself, planted a magnolia tree, and got a Shop-Rite supermarket to donate benches. He also installed the sign with a quotation from the Quran: "Every Soul Must taste of Death, then to us you will be returned."

Near the sign is a small box with a petition that visitors and passersby can sign. The petition (which I signed months before I met the couple) is addressed "Dear Government Body." It calls conditions in Mount Moriah "a very serious problem and a moral issue as well" and asks for the city to "give the dead the respect they deserve." Muhammad expressed concern that his petition may not have been worded right, that he might need an attorney's help. He said he was "just trying to guess and put words together or, you know, crying out for help. . . . I know that what I'm doing is not the long-term solution. I can be gone, my health can be bad, whatever. . . . It'll be just as it was when I first came, looking like a jungle."

In April 2021, I returned for the first official workday of the spring at Mount Moriah. Along with regular volunteers, members of a Girl Scout troop came out with parents and scout leaders. They practiced citizen science, identifying trees for a crowdsourced Philadelphia tree map.[52] Members of the public could register online, and many of the participants were visiting the cemetery for the first time. An Eagle Scout troop also had its own separate tent, with a project removing the eggs of spotted lanternflies from the trees. The cemetery was busy.

While I was on my way to the cemetery for the 9:00 a.m. workday check-in, I got a text from Naji Muhammad. He said that he had arrived at the cemetery and was working in the Springfield Avenue section. I had to decide where to go first, how to navigate my relationships to these two very separate efforts.

I rode my folding bike over to the Springfield side. It was less than a half-mile ride from the Yeadon entrance, where I'd started, but the curve of Cobbs Creek Parkway and the speed of the cars made for a frightening crossing. The path alongside Springfield Avenue was strewn with rocks and trash, forcing me to get off my bike and walk it.

When I reentered the cemetery, Muhammad was there on an orange ride-on lawn mower, making tight turns as he cut the grass. He wore light blue coveralls, work gloves and boots, a sun hat and a mask.

When he pulled up in front of me on his mower, he told me it was his first visit of the season. He would need to come back every two weeks to keep the section mowed. I asked what he thought of the state of the cemetery, whether there had been any notable changes since we last talked on that cold day in January 2020, just a few weeks before COVID-19 lockdowns began.

He pointed at two flat grave markers on the ground, which he said had been placed there recently. They were more signs that, while all of Mount Moriah is technically inactive, some people are still making changes, marking graves. He said the markers' location may not be at precisely the right place of burial—not "legit"—but that installing them provided people with closure. The markers were not dug into the earth to lie flat, as is common, but rather were lying on the surface of the ground. Strangely, when we approached, we found that both were for the same person—though made of different kinds of stone, one with a portrait carved into it of a bearded, smiling young Black man wearing a kufi skullcap.

When I asked about his thoughts on Mount Moriah's upkeep in general, Muhammad said, "Everything is the same. I don't get no call from nobody." The last time he put out a call out for people to come out and help, in 2019, no one showed up. He was now resigned to doing the labor himself.

Muhammad theorized that the Friends of Mount Moriah saw his work and figured that since the Springfield Avenue section was already being maintained, they didn't need to worry about it. He pointed to a section right nearby, just a bit up the hill from us, where someone had done some clearing, stopping short of the area where we were standing.

I was surprised at the persistence of the notion that the Friends were ignoring or avoiding Muslim graves. Over the years, I have watched them come quickly and enthusiastically to the aid of Muslim mourners seeking information about their dead. At least one member of the organization, Al Wilson, has photographed and shared, with reverence, the inscriptions from Muslim graves in his regular updates from the cemetery.[53] I reminded Muhammad that, as Paulette and other members of the Friends had described at the 2017 public meeting, they had a plan determining the order of the sections they were clearing. I said there was a "schedule." It was not exactly the right word; but that's what came out.

With a rueful laugh, Muhammad gestured around us at the graves facing Springfield Avenue. "It's not in the schedule. . . . When this section come up, it's not in the schedule." I asked if he would trust others to care for the area where his son is buried. "It's not about trust," he responded, "it's an all-hands situation. . . . It'd be nice to come here one day and look, and it's done." As much as he'd prefer not to go it alone, Muhammad said, "My deeds are recorded with God, and it's all right."

I wondered if I could do something productive with my ability to cross these cemetery boundaries. The Friends had a welcoming table set up just a short walk from where Muhammad and I were standing. I gave him Jenn O'Donnell's name and told him that it might be worth stopping by the table on his way out, just to have a conversation. He never did.[54]

On the other side of the cemetery, a couple of hours later, I suggested the same thing to Jenn. I asked whether a simple phone call to Naji Muhammad could clear the air. I was really meddling now, and uncomfortable about it.

As adamant as Muhammad was that the Springfield Avenue section "wasn't in the schedule," Jenn was equally certain that the Friends' plan for clearing the cemetery had already been explained to him. If Muhammad were to repeat the same kinds of accusations now that he made at the meeting in 2017, she said, he would not get a kind reception from the people putting hours of work into the cemetery every week with the Friends. That meeting, and the entire strategic planning process, seemed to have exposed wildly divergent narratives about Mount Moriah without providing any clear process for hashing them out.

The strategic plan calls for more frequent communication to the public, and more representation from different stakeholder groups on the Friends' board. Vaguely, it also suggests they "discuss a plan for creating more unity and central-ization among those interested in the future of Mount Moriah."[55] When I spoke to Ken Smith in 2021, he said the Friends were clearing three of the four histor-ically Muslim sections of the cemetery. Beyond that, his approach to inclusion was more passive than what the strategic plan envisioned: "Everybody is always welcome to go ahead and come out. . . . We're always open to having them a part of our organization."[56]

In March 2022, Muhammad posted on Facebook that he was moving out of state. "I'm at the end of the road, I will not be able to continue to maintain Mt. Moriah cemetery. . . ."[57] At the time I interpreted "the end of the road" as the end of his cleanup efforts, since he would now be too far away to work in the cemetery regularly. I didn't recall his words from that day in January: "I can be gone, my health can be bad, whatever. . . ."

When multiple subsequent attempts to reach him failed, I searched for him on Facebook. I saw that the couple had moved to a house in Delaware, where they were caring for one of their grandchildren. Muhammad was planting fruit trees.

On May 8, 2022, he died.[58] "The end of the road." Without Naji Muhammad's care, his son Hakim's grave will need tending by the Friends of Mount Moriah. It will have to be in the schedule.

In July 2022, the Friends got a Facebook post from someone whose cousin was buried in the Springfield Avenue section, inquiring as to why it was so overgrown and whether donations could be directed to replace Naji Muhammad's efforts. A few weeks later, Ken Smith wrote to say that the Friends had just mowed. When I visited in November 2022, about half of this section—including the area around Hakim's grave—was looking clean and well tended. The other half was overgrown. But when I came back in April 2023, the whole section had been swallowed up again, with almost none of the markers visible unless I pushed away the grass. One of the few exceptions was Hakim's

FIGURE 3.3. A black-and-white sketch. In the foreground, the author, wearing a puffy jacket, mittens, and winter hat, gestures while holding a notebook. Naji Muhammad stands nearby, thin, wearing a light hooded sweatshirt and baseball cap, his hands in his pockets. Parked cars, buildings, and the tops of trees are visible behind us. Drawing by the author from my interview with Naji Muhammad in Mount Moriah Cemetery on January 20, 2020, based on footage taken by Inez Muhammad and posted on Facebook.

flat stone marker, where the grass didn't reach so high and the inscription was still easy to read. As if all of Muhammad's care over the years was exerting some lasting influence.

During all this time, his petition remained in its box at the street entrance, awaiting more signatures, never sent.

I MADE A PATHWAY
(Naji and Inez Muhammad, Mount Moriah Cemetery, January 20, 2020)

Naji
I used my residential lawn mower
I just made a pathway to where my son's remains—
the remains of my son. I made a pathway,
and I made it not just in a small section.
I did a big whole section there.

But it was only maybe two years later I realized that it was abandoned,
and I couldn't really recognize this area at all.
I thought it was at the wrong place.

Every now and then, you'll see,
someone will come and just do their loved one,
just a small portion, and that's it.
And I said, "Wow, you know,
you got to do better than that."
I've just been doing the whole thing.

Inez
A lot of us have lost our sons
to the street violence
and a lot of them are laid here.

So it holds a special place to a lot of parents
that went through that.

The neighbors, they really admire Naji.
Because can you imagine getting on your deck
and seeing this thing full with weeds?
It was past our heads.

All the people that could not find their loved ones,
now they come up,
and I just saw a rose
on someone's grave.

Before they wasn't even able to do that,
and sometimes we come up here
and it's balloons, you know,
because they put balloons out
on their loved ones' birthdays
or teddy bears. And they were not able
to acknowledge their loved ones
before.

Naji
So people is constantly trying to find loved ones.
Some of them don't know
where their loved one's at, you know,
and they're still getting headstones.

That one is new with the flowers, that one: new,
that one over here, that one is new.
The one all the way over there with the blue,
that's new—
she had got that last year,
that's new.

Inez
Isn't that the one that couldn't find her son?
I think that's the one.

Naji
There's a lot of other cemeteries like this.
Somehow it seem like people don't really care
about dead people. They don't. After you're gone, man,
you're just forgotten. They'll just think about you
every now and then. And that's it.
The living have to actually give them that respect,
and that's what I've been doing

for the remains
of my son
and for the whole cemetery

Springtime come again
I'll be right at it
again

A House That's Gone Now

Poems

TOOLS

A trowel is a tool
for digging headstones out from the dirt.
A probe can help you find
where to dig next

A chainsaw is a tool
for felling dead trees
chopping them up
and removing them
so they don't fall
on the dead buried beneath

A clipper is a tool
for making graves reappear
and a simple bucket of water
reveals a name that was lost

I'd like this book to be a tool
but I'm not sure what it does—
if it's a sandwich to keep you going,
or a tent offering shade and pause

Or if, like the trees,
alive or dead,
it's not a tool at all
but a presence, a sentinel

This book was mine for so long
I am ready
for it to be yours

WORKSHOP
Down the steps
past the laundry room
lemon and electricity scent
past the black and white swivel chair
and the temptation of Grandpa David's violin

to the darkest part of the house
where it is always cool

smell of motor oil, wood glue, metal
smell of things he knows how to do and I don't
never will

If it is time to eat, as it is so often here
if the cousins arrive
if it's time for a bath
for the nicer clothes we wear on holidays
even when we're not going to temple
I must go up to it
it doesn't come down here,
to the workshop

I am forty-two
writing this book
in a house full of people
who can't go to work or school
moving my computer and books
from dining table to office
to front porch to insomnia
on the downstairs sofa at night

But where I want to write this
is in his workshop
in a house that's gone now
sold and scraped:

a workshop like a cabinet of wonders, like a secret
and also like a missing grave

REVISION IS NOT FIXING
Revision is not fixing,
or setting names and meanings in stone.

Revision is broken world thinking:[1]
Here is this boat, it's smashed.
What do we make out of it? Is there a future for it
as a non-boat that still remembers,
can still tell the story,
of its days on the sea?

Of the changes in the water,
and how it felt itself
starting to sink?

Here is this past: it's both terrible
and utterly ours. We own it
so much more than we own our bodies
or our words. How do we live with it?
How do we pass it down

in a way where it doesn't twist, tense, and tighten,
trapping us in narrow places?

When I was three or three-ish, we visited my grandparents
in Fair Lawn. During a long meal,
I went out to the car unnoticed. I took the coins out
from where they were stored for paying tolls.
I inserted them into the heating vents,
cassette deck, every slot I could find.
All the shiny money
into all the narrow places.

When the adults discovered what I was doing,
I was removed from the car by quick, angry hands.
But I was spared any spanking or screaming.
I still got my dry *mandelbrot* cookies, my afternoon cartoons.

My grandparents knew what really breaks a world
and they had made their revisions
already.

Part II

REVISIONS ("IT WILL NEVER END, THAT WORK")

Repair inherits an old and layered world, making history but not in the circumstances of its choosing. It accounts for the durability of the old, but also the appearance of the new....

STEPHEN J. JACKSON, "Rethinking Repair," 223

All these stories of mourning, erasure, and partial repair: Why have I been looking for them my whole life? What do I want from them?

My field notes, April 2, 2021

FOUR

Pathways to Revision

HERE'S THE THING, AND HERE'S YOUR KNOWLEDGE
(Lisa Y. Henderson, Lane Street Project, February 9, 2021)

I was born in 1964. We're obviously
almost ten years past Brown v. Board at that point,
but I was born into a pretty rigidly segregated world.
I started first grade in the first year
that Wilson County complied fully with integration orders.
So, you know, I grew up in this kind of liminal space
between this old order and this new order.

Part of what I want to do is capture some aspects of history
before they disappear. I just feel like, when you have documents
or other sorts of artifacts, you—you know, I'm not an archaeologist,
but I know you sort of look at things, and you try to create some context.
Like: *What am I really seeing?* And sometimes it seems like
there's this sort of gap, like a synapse, between *here's the thing*,
and *here's your knowledge.* And sometimes I feel like I'm right there.
Like I can recognize this thing in a way that maybe someone
ten or fifteen years younger than I wouldn't recognize it,
and I want to preserve those connections.

The way [the Lane Street Project] is resonating,
particularly with younger people,
has been pretty amazing to me. These are people
who have come back to Wilson for the most part,
people who've gone away to school and who chose
to come back, and have lots of ideas
about what they'd like to see happen in Wilson
and lots of ideas about what should—
what we should value,
you know, what we should protect.

And I think also, and I'm speaking
as a person a generation older than they are . . .
you are at that age where you kind of start thinking about:
Who came before me? I think for most people
it takes a minute to kind of think of yourself
in a context larger than, say, your immediate family
and to consider your place in a lineage.
They're at that age
where they're starting to think about their own legacies,
what they've done,
what they want to do.
Looking around and wanting
to be inspired.

In January 2020, I had lunch with Jenn O'Donnell at a Mexican restaurant in the Philly suburbs, about five minutes from Haverford College, where we had met. We were on the Main Line, a string of historically wealthy towns stretching to the northwest of Philadelphia. At the time, Jenn was the board secretary of the Friends of Mount Moriah; she would later become, in rapid succession, vice president and then president. I'm used to seeing Jenn amid the green expanses and gray monuments of Mount Moriah, or the light stone of Haverford College buildings. The bright yellows, reds, and greens on the walls, tablecloths, and dishes at the restaurant were a bit disorienting, especially in midwinter.

As we ate, Jenn reflected on some of the challenges of organizing cemetery citizens: "You're talking about people who all arrived at this place for different reasons, who maybe would not in any other context find themselves spending time together or working together. Who maybe have different goals and different hopes for the work that we're doing. And trying to keep all of those differences in mind, while keeping everybody motivated and moving . . ."

Marginalized cemeteries create odd fellowships, which is both a beautiful and a challenging thing. I met cemetery citizens who were looking for a way to spend time outdoors while doing some good for their communities, and who put long days of physical labor into clearing and maintaining cemetery plots. I met cemetery citizens who were passionate about honoring veterans, or about power tools. Others had started coming to the cemetery through their own efforts to discover their ancestors; they soon found themselves with expertise they could use to help other descendants do the same.

What people *do* as cemetery citizens, and feel like they do well, often shapes their stories about what the cemetery needs most: what kind of damage or injustice it embodies and what revisions would be an adequate response.

For writers, revision begins with close reading. What is this thing in front of me? Where does it need to grow, shrink, or change? You can't revise something you haven't looked at and interpreted; your revision is built on these insights. Cemetery citizens also start by reading the landscapes of the dead and then deciding what needs revision. In the process, they build theories about what is broken and how it needs to be fixed, what stories should be shared. I agree with Jenn that people come to marginalized cemeteries with "different goals and different hopes." But I'm equally interested in the different *meanings* they make once the work has started: for themselves, the burial grounds, and the dead.

There are patterns to the ways people see a marginalized cemetery. They flow across the places I studied: not as exact duplicates but as echoes, changing slightly as they go. The tensions between cemetery citizens often start with their fundamentally different interpretations of the burial landscape around them, what the dead deserve, would have wanted, or are still crying out to have restored. I call these different visions "pathways to revision." The phrase is inspired by Naji Muhammad's story of how he had to clear his own pathway to his son's grave in Mount Moriah.

Spend an hour with Lisa Y. Henderson, Alex Green, or many of the other people whose voices appear in this chapter, and you will be reminded that one person can see through multiple lenses at once: that different pathways to revision can overlap and combine.

FIGURE 4.1. A simple black-and-white sketch of two volunteers working at Geer Cemetery. Both have long hair tied back. They are crouched down near one another weeding, their heads close together. Drawing by the author, November 13, 2022.

They can pull apart or reinforce each other. But the pathways that I describe here, as they have surfaced in my research, are meaningfully distinct. Some of them grow from experiences that not all cemetery citizens share: for example, for someone to experience a marginalized cemetery as a painful and powerful (even *empowering*) place to mourn, they must have an intimate connection to the dead who are buried there, or some other loss that they carry with them into the burial ground.

In *Death and Life in a Southern City*, Ryan K. Smith explores a variety of ap-proaches to cemetery reclamation. With a historian's eye, he describes three "waves" of historic preservation in Richmond. The first, "traditionalist" wave was led by Whites and largely conservative, determining that Revolutionary and Civil War landmarks and historically well-resourced cemeteries were "heritage worth saving" while ignoring spaces that held meaning and sacredness for non-dominant groups.[1] The second wave—which was there from the start, contesting the traditionalists and gradually gaining force—developed among preservation activists who have "sought to put marginalized sites on par" with the histories that had already been elevated in our national memory landscapes. In advocat-ing for various Indigenous, African American, and Jewish sites, they argued that "preservation could pose radical ends."[2]

The third wave of cemetery preservation is an outgrowth of this more radi-cal tradition, one facet of a larger struggle over whose story gets told and whose does not. However, in contrast to the second wave efforts, the leaders are often newcomers and more transitory figures: "students, transplants, artists and poli-ticians without previous ties to the city."[3] In cemeteries, especially, the intensity of their efforts can seem surprising and "enigmatic." According to Smith, "Some participants can be slow to express what has brought them to work every week for a decade at a cemetery where they have no relations."[4]

To understand these people, and the energies they bring to cemetery work, we need to pay particular attention to notions of belonging and kinship that don't fit neatly into the categories of descendant or non-descendant, insider or outsider. Some volunteers don't arrive at a cemetery with a clear plan to become a "regular" at workdays; they don't have a tidy explanation of the meaning the work has for them. Rather, they find meaning and belonging as they go, hand to earth or poring over archives in the local library, revising the present as they apply new ideas to the interpretation of the past.

In his novel *The City & The City*, China Miéville imagines two distinct cities located in the same physical space.[5] The two cities have different languages, foods, and cultures. It is the work of citizens, in each respective city, to inhabit their own city while actively "unseeing" the other: they must seem, even to themselves, not to hear cars and conversations that are well within earshot, not to notice smells that waft from one city into another. Miéville creates a vocabulary for how space is divided in this complex, layered world. Some large areas belong wholly to one city or the other, while others—down to different blocks of the same street—are "crosshatched," nearly contiguous. These spaces, even more than others, must be governed by rules and practices that keep the citizens of one city from straying into the other.

Though there are no formal borders or secret police enforcing them, I have come to think of marginalized cemeteries as being crosshatched too. Cemetery citizens converge in the same place and catch glimpses of each other's points of view across visible or invisible boundaries. They may acknowledge these differences and seek to work through them. Or they may learn, like the citizens of Miéville's city, to "unsee" the troubling or unwanted differences that are right in front of them.

Because these are places of the dead, a crucial part of the cross-hatching is that in each of these overlapping ways of seeing a cemetery, the dead *mean*, *need*, and *do* something different. They are stories to tell, sacred ancestors, or kin. They are people who left behind unfinished projects. Sometimes they are even allies in political struggle.

Cemetery Anti-Politics

Soon after George Floyd's murder, Debra Taylor Gonzalez-Garcia, the Friends of Geer Cemetery president, called me to discuss the organization's response to the nationwide protests. Some board members, including me, had been suggesting a statement of solidarity that would connect the cemetery and its many histories with the ongoing struggle for peace, justice, and Black lives. But Debra was worried. "There's always a backlash," I remember her saying. She didn't want a published statement to draw unwanted attention to the cemetery and make it a target for vandalism. I was happy that she trusted me with her concerns. But it made me see my earlier enthusiasm for a public statement in a new light. I hadn't perceived the same vulnerabilities that Debra, as a Black woman, could feel so acutely—vulnerabilities that extended from her body into the space of the cemetery.[6]

Meanwhile, I spoke with many cemetery citizens who reminded me of the "enigma" that Smith describes, pouring hours of hard labor into cemeteries without necessarily having a lot to say (at least to a visiting researcher) about what was driving them. They were, for the most part, White people in their fifties or older. One straightforward reading of their silence and avoidance is that they were uncomfortable talking about race. Geer and East End exist because of racial segregation, and Mount Moriah offers many reminders of the de facto segregation that still exists in our country today. But it is possible to spend time in all these places without engaging deeply with the forces that shaped them.

To some of my interlocutors I may have been an intimidating audience on questions of race and social justice, since they are topics I teach and write about in a university setting every day. These cemetery citizens may have been afraid to get things wrong when the pain, the passion, and the stakes were all so high. I know the feeling because I shared it. Shouting slogans at protests was relatively easy, while standing in front of a classroom of young people—or finding the right words in Friends of Geer meetings—often felt hard. In their reticence, some of the White cemetery citizens I interviewed may also have been striving for humility, wanting to allow others—especially Black leaders—to be the voices and visible representatives of these projects.

I acknowledge all these possible reasons for guardedness and avoidance in the encounters I had with other White cemetery citizens, drawing attention to the silences without having an answer for all of them. But I also want to look at the ideas these people *did* share: the content that was cross-hatched around the silences. Like denizens of one of Miéville's two interlocking cities, they had their own rich experiences of working in cemeteries, and a lot to say about why revisions to these spaces mattered, even as they worked to "unsee," or at least avoid, other topics.

When interviewing people who volunteer at Mount Moriah, I asked them about the tensions that had surfaced there, since members of Philadelphia's Black Muslim community had cast doubt on the Friends of Mount Moriah's fundraising practices, and whether the organization was really concerned about their loved ones' graves. One volunteer told me, "It doesn't matter what religion you are, if you've passed and you have people who love you, they should be honored like anybody else."[7] I heard things of this sort often: heartfelt and stirring, but also avoidant. They reminded me of the community meeting about Mount Moriah back in 2017, and one White speaker's response to accusations against the Friends: "All headstones are gray," he said, and his attitude toward every grave would be similarly equal.

This kind of universalism—sometimes presented in the language of "colorblindness"—produces a strange irony. When cemetery citizens' vocabulary becomes more expansive and universalist, it also offers a far more circumscribed view of the relationships between cemeteries and the world around them.[8] On the one hand, these volunteers are constantly confronted, in the most concrete ways possible, with the inequities that make marginalized cemeteries different from other burial grounds nearby. The workdays where I met them would be unnecessary if the cemeteries had professional maintenance, if they weren't used to dump trash or left to the weeds. While these "colorblind" volunteers did compare marginalized cemeteries to some other baseline of a "normal" cemetery, they tended not to talk about the contested memory landscapes around them: the Confederate statues on Monument Avenue in Richmond, the destruction of Hayti or Jackson Ward, redlining in Philadelphia. Rather than reference racism or other forms of oppression, they spoke more generally about what a cemetery "should" look like, about the dignity and memory owed to all the dead. They wanted to deal with concrete problems (weeds, trash, and toppled headstones) only within the bounded space of the cemetery, but to frame that work in the broadest terms—abstracted from specific histories, identities, and forms of violence.

I spoke to many volunteers who looked askance at meetings, and joked about having their arms twisted into board service or other administrative roles. They avoided or denigrated the spaces where conversations about contentious issues, and about the context around the cemeteries, were likely to consume hours and emotional energy. "I like to stay out of the politics," said one volunteer, referring to himself as a "boots on the ground" person.[9] Unlike a cemetery workday, meetings and media appearances seemed like spaces where other "agendas" could take over—where politicians, and other cemetery citizens, might use the burial grounds for self-promotion or pet causes.

Avoiding politics, criticizing politics, labeling others as too political—these are all, at bottom, political strategies. In a classic study of international aid projects in Lesotho, anthropologist James Ferguson used the term "anti-politics" to describe how they were designed to keep questions such as the roots of poverty and inequality out of bounds. Development "experts" separated politics from technical expertise even as they expanded their own bureaucratic power over the lives of others.[10] White volunteers who refuse to talk in anything beyond broad, universalist terms about the forces acting upon the cemeteries where they work—framing politics as a distraction from the "real work" that needs to be done—may be keeping themselves comfortable while making it harder for others to feel seen, welcomed, and understood. I recall again my conversation with Debra in late spring of 2020 and the vulnerability she expressed. Debra's way of seeing a cemetery is no more or less political (and no more or less rooted in the daily realities of living in her body) than the discomfort some White volunteers might feel when the conversation moves from cemeteries to the life-and-death struggles all around them.

An Outdoor Archive

In March 2021, nearly a year after COVID lockdowns began, Debra joined me in a videoconference for a formal interview. I asked her when she got interested in genealogy research—a passion she has pursued for over thirty years. Debra recalled:

> I was always interested, even when I was young. I mean I always loved history and I spent a lot of time at the library, at home, just reading. But the thing I—and I kick myself all the time now—was I never asked questions. The way I was brought up, you just didn't ask your elders a lot of questions. And a lot of times they would shoo us away when they were going to discuss something. You know: *go outside, do this, go away.* There were things they didn't really want to talk about or share down. I'm sure I would have learned a lot of things.[11]

As an adult, Debra circled back to those questions she had once been too afraid to ask. At the same time, the internet of the early 1990s was opening new doors to people seeking information about their family histories, with census records and other primary sources becoming available on the web. "I started learning how to do, *really* do genealogy," she recalled.[12] Her curiosity expanded out from her own family history to the larger project of reassembling narratives of African American lives, eventually leading her to Geer Cemetery, and a leadership role in cemetery work in Durham and beyond.

While church founder Millie Markham initially sparked her interest in Geer, Debra now speaks with special passion about Abner and Emily Banks. The Banks formed a family while enslaved at the Cameron-Bennehan plantation, with no legal recognition or protection for their union. After Emancipation, they were legally married. They stayed together for over sixty-three years (until Abner Banks's death at age ninety-three). A tall, elegant headstone, with both their names carved into it, still stands at Geer Cemetery near the grave of their son, Fendell.[13] Debra told me:

> I'm attached to the Banks—I got attached to Abner and Emily because to me they tell the story of a family. Even people who have been enslaved for a great part of their life . . . How they form families, and these families didn't just fizzle out because Emancipation—they weren't forced families. They were families that were built on love, on mutual love and respect for each other.

One way to see a marginalized cemetery is as an outdoor archive, full of histories that are still in danger of being lost.[14] These are individual life histories, but also stories of family units that persevered, as in Debra's example of the Banks, and of the organizations and networks that fostered Black "survivance"— "moving beyond . . . basic survival in the face of overwhelming cultural genocide to create spaces of synthesis and renewal."[15]

Cemeteries also record the former lives of our cities and neighborhoods. Lisa Y. Henderson, the founder of the Lane Street Project in Wilson, North Carolina, told me:

> Wilson was really hard hit by the crack epidemic of the 1980s. I mean, it really tore through the landscape like a forest fire. And it not only disrupted the community in terms of mass incarceration and addiction and those sorts of ills. It literally changed the landscape. Green Street was the main sort of middle-class residential street, the showplace street of East Wilson. And to ride through East Wilson now . . . it's just these empty lots. And so I think it's hard for people who grew up seeing this to think that there was ever anything different.[16]

The three African American cemeteries on Lane Street in Wilson—Rountree, Odd Fellows, and Vick—contain stories of what Green Street and its surroundings used to be, inevitably leading to the question of what happened to that place, how the landscape was emptied, effaced. These are histories of neighborhoods and generations, windows into erased pasts. As Lisa sees it, they are also reference points for imagining new futures: what to value and protect, but also what can inspire.

In Debra's and Lisa's words, we see a shared grief over what can never be recovered: the questions Debra never asked her elders, the weight of responsibility Lisa feels as she tries to fill the "gaps" or "synapses" that provide context and history for the cemeteries in Wilson—things she knows the next generation will no longer be able to see as vividly. It is no coincidence that these two voices belong to Black women—inheritors of a tradition of memory-keeping, storytelling, and public mourning.[17]

For those who see a cemetery as an outdoor archive, the clearest pathway to revision is preserving the space while also gathering up its stories and sharing them down to future generations. These cemetery citizens are mindful, like Lisa, of the gaps between what once existed and what can be described today: the thing and the knowledge. As Brian Palmer says:

> We have learned one lesson that now sustains us: It's the looking that matters. . . . The looking—the process of researching, visiting, interviewing—itself strengthens and affirms our faith in the power of our past and in the people whose stories we're telling. And we have become part of a diverse and diffuse community of searchers, amateur and professional, gathering textual and physical fragments that allow us to tell truer stories of the American past.[18]

A Sacred Space

A cemetery is a sacred space, which "order[s] relationships between the spiritual dead and the secular world of the living."[19] In a cemetery that has been marginalized, degraded, and desecrated, cemetery citizens look for ways of reclaiming sacredness. "[E]very space is potentially sacred depending on what story you tell about it," said Yoni Kadden, a history teacher at Gann Academy in Waltham, Massachusetts, who has been involved in teaching and research at MetFern Cemetery.[20] Kadden echoes poet Wendell Berry's notion that "there are no unsacred places."[21]

In Geer Cemetery and other African American burial grounds, cemetery citizens have organized libation ceremonies to remember the dead and mark birthdays, death dates, and other key events. Libation is an ancient ritual originating in the Nile Valley, later practiced by enslaved people at their loved ones' graves in North and South America and the Caribbean. It is now part of the large constellation of ideas and rituals from the African continent that many African Americans are reclaiming and adapting.[22] In a libation ceremony, participants pour water or alcohol on the ground as an offering, accompanying it with a verbal prayer or invocation that names the ancestors and sometimes petitions them for assistance.[23]

In June 2019, we held a Restoration Awareness Ceremony at Geer. Along with a demonstration of headstone repairs, the event featured a libation ceremony for all the ancestors in the cemetery. It was led by Dr. E. Victor Maafo, a Durham icon now in his nineties. Dr. Maafo, who immigrated to Durham from Ghana, has worn many hats: working for North Carolina Mutual Life, teaching economics at North Carolina Central University, and serving as the pastor of a Methodist church. A hush came over the crowd as Dr. Maafo said a prayer and poured water over the graves (a practice of the Akan people that is also carried out at weddings, funerals, dedication ceremonies for new homes, and other occasions). In my notebook I did a quick sketch of two young people who quietly clasped each other's hands.

A libation ceremony at Geer is an attempt to draw multiple threads of ritual and sacredness together. The people who buried their dead in this cemetery were, to a large extent, deeply Christian in their spiritual beliefs.[24] Many of Geer's visible headstones mark a clear separation between the earthly and the divine, the living and the dead: "A brighter home, where grief cannot come" (Lillie Bailey, about 1884–1922); "May the resurrection find thee on the bosom of thy God" (John Tuten, 1889–1925). They project a Christian confidence that all the righteous dead will be reunited someday in a better place. The libation ceremony Dr. Maafo led, by contrast, reflected the belief that the ancestors are here with us now.[25]

Some people have reacted to the popularity of libation and other reclaimed rituals with skepticism. In his essay "Things Which Don't Exist," Kyrie Mason writes, "The gag of reclaiming Yoruban religion or Griot traditions or West African heritage foods by Black Americans is that many of us are as foreign to those things in our current modalities as any other *westerner*; we learn about them on an intellectual level, and there is little retention in the body, but still it's all only resemblance, resemblance far removed from context and grown out of an absurdist, purgatorial condition."[26] The literary critic Henry Louis Gates Jr. worries that "an excess of kitsch substitutes for substantial reflection about the meaning and import of the burial sites."[27]

During a different libation ceremony at Geer, marking the anniversary of the North Carolina State Senate's ratification of the 13th Amendment (abolishing slavery nationwide) in 1865, Dr. Maafo rejected the notion that libation was really so distant from the Christian traditions of those buried at Geer:

> I would like to let you know that the word "libation" in my culture is ancestral prayer. We believe in a supreme God. We believe in a supreme being. The word God has come in because Christians believe that—we Christians believe that God is our Creator and he has retained permanence in all that we do. But my people believe that there is a supreme being who created these trees and rocks, and unfortunately when the Western missionaries came, they said, "These people in their ignorance worship trees and stones." That's not correct. We give credit to who created those things. It's not ignorance. It's knowledge. . . .
>
> We pour the libation and we say our prayers for the dead, the living, and the yet unborn. From a Christian point of view, it is the Father, Son, and the Holy Spirit. . . . This is our tradition."[28]

Dr. Maafo draws on his own immigrant, hybrid identity to offer a vision of underlying unity. That holism likely resonates for some, while for others it forgets too much about the violence with which Christianity was imposed on colonized people, the subjugated forms of knowledge in African traditions that do not fold as neatly back into Christian monotheism as Dr. Maafo might wish. Libation remains complex, sacred, uncomfortable, and resistant—as thick with meaning as a ritual can be.

FIGURE 4.2. Black-and-white sketch of Dr. E. Victor Maafo, a Ghanaian-born Durham pastor and educator, conducting a libation ceremony for the Pearson family and other ancestors at Geer Cemetery on December 4, 2021. He is an older man wearing sunglasses, with a long cloth draped over his shoulder. He stands next to a large headstone (belonging to George W. Pearson) and holds a small drinking glass in the air. Drawing by the author, May 2023.

As with any other kind of revision, there is no going back to the original—no easy way to reaffirm the sacred in the precise way the dead and their communities might once have done. New pathways to revision must be found. The idea of the sacred is transcendent, but the project of reestablishing it in space is a worldly negotiation, fraught and full of life.

A Field of Struggle

For Jarene Fleming, an African American Richmonder with ancestors in the ground at East End and Evergreen, cemeteries have been fields of struggle from the start. In fact, sometimes the struggle threatens to overwhelm the other ways in which she'd like to relate to her ancestors' graves.

When I met Jarene in October 2017, she was doing laundry in the upstairs apartment she rents out on Airbnb. Her hair was back in short braids, and she moved gracefully through the space, gathering laundry as we began to talk. Jarene grew up in Richmond, then left for most of her adult life. She came back in 2015 with her two kids. She now works as the breastfeeding coordinator for the Virginia Department of Health.

Jarene has done a lot of research on her family's history. She can name ten relatives buried in East End and Evergreen. But her first visit to the cemeteries was in her mother's womb, when the family came out to bury Jarene's father, Reverend James Fleming Sr., in a plot at East End next to her grandfather, Archer Coles. These graves are still visible. Others, such as those of Jarene's great-grandparents, are somewhere in Evergreen, lost beneath the overgrowth.

The last of her family to be buried in the cemeteries was her grandmother, Mary Christ (Carter) Coles, who died in 1980 at age eighty-six. A photograph Jarene shared with the Friends of East End shows a young Mary Coles, face serious and a dramatic part in her hair, a dimple just visible on her chin.

Jarene attended some of the early workdays at Evergreen, back when park ranger Jim Bell was organizing cleanups. Even when she lived elsewhere, she would come down to clear her family's graves or hire someone to do it. At her house, she showed me a video on her phone: a crowd of her family members, multiple generations gathered around their ancestors' graves, singing the spiritual, "I Said I Wasn't Gonna Tell Nobody." The song was a favorite of her father's.

"Just in my lifetime I've seen the property make steps forward and then the forest takes it back, and volunteers come in and clean it up, and then the forest takes it back," Jarene said.[29] She grew up near an open field that, she learned as an adult, had once been a playground with an attendant on duty and play equipment; the city tore it down as the neighborhood was transitioning from White to Black. She recalled, "[I]t would make me, like, sick to my stomach when I would come out here with my family, bag up trash, clean off, and then we would drive out, make a left, and drive past the Confederate cemetery [at Oakwood] that was just like manicured and beautiful all the time. It just—you know, it's just such a huge disparity visually. This has been a legacy of racism, disenfranchisement, and disinvestment."[30]

Jarene's vision for her city, which she shared with me years before the murder of George Floyd and the removal of Confederate monuments, was to see the statues commemorating traitors and enslavers "just fall into neglect"—the same thing that has happened with grave markers at East End and Evergreen.[31] She wanted the world to see that Black people aren't the only ones whose memory landscapes decline or disappear when there is no public support for them. "The story that's being told about these cemeteries is distorted," she said at the 2020 online meeting after human remains were discovered in a ravine at East End. "It makes it sound like they've been neglected, abandoned, and forgotten—they've never been. What has happened is that they were continuously under-resourced."[32]

Jarene would like to be sure people visiting the cemetery don't just see the names of people buried there, but also all the civic associations they formed. She imagines additional markers at the cemetery with this kind of information, or an app that people could use to learn about people's histories as they walk through the cemetery: "I'd like to . . . put Eagle Scout, Scout Leader . . . fifty-five years as a secretary at the school," she told me. She has contributed material to the Friends of East End for the website where they share these kinds of stories.

About the work she's done in the cemetery over the years, Jarene said:

> Part of my involvement is wanting to see justice
> so that future generations
> won't go around the corner
> and see woods

For Melissa Pocock, the journey to understanding East End as a field of struggle took longer, but was life-altering. Melissa, a White woman and longtime Friends of East End volunteer, sat with me at the kitchen table in Erin Hollaway Palmer and Brian Palmer's house in Richmond one afternoon. We had all spent the morning working at the cemetery, then ordered sandwiches to bring home. Melissa described how her ways of seeing East End had changed as she participated in the revisions there.

Melissa had graduated from William & Mary, where she focused on archaeology and museum studies. But her day job wasn't related to these interests, so she had her eyes out for ways to pursue them outside of working hours. She came across a request for help on a neighborhood blog—a post by John Shuck, who was coordinating volunteer efforts at East End. As Melissa recalls:

> [I] came out the first day, spent several hours, thought I was doing great. He [Shuck] told me where to go pull the weeds and I was like, "This looks great! I'm doing such a great job." And he comes back and he's like, "That is all poison ivy. . . ." Came back head to toe poison ivy, had to go get steroid shots, but been back every Saturday pretty much since. . . .

Melissa laughed off the poison ivy but soon turned more serious: "I think when I first started going out there, I didn't entirely grasp that it was . . . the African American cemetery. When I was pulling weeds, I was just thinking about it as a place, as a cemetery. I was just trying to make it clear, just clear the site so I can find headstones, so we can uncover them."[33]

She kept showing up Saturday after Saturday, forming a close friendship with Brian and Erin:

[T]hey really sparked my interest to take a closer look. . . . Now, it's completely different. It's almost less about the weeds or the physical landscape. It's a lot of the questions *why*, and *how could this be*, is really now at the forefront of my mind. Versus: *Oh no, the weeds are growing back in this particular spot.* . . .

Working at East End, there's a lot of time to think to yourself. You're pulling vines and then connecting with the person who's buried there, even if you're imagining what their life would be . . . trying to see how Virginia was, the world was, and coming up with the story. Wondering what this person did, or: *Oh, they worked here at Philip Morris,* so we could connect better with the person they are, even if it's made up in our heads a little bit. I would never be able to fully appreciate what [the people buried at East End] went through, and how completely different it would have been for me living at that time that they were alive, and how I would have probably acted. It's not pretty.[34]

Volunteering in cemeteries can give people a shallow sense that they are "doing good," or combating racism, without having to deal with living people or learn about the structures that perpetuate racial inequality. Some of the "colorblind" volunteers I met in my research offered examples of this thin form of cemetery citizenship, exiting conversations about the social and political meanings of the cemetery spaces that they were clearing, working more as landscapers than reclaimers. But Melissa embodies a different possibility, a different pathway to revision. For her, the "physical landscape" of East End gradually transformed from a place to "make . . . clear" into a set of questions; and the answers to those questions were sometimes uncomfortable, "not pretty." East End became a place where Melissa could "think to herself," in those quiet moments, about her place in history—and then act. In the past few years, she has become a more vocal advocate for East End and served on the Lemon Project Committee on Memorialization at William & Mary, addressing the college's entanglements with slavery and Jim Crow.[35]

A Painful and Powerful Place to Mourn

Weeds, trash, and speeding cars can be desecrations. They don't alter the fundamental nature of a burial ground; but they obscure, damage, and vandalize it. Just as we know that violence is present in structures and not just individual acts, we can also think of desecration in cemeteries beyond its most obvious forms, such as people spraying graffiti or toppling headstones. We can think of vandalism, like violence, as structural.

As Naji and Inez Muhammad toured me around the section of Mount Moriah where their son Hakim is buried, they showed me how a neglected cemetery becomes a desecrated, painful place to do the work of mourning. Amid the indignity of neglect and overgrowth, trash and weeds, the dignity of mourners—and of mourning itself—comes into even sharper relief. Marginalized cemeteries are places to mourn, but they can also build an unexpected form of power. No one should have to experience the compounded grief this couple felt—robbed of their son, and of the dignity they wished to give him in burial. But there was also an unmistakable kind of agency and authority in the way they told their story and interpreted the landscape for me: "That one is new with the flowers, that one: new, that one over here, that one is new."

On January 26, 2020, Keisha L. Phillips posted a message to the Facebook page of the Friends of Mount Moriah. She included photographs: a wreath on the ground with a bouquet of red roses laid neatly atop it; a blurry image of an infant wrapped in a white, blue, and pink hospital blanket with tags above her crib, and two tiny stamped footprints, right and left. Phillips wrote:

> I would like to take a moment to send a special thank you and appreciation to Steve Martin. Your act of kindness yesterday meant so much to me, I am forever grateful. In yesterday's pouring rain, you waited for [me] to arrive to locate my only child's grave. Thank you to everyone whom made this possible. I am truly grateful [three heart emojis]. Assitan Leila died shortly after birth, she was buried 2 days later. I tried getting a stone laid but I couldn't reach anyone at Mt. Moriah to make it happen. Yesterday, I laid a wreath with [roses] for my baby. I had tears but these were tears of relief, finally I had an idea of where she is resting. From Allah we come and to Allah we shall return. Salaams

Ryan K. Smith, in his work on African American burial grounds in Richmond, talks about people "wrenching dignity from their situation."[36] It's a good phrase. We generally don't have to wrench something unless it is being gripped tightly on the other side. But we also wrench things away with sudden force. When I first read Phillips's post, it was like someone had quietly but swiftly scooped the air out from my lungs.

People trying to mourn in desecrated landscapes can reassert their dignity in slow, humble ways, like Naji Muhammad with his signs and petitions, his nagging worry that there was something more proper, more legalistic he could be doing for the cemetery. They can do it in more sudden ways too. They can go out to an unmarked spot, like Keisha L. Phillips did with Steve Martin, and mark it with a red wrenching of roses.

A Place of Then and Now

Preservation, reclamation, revision. Each of these terms has its uses, its subtle differences from the others. But all of them suppose the existence of a "past" or "history" that is distinct from the present, available to be preserved, reclaimed, or revised.

The dead are gone, or some people believe that to be the case. But are the worlds they inhabited, the violence they experienced, or even their fates after death so distant? Are the lines between past and present so clear? No one troubled these boundaries for me more than Alex Green, who has spent years researching people who were incarcerated in institutions due to their perceived disabilities or mental illness, then buried under nameless, numbered stones at MetFern Cemetery. Alex makes urgent connections between the precarious present and how we interpret the past: "Having a claim to a disability history is really a claim to disability rights."[37]

People can see cemeteries as outdoor archives, sacred spaces set apart from the world around them, or painful and powerful places to mourn what is gone. But for some cemetery citizens, the places of the dead feel like a field of struggle not just over the meaning of the past, but for their own basic dignity and survival today. Another way to see cemeteries is as part of our present—"as now, not as then."

THE POSSIBLY TAIL END, BUT POSSIBLY IN THE MIDDLE
(Alex Green, disability historian and MetFern
Cemetery advocate, January 27, 2021)

When I walk around [at the Fernald School]
I think: the names of these people,
the lives of these people you've been researching,
these are their footsteps, these are their places.
Look around
as though they were here.

Think about it as now, not as then.

We've got these two sort of rising/falling things,
which is my own reckoning with my own sort of issues,
because I can't seem to keep them back the last few years
and then kind of reckoning with what
that forces me to reinterpret about this place.

At the possibly tail end,
but possibly in the middle
of just a colossally altering bloodbath
I know that . . .
I know that any optimism with which I taught
a differentiation between past and present,
and a kind of evolutionary arc of history
is gone from this year.
Like, it's just totally obliterated.

Between the COVID response
which is inherently,
repetitively eugenic in mindset
and the concurrent mass level of—
what do you want to call it?

—*extrajudicial killings* of people with mental illness
around the country, by police

I don't know, I feel extraordinarily more vulnerable
and I guess in a broad way,
though I've not thought a lot about connecting myself
to the folks in MetFern,
I see my own vulnerability.

It's like the end of *Amadeus*
where you've watched this whole thing of this great individual,
and then he gets chucked in a ditch, right?
In an anonymous grave?
I see ...
I see that more. Like I could do just fine
in this world,
and still end up in the ditch
and, I don't know, maybe some of that's age, too, but ...

It's bad out there.
It's really bad out there.

FIVE

Revising How We Belong

I SEE MY FAMILY THERE
(Debra Taylor Gonzalez-Garcia, Friends of Geer Cemetery, March 5, 2021)

I'm not a North Carolina native.
I finished high school in Virginia
and then I came down here
to North Carolina Central University.
I had spent most of public school being
like the only African American
in my class. I was on the gifted track,
and unfortunately they don't put too many African Americans
in those tracks. The only time I would be in class
with the others was like P.E. or some class like that.
I really didn't know my culture
or African American culture. It was a little difficult
fitting in. I got down here and it was really hard
the first couple years. I almost transferred
and I didn't. I think what really helped
was I was a math major
and it was a very small number of math majors.

I see my family [at Geer].
I see their stories there.
That's how I relate to that cemetery now.
They're not my people, but they are my stories.
I see my family in some of those very situations,
those timeframes,
and all of the complexities.

I've got situations in my own family where it's so confusing
and some of that's coming from the results

of being enslaved and trying to find
your own identity and your name.

My great-grandfather, who was born about the same time
as P. W. Dawkins, kind of went through
some of the same journeys. And this
I don't know how, but he ended up going
to Lincoln University.[1] He got not only one degree,
two degrees—
he got a law degree. And yet the best
he could be was a teacher in the colored school,
where maybe the African Americans, you know,
would call him "Professor Becks," but I'm sure
that's where it was limited. I look at pictures of him,
and one is when he's young and he's all kind of dressed up.
It's one of those studio pictures. And then there's one
when he was older, and I just look in his eyes
and just see, like, you know—is he?
                    Did he . . . ?
                    I feel like he was beaten down.
                    I feel like that's what I see
                    in his eyes.

I can't help but wonder
what he thought his potential was,
and he couldn't reach
that potential. When I looked
at his school records, both he and his brother
were like in the top five of their class.
They would be selected to do things.
And it's like, you know,
                    damn.
You really do wonder what kind of greatness
they could have achieved with that.

So I do, I see my family stories through
some of these stories,
as sad as some of them can be.

Forms of Belonging

In her book about African American cemeteries in Virginia, *Hidden History*, historian Lynn Rainville recounts a series of interactions she had in 2008 with a woman named Leah, a White archaeologist and collaborator in Rainville's cemetery preservation work. Leah and her husband were living near a small African American cemetery in Crimora, Virginia. A crew from the electric company had recently driven heavy equipment over the cemetery to prune limbs from nearby trees and preserve the power lines underneath them. In the process, they had damaged several headstones and "created deep ruts in the middle of the cemetery."[2]

Leah called the company and the sheriff's office, hoping to put a stop to the damage. They gave her the runaround. So Leah and her husband planted flags to mark the cemetery and began organizing with neighbors to protect it. "A week after her original email," Rainville writes, "Leah left a message on my answering machine, sounding very frustrated and worn down. While she and her husband Joey had spent dozens of hours trying to rally support to protect the cemetery, only a handful of groups expressed an interest in her mission. Her last sentence was 'I'm not sure why I should care about this cemetery any longer.'"[3]

Leah's only connection to the cemetery was because of where she'd purchased a house, in a historically Black neighborhood that had already lost many of its original families and landmarks. Why should she fight uphill battles over a seemingly abandoned burial ground more than a century old? Was it an appropriate role for someone with so little connection to the people buried in there?

Leah overcame her moment of doubt and went on to make a real difference in protecting the cemetery in Crimora.[4] What makes others do the same? Rainville offers her own set of answers: she emphasizes all the painful and inspiring "hidden history" in these outdoor archives, the power of cemeteries as "instructional spaces that, if read correctly, have much to teach us about our social and moral values and our shared history."[5]

Rainville's answer focuses on the interpretive value of these spaces, but I want to emphasize relationships instead: relationships between living people, and between the living and the dead. While values may initially bring people to work in a cemetery, relationships are what sustains the work—or makes it unsustainable. Throughout the previous chapter, cemetery citizens gave voice to some of these different kinds of relationships, all of which served as different pathways to revision. There was the charge Lisa Y. Henderson got from seeing how the work in Wilson, North Carolina's African American cemeteries was "resonating" with and "inspiring" a younger generation; Jarene Fleming's concern that future generations not "go around the corner" at East End and Evergreen "and see [only] woods"; Melissa Pocock being inspired by her Friends of East End colleagues Brian Palmer and Erin Hollaway Palmer to "take a closer look," asking more profound questions about what she was seeing at East End. Melissa also found herself "connecting with" the people buried there as she tended their graves and learned their histories.

Cemetery citizens include descendants and non-descendants, people with longstanding roots in the region and newcomers. They are people who share marginalized identities with the dead, and people from different, sometimes much more privileged, backgrounds. One of the main goals of my interviews was to find out how cemetery citizens answer this question for themselves: what story they tell themselves and others about all the hours and effort they put into cemeteries, why they care. Most often, they did this not in a language of abstract values but a language of connection, exploring forms of belonging between them, the cemetery, the dead, and each other.

Circles Around Cemeteries

In 2017, I taught a course at Haverford College called "Human Rights and the Dead." One of the first readings was historian Antoon De Baets's thoughtful, ambitious article "A Declaration of the Responsibilities of Present Generations Toward Past Generations."[6] The article offers reasons why we (the "present generations") still owe respect to the dead, whom De Baets calls "former human beings."[7] It then uses key human rights documents to outline a series of responsibilities that we should uphold, from treating dead bodies with dignity to investigating genocide.

After we talked about the article in class for a while, one of my students, Itzél Delgado-Gonzalez, spoke up. As I recall now—and I regret not taking better notes when my students say brilliant things!—she said, "I don't recognize any of this. To me and my family, the dead aren't 'former human beings,' they're ancestors. And they're still here with us."

It was an important moment for everyone in the class to see how De Baets's expansive, deeply ethical writing was still based on a set of assumptions tied to his own culture and the transnational "human rights culture" he has contributed to building. That even in the room where we were sitting, we had not yet heard all the voices or considered all the possible ways of knowing the dead.

I got in touch with Itzél, now a PhD candidate at NYU, to see how she remembered the conversation. She texted:

> I really can only (and definitively) remember that I thought of time a little differently because thinking of the dead in connection to the past and of the living in connection to the present didn't explain how my family and I are able to communicate with our deceased loved ones in the present through dreams. . . . There's an ongoing presence to them that I have been taught to watch out for. I definitely stand by that it's possible to continuously engage with our dead. And this definitely comes from my mother's side of the family. I wouldn't be surprised if it's a Mixtec way of understanding time, death, and the presencing of the "past."[8]

One day I texted Yamona (Mona) Pierce, a cemetery citizen friend who is working to preserve and protect Pierce Chapel African Cemetery in Harris County, Georgia—a burial ground founded around 1828 that is home to at least five hundred enslaved people. Among them, according to relatives, are Mona's great-great-great grandparents. Yet Mona was treated "like a trespasser" when she first came out to visit the cemetery, which she soon discovered had been partially destroyed by the local power company and a cable provider as they bulldozed to make room for utility poles.[9] In my message, I complimented Mona on her "efforts to honor the dead." In her reply, she changed

FIGURE 5.1. Black-and-white sketch of a volunteer raking leaves at Pierce Chapel African Cemetery in Harris County, Georgia. They are wearing a long sweater, with their hair in a bun and a focused look on their face. In the background is a split-rail fence with a person in a baseball cap leaning on it. Drawing by the author, November 2022.

the vocabulary: she described her work as honoring her "ancestors." Mona's gentle correction hinged on a subtle but important difference. "The dead" seem definitively gone, on another plane, honored only as memories. The ancestors are maybe not-so-gone, their fates more actively entangled with ours. They are not objects to be honored, but subjects that welcome—and perhaps even demand—the return of their dignity.

Whatever vocabulary they use, and whether they think of the dead as present or not, the richest and most resonant work of cemetery citizens has the dead at its center. Their presence may be shimmering, indefinite. But it informs an overall ethic of revision, as well as the practical decisions that cemetery citizens make. Some of the greatest failures in cemetery work, by the same token, occur when the dead are displaced, taken for granted, flattened into simplistic symbols, or used instrumentally.

An obvious starting point for an ethic of cemetery revision is that those with the most at stake should have the most decision-making power. But the histories of marginalized cemeteries are often the opposite: the people with the closest ties to both the land and the dead have spent decades feeling silenced and disempowered. In those cases, the first step in revising a cemetery—or any space of historical significance—is to change who is at the table when decisions are made, whose voices are heard. Among the most important developments in historic preservation in recent decades is this reconfiguration of power. All over the world, challenges have emerged to the paternalistic and custodial control and interpretation of human remains, artifacts, and heritage sites by colonizing institutions.[10]

In cemeteries that have no clear ownership or caretaker, there are also quiet, everyday ways in which kin and descendants exert power. In the Springfield Avenue section of Mount Moriah Cemetery, which for years he tended alone, Naji Muhammad did not ask for the right to decide what trees to plant or what signs to put up. His son was buried there; so he took direct action as a mourner, someone attending to a space abandoned by its formal caretakers.

Do family ties create moral authority over the places where one's dead are laid to rest—a sort of de facto ownership that goes beyond holding a deed to individual plots? An ownership that defaults back to kin when a cemetery is abandoned by its owners, as is the case in Mount Moriah?

Marginalized cemeteries, as noted earlier, are almost never truly "abandoned." Whether perceived by outsiders or not, they almost always have concentric circles of care around them.[11] At the center of the circles are the people who have the most at stake in the conditions and fates of these burial grounds. Those people are dead; they are buried in the cemetery's soil. While others might argue over whether the dead are present or not, have "interests" or not, many descendants and other cemetery citizens work, hope, and hurt because they believe the answer is yes.[12] Questions about the dead, what they do, or what they mean can be addressed in philosophical tracts; but they are answered with far more consequence in real spaces, as people co-construct—and then revise—their relationships to the dead.

Moving out in concentric circles, next come mourners and descendants—"folks with people in the ground," as Brian Palmer said.[13] Then there are people whose care for a cemetery is bound up with geography and structures of political responsibility. Leah, Lynn Rainville's friend, wound up fighting to preserve the African American cemetery in Crimora because, in addition to her professional concern as an archaeologist, she lived nearby. City and county agencies sometimes (and to varying degrees) put labor and other resources into these cemeteries, as do organizations that are invested in the overall conditions of a city's historic and green spaces (such as Keep Durham Beautiful, which often co-coordinates workdays at Geer Cemetery). Increasingly, groups of local university, faculty, and staff, such as the East End Cemetery Collaboratory and the Durham Black Burial Grounds Collaboratory, partner with organizations of other cemetery citizens and try to foster connections between students and the burial grounds.

On a workday at East End in March 2019, a yellow Volkswagen Beetle rolled up to our group of volunteers. A neighbor had come by to hand out granola bars and two-dollar bills (for good luck). Another time, it was McDonald's breakfast sandwiches. The circles of care included people caring for the cemetery, and people who wanted to care for cemetery citizens.

To some, the circles widen out much further: the idea behind the international "sites of conscience" designation is that all of humanity, geography aside, has a stake in landscapes of mass violence, tragedy, or injustice.[14] Recent attention to Indian Residential Schools in Canada and the United States, as well as former asylums and carceral institutions, has been putting overlooked sites of complex, structural harms onto revised maps of our collective conscience.[15] A

2022 summit on African American heritage sites and descendant communities, held at Thomas Jefferson's historic home at Monticello, named African American burial grounds as sites of conscience.[16]

Cemetery citizens come together from different locations within these circles: descendants working alongside neighbors, volunteers from local colleges or Scout troops joining them for a single workday, or for years of workdays, before they depart. Perhaps more importantly, some cemetery citizens move between the circles, challenging the framework I've just described. Their sustained work in a cemetery, and engagement with what Itzél called the "ongoing presence" of the dead, makes for a less straightforward connection or stake than direct descendants have; and yet it speaks to a far richer connection than that of other concerned neighbors or preservation advocates. These cemetery citizens invite us to reexamine the logics of kinship and belonging at work in marginalized burial grounds, and sometimes even our ideas about who mourns and remembers in these spaces.

"Our Familial Ties, Our Ancestral Ties, and Our Community Ties"

The centrality of descendants—and the real power they do or do not have in the interpretation and uses of cemeteries and other historic sites—has been particularly important for African American placemaking in the United States. The norm, when it wasn't complete erasure, has often been to focus on flattering portrayals of White enslavers at their plantations and historic homes while "fail[ing] to provide representations of enslaved people as multi-dimensional, complex individuals with agency, and with important identities beyond their labor."[17]

Friends of Geer Cemetery president Debra Taylor Gonzalez-Garcia often reminds people that the organization doesn't own the burial ground in a legal or moral sense. The cemetery "belongs to the descendants," and the ultimate plan for how it looks and what happens there should be shaped by them.[18] Geer has a descendant outreach committee, which is trying to locate family members of the people buried at Geer based on ongoing research, as well as outreach to local churches and other groups.

In one of my conversations with her, Friends of Geer vice president and descendant DD Barnes expressed many of the hopes and frustrations that come with this work. She pointed out that only a few descendants are regularly involved in the organization: "It's got to be tons of descendants in Durham. It's got to be. We know there are some people who are not going to be interested because they could care less about a cemetery. But there are people out there that are interested in it."[19] DD cast descendant involvement not only as a necessary component of any decisions made about Geer's future, but also as part of a responsibility to past generations: "They worked hard and they did everything that they had to do because I'm sure that they were thinking about their future, their children's future, their grandchildren's future, and how they can make things better. And to me, it's our responsibility to try to uphold their dream and make sure that they're recognized, or they're remembered for the work that they did."[20]

New York City's African Burial Ground sparked important changes in who is considered a descendant of African American heritage sites. The eighteenth-century burial ground holds the remains of an estimated fifteen thousand Africans, both free and enslaved, and a much smaller number of poor Whites. Though already recorded on maps and known to historians, it entered public consciousness when the U.S. General Services Administration moved to construct a thirty-four-story office building that threatened to disturb the site, bringing a wide array of New Yorkers together for its preservation.[21]

Michael Blakey, an anthropology professor at Howard University at the time, became the director of scientific investigations there. In that role, he invested the idea of the "descendant community" with new meaning. Blakey had been influenced by his conversations with Native Americans and his support of NAGPRA, the Native American Graves Protection and Repatriation Act, which passed into law in 1990.[22] The descendants connected to the African Burial Ground, he said, should be thought of as having a similar status to Native American groups as the most legitimate stewards of any ancestral remains; their voices should have a more-than-equal status.[23] Blakey described descendants as the "ethical client" for any research that would be conducted.[24] These clients, he argued, must be allowed to determine what questions researchers ask: "we might offer our skills as a service, working *for* descendant stewards of their ancestral remains and sacred sites. We would ask them for questions that they — as our ethical client — might need our empirical methods to answer."[25] Crucially, Blakey's model of informed consent also means that descendants have "the ability and opportunity to say 'no.'" As he likes to point out, the best way to preserve an archaeological site is not to disturb it at all.[26]

But who *were* the descendants of the thousands of people in this Lower Manhattan burial ground? Blakey argued that all people of African descent, especially those who had protested the General Services Administration's "bureaucratic arrogance" in dealing with the mass grave, were a descendant community.[27] NAGPRA's language of "cultural affiliation" acknowledges "a relationship of shared group identity . . . between a present-day Indian tribe or Native Hawaiian organization and an identifiable earlier group."[28] Blakey and his coauthor, Cheryl LaRoche, argued that, similarly, "all African Americans are culturally affiliated" with the African Burial Ground.[29]

The principal difference between NAGPRA and African American claims on their ancestral remains, for Blakey, is not a moral one but a procedural challenge: Native American groups can turn to tribal councils or similar structures to navigate NAGPRA claims, whereas African American communities generally don't have the same kinds of "decision-making polities" already in place for cultural heritage issues.[30] Nevertheless, the key element in being a descendant, aside from ancestry, is care. Once descendants care, he argues, you can do harm to them by mistreating their ancestors. Their needs thus have a clear place in an anthropological ethics whose first principle is to "do no harm."[31]

Blakey was among the authors of *Engaging Descendant Communities in the Interpretation of Slavery at Museums and Cultural Sites*, drafted during the National Summit on Teaching Slavery in 2018. The report is called "the rubric" because it includes a series of measures to evaluate a site or institution's collaborations with descendants and incorporation of descendant voices.[32] The gold standard, for places that interpret slavery and its legacies, is to have descendants "inside the organization instead of outside."[33] As Antoinette Jackson, the founder of the Black Cemetery Network, puts it, "Descendant knowledge needs to be on the same plane with archaeological and historical knowledge." (In her book *Speaking for the Enslaved*, Jackson also proposes that enslaved people's "everyday acts of living" such as "working, establishing families, raising children, caring for elders, and growing, harvesting, cooking and sharing food" are important sources for interpreting these sites of enslavement—a method I witness regularly at Stagville State Historic Site, in Durham, where I take my students.)[34]

"A descendant community can include those whose ancestors were enslaved not only at a particular site, but also throughout the surrounding region, reflecting the fact that family ties often crossed plantation boundaries. It can also welcome those who feel connected to the work the institution is doing, whether or not they know of a genealogical connection," the *Engaging Descendant Communities* report states.[35] This broad definition of descendant community, embraced by activists and scholars at the African Burial Ground and other sites, has deep roots in African American history: in the terrible disruptions and separations that enslaved people and their families endured, and the forms of kinship they created in response.[36]

Descendant communities are not static entities.[37] Peighton Young walked me through some examples of why the concept of a descendant community "has to be malleable enough to be locality and regional specific."[38] Peighton is an activist and PhD student in history at William & Mary. They work at American revolutionary Patrick Henry's Red Hill plantation in Brookneal, Virginia, where Henry enslaved at least sixty-seven people; Peighton's job there is to expand African American interpretive programming.[39] They now also serve as the public representative of the Descendants Council of Greater Richmond Virginia, which formed amid concern about the Enrichmond Foundation's stewardship of East End and Evergreen cemeteries.

The Descendants Council was meant to operate independently of any cemetery reclamation organization, representing the voices of concerned people with ancestors buried in the cemeteries. It included other key African American voices, such as the public historian and preservation activist Ana Edwards. These descendants and advocates, along with other members of Richmond's Black community, sent an open letter to Governor Ralph Northam after a February 2021 announcement that the Virginia Outdoors Foundation would be giving Enrichmond another infusion of cash. The letter called for the state to present all materials related to its decision to fund Enrichmond and demanded increased vetting of the foundation's handling of cemeteries as cultural landscapes, in addition to more dialogue with families—a chance to "pause, reflect, and reset."[40] Over thirteen thousand additional people signed a related petition in support.[41]

It had impact. The City of Richmond soon announced its decision to deny Enrichmond's application for a right of entry to the "Colored Paupers" cemetery and turn down its application for additional funding for the coming year. The city itself would step in to do some of the work Enrichmond had proposed.[42] As with every piece of news, this one caused bitter disagreement, including among descendants and other African Americans in Richmond.[43]

To date, the Descendants Council has focused its efforts on the crisis at East End and Evergreen. But its mission is ultimately to help mobilize descendant voices for African American heritage sites throughout the region. Like the Montpelier Descendants Committee, which fought for decision-making parity with the historically White Montpelier Foundation, it addresses the lack of a democratic, decision-making structure for African American descendants that Blakey noted in his comparisons to NAGPRA.[44]

Peighton represented the Descendants Council in conversations with the late Congressman Donald McEachin of Virginia, voicing the council's position that the African American Burial Grounds Preservation Act—which McEachin cosponsored—must incorporate language to empower descendant communities and protect their interests from property owners.[45]

I spoke to Peighton via Zoom on a summer day, taking in their relaxed, matter-of-fact delivery of profound insights. In Peighton's view, Richmond, a large metropolitan area with many African American cemeteries, has a widespread and heterogeneous descendant community, including "the biological familial descendants of the people buried in the cemetery. It's the broader Black community who has descendant connections to other historic Black cemeteries in the area. It is including the Black community at large in Richmond in the metro area. And it includes the third-party reclamation organizations in the area."

By contrast, Peighton said, the descendant community around the Quarter Place cemetery in Brookneal, a burial ground for people enslaved at Red Hill, would include direct descendants and members of local Black churches: a smaller, "more tight-knit body" with lines of connection that are easier to trace. While flexible and evolving, Peighton's description of the descendant community seemed more bounded than Blakey's "cultural affiliation" approach. It was shaped by specific geographies, congregations, and institutions.

In communities whose histories have been marginalized, unrecorded, or erased from the archives, lines of descent can take a long time to become clear. Brian Palmer had been working at East End for years before his wife, Erin, discovered two distant relatives of his that are buried in the cemetery: Mary (Druitt) Fauntleroy, and an infant boy, Henry Lee Tunstall. Brian's place in the concentric circles suddenly shifted—he moved closer to the center, with other descendants.

In some cases, descendant status can only ever be a best guess. A definition of descendants and the descendant community must take this uncertainty into account. In a 2021 public relations video, Enrichmond allies Veronica Davis, Viola Baskerville, and Delores McQuinn indirectly criticized the Descendants Council as "individuals and groups with no real ties or proof of ties to descendants buried in the cemetery disrespecting the legacy of those who began the process of making the cemeteries look like what they look like today."[46] Peighton's own story complicates this narrow, show-me-your-family-tree approach. They have a great-great-great-grandfather buried at Woodland Cemetery and believe that his wife may have been buried at East End or Evergreen, near the family home. "It's just a very weird messy thing," they said. "But honestly, I think it's illustrative of the complications that can go on when Black people are trying to figure out where their relatives are, especially at some of these cemeteries."[47]

Peighton acknowledged that any descendant community—especially one working with a broad definition of that term—will have disagreements. They mentioned the Descendants Council's "growing pains" as it seeks to maintain a democratic process: the majority rules, they said, but "we try to stay away from the forty-five percent versus the fifty-five percent split."[48]

Direct descendants may be considered the most important voices in a cemetery's fate; but they are not always the people most active in reclamation efforts. They may be geographically dispersed, with full and complicated lives. Or they may simply not have the time or interest to get involved with a neglected, overgrown cemetery. They may not be connected to family history or have strong sentiments about the dead. Being a descendant shouldn't translate into an obligation to feel a specific way: it grants people special stakes, and a more-than-equal voice should they choose to use it, but doesn't force them to do so. Descendants can find themselves deep within the concentric circles of cemetery ethics while retaining the right not to put the cemetery—or the dead—at the center of their own lives.

The sense of shame that hangs over many of these cemeteries can also be an obstacle to descendant involvement. Brian Palmer describes encountering a "trap of shame and desperation" when he first came to East End, walking among the graves of people that Whites despised so much they could not bear the thought of being buried in the same soil. For Brian, paying close attention to the headstones themselves—the "love and care" inscribed on them, as well as the wider social worlds they reflect—enabled him to "pierce" the sense of shame.[49]

Reverent references to the descendant community risk becoming their own burden on people who do not feel a particularly sacred or emotional connection to their ancestors.[50] I first met Evergreen descendant John Mitchell at a museum event dedicated to Richmond's African American cemeteries. In prepared remarks, he pushed back against the dominant tone of reverence for the dead, with its politics of respectability. He rejected the "boring myths about those lives we extoll in our sacred grounds" and called for the bootleggers and money launderers to be remembered along with everyone else:

> They were real people. They were fighters and revolutionaries. Artists and writers . . .

> They were not boring. They were not goody-two-shoe, by-the-numbers people. Hell . . . some of them even ran numbers. Some of them ran fast and free. . . .

> They sang; they danced. They kissed and cried. They rode fast horses and drove big cars. They were beautiful, creative and wore sexy dresses.

> Get that old time vision of them out of your mind. They were, as my Uncle Billy would say, "tall, tan and teasin'." They were the realest of the real.[51]

"They're Not My People, But They Are My Stories"

Descendants have a special kind of moral authority over cemeteries; but intimate connections can be made through other means. Friends of Mount Moriah president Jenn O'Donnell told me that she did "a fair bit of her grieving" in that cemetery after the death of her brother, about a year after she began volunteering. Jenn's brother is not buried in Mount Moriah, or even nearby. She described her struggle, in a culture that often shuts down expressions of grief, to find space for speaking her feelings and having them recognized. Cemeteries—and being in community with other cemetery citizens—offered her space to connect with her distant dead.[52]

While Jenn widens our sense of who might connect with a cemetery as a mourner, Debra Taylor Gonzalez-Garcia further complicates the boundaries between mourner and descendant, descendant and non-descendant. In the poem that opens this chapter, "I See My Family There," Debra compares a man buried at Geer, P. W. Dawkins, to her great-grandfather on her mother's side. Dawkins was a prominent educator who graduated from Hampton Institute (now Hampton University), a historically Black institution. He later became the principal of Durham's West End Graded School, a segregated school for African American children.[53] Debra's words—some of them spoken as a sudden wave of tears came upon her—describe an intimacy with a dead man she never knew, in a place far from her family home.

Debra's relationship with P. W. Dawkins and the other dead at Geer Cemetery goes beyond what the term "cultural affiliation" can convey. It is based in specific stories, places where the outdoor archive of Geer overlaps with her own family history. The cemetery becomes a place for honoring P. W. Dawkins and her great-grandfather, linked by "some of the same journeys," their frustrated potential hitting the walls erected by White supremacy. At Geer, Debra mourns the violence and the constraints her own family lived with in Virginia, the greatness beaten down.

This type of intimacy and kinship, based on shared stories rather than lines of descent, also emerged in my research on psychiatric hospital and disability institution cemeteries. The rows of numbers in these burial grounds are not merely a technology of anonymity. Like an outdoor spreadsheet in stone, they make burial into a final and efficient bureaucratic procedure. Somewhere between an unmarked mass grave and a traditional cemetery, they offer a single form of belonging in death: belonging to an institution. As disability scholar Jennifer Natalya Fink explains, in most families, "Disability is erased, repressed, covered over. Families de-lineate—destroy the connections between generations of disabled people, their families, and their caretakers."[54] These cemeteries help de-lineate the dead from their families, while carrying their institutionalization onward past their death.

Ex-patients and other activists act as a descendant community for the institutionalized dead. They re-lineate them, making chosen families, as queer and disabled people have long done for their survival, safety, and joy—but also chosen *ancestors*.[55] Pat Deegan, an early pioneer in psychiatric hospital cemetery revisions, writes:

We declared kinship with those who, like us, had been patients at the State Hospital. It was a kinship born, not of blood, but of intention and recognition of a common experience. It was said that those buried beneath the numbered markers had no family. So we stood up and said, "We are their family. We are their mothers, fathers, sisters and brothers. We will remember their names."[56]

In this way, ex-patient activists made kin out of what the medical profession has often treated as a population—people whose common experiences could be categorized, analyzed, and treated, but not form the basis for a shared identity.[57]

Disorganizing Descendants

As Peighton Young explained, an important challenge for cemetery citizens is matching a complex, flexible definition of the descendant community with decision-making procedures that are recognized as democratic and legitimate. It's a challenge that the Enrichmond Foundation repeatedly failed. Carrying out a performance of descendant organizing without substance behind it, the foundation caused unnecessary pain and confusion for the descendants it claimed to be treating as ethical clients.

On July 17, 2021, a powerful summer storm blew through Richmond. It felled trees in the cemeteries and knocked over grave markers. Three days after the storm, Enrichmond placed a lock on the gates to East End and Evergreen, with a sign indicating that anyone wishing to visit—including descendants seeking out their ancestors' graves—should contact the new "community ambassador," John Mitchell.

In late 2021, Enrichmond replaced its impromptu barriers with more permanent-looking cattle gates. East End and Evergreen were the only major cemeteries in Richmond where access continued to be restricted to this degree. Mitchell could not offer a coherent explanation of who was responsible for locking up the cemeteries—or who could open them back up.[58]

On a Zoom call in September, Mitchell shared that the storm had disturbed more than grave markers.[59] Almost precisely a year after the remains of dissection victims had been exposed in a ravine, descendants were informed once again that the dead of East End and Evergreen were not safe below ground.

The remains of one or more people, entangled with the roots of a fallen tree, had been unearthed when the tree fell. Archaeologists would have to excavate them, avoiding the use of any heavy machinery that could damage other graves. As with the bones found in the ravine the previous year, it was highly unlikely that these skeletal remains, in an area with an unknown number of unmarked graves, would be identifiable.

Mitchell said that descendants would be responsible for deciding on the procedure from there. How should the remains be treated? Should they be placed in some sort of box or coffin, and then reinterred? Should there be a ceremony— and if so, what kind, with whom present? The archaeologists would take care of the technical aspects of this difficult excavation, but the descendants would have final say on how to treat the remains respectfully.

As many of the descendants at the meeting pointed out, the problem was that it was unclear how a decision-making body of descendants would be formed, and why it should be considered legitimate in making these kinds of painful decisions.[60] These were concerns Jarene Fleming had shared with me nearly a year earlier, when she was describing her time serving on Enrichmond's ExPRT committee of descendants and other stakeholders:

> I've been a part of a lot of organizations that start from the ground up, but I would have thought that the group itself would have developed our own bylaws and protocols.... You have to set ground rules and communications, and you also have to build trust in order to do this really sensitive work. And nobody seemed to realize the importance of that at all.[61]

The Zoom meetings about the newly unearthed remains generally had ten to twenty attendees, invited by Enrichmond representatives. The foundation's allies had already been implying publicly that the Descendants Council of Greater Richmond Virginia was illegitimate; meanwhile, in what seemed like a classic attempt to "divide and rule," Enrichmond was advertising on Instagram and elsewhere for people to join its own new Family Council.[62] (The "Cemeteries at Evergreen" website had multiple buttons inviting visitors to "Join the Family Council." You would then be prompted to specify your relationship to the cemeteries: "a descendant of family buried in the cemeteries," "a descendant of family connected to families buried in the cemetery," or "members of the community that feel a strong connection to the cemeteries." I inputted my contact information and identified myself as part of the latter category, but never received a response.)[63]

At one of these meetings, Jarene Fleming asked, "Are you saying that we, the twenty people who are on this call, have the power to make the final decision about what's going to happen with these remains? . . . Who is the 'Family Council'?" The vague answer she got was that Enrichmond wanted to empower descendants, as represented by the people invited to these meetings. "You tell us what to do because we want to do what you want to do," is how Mitchell put it.[64] Their power—or burden—would apparently include determining the membership, structure, and decision-making procedures of the Family Council. It was a perfect loop: the Family Council would be whoever this group decided it should be, legitimized by whatever procedures they created. Why? Because they were the Family Council.

Mitchell apologized for making the group into "guinea pigs" and talked about coming up with a charter in future meetings. Jarene continued:

> I've never heard of the Family Council before this week so that's why I was asking. . . . You could ask the churches, the seven historic churches in downtown Church Hill. You know, put it in a newspaper that you need to call a public meeting, and give people time in that manner. But I want to know, is there a magic number? Is it fifteen? If you have twenty people to vote?
>
> You put the burden back on the people who were in attendance on Tuesday, to reach out to peers, friends and family, and other descendants that we know, instead of doing the really good community engagement work that needs to be done around the cemeteries. That hasn't happened.[65]

In early 2022, without having resolved these questions about the Family Council, Enrichmond had the archaeologists begin excavating the remains from the fallen tree. At the time of this writing, they remain in the custody of the Virginia Department of Historic Resources; but because of Enrichmond's collapse, the archaeology firm has barely been compensated for their work.[66] A gaping hole now marks the spot where the excavation took place.

After executive director John Sydnor's departure from Enrichmond, the Virginia Outdoors Foundation hosted a meeting in which J. David Young, Enrichmond's board chair, called for "real partnership" and "a new day" at the cemeteries. This kind of gesture made it even more shocking when Enrichmond fell apart one month later.[67] But at this meeting, confusion about descendant engagement continued to be front and center.

J. David Young questioned the justification for "two descendants councils of the same space," referring to both the independent Descendants Council of Greater Richmond Virginia and Enrichmond's Family Council.[68] Peighton Young explained that the Descendants Council was not for East End and Evergreen descendants alone. It offered a support system to African American descendants and descendant communities throughout the region, including areas where people felt they did not yet have an organization representing them.[69]

The inconclusive conversations that autumn had dealt with numbers: how many descendants were enough to make decisions that matter? Now the issue became the scope of the descendant community. John Mitchell expressed concern that the group included people who were not "descendants of Evergreen" (he likely meant both East End and Evergreen, as many people do when they talk about Evergreen Cemetery). He called for a "structure that actually matches the specific status of Evergreen"—not one based on the Descendants Council or other models. Decades of "intellectual power" have been generated at the African Burial Ground, Montpelier, and at Richmond sites such as the East Marshall Street Well—most of it by Black activists, scholars, and preservationists.[70] Yet in his short time as Enrichmond's community ambassador, Mitchell seemed determined to start from scratch—even as he offered no vision of what that process should look like.[71] Mitchell has rich intergenerational ties to the cemeteries, but kept ignoring the fact that preservation efforts in African American cemeteries have a history too.

In response to Mitchell's distinction between "descendants of Evergreen" and a wider descendant community, Peighton reminded him, "our ancestries are complicated. And I guess what I'm saying is that sometimes those boundary lines are a bit more blurred than I think some people may realize. . . ."[72] Later, Peighton elaborated on this point: "Sometimes our ancestors were laid to rest here under less celebratory or favorable circumstances. Some of us only have oral histories from our family elders to tell us where their loved ones were laid to rest. Some of us will never find our ancestor's burial card or plot information because it's somewhere lost in an archive. Some of us can't find our relative's plot because our families didn't have enough money to buy them a stone. This is why I ask that people be mindful about the way they try to label what a descendant community is."[73]

In the meeting hosted by the Virginia Outdoors Foundation, Peighton talked about descendant community in a way that differed radically from what anyone else had said in a year of Zoom discussions about East End and Evergreen. Rather than basing legitimacy exclusively on lines of descent, they emphasized solidarity and relationships that evolve through the hands-on work of revising cemeteries. "There is a genuine love there . . . that's something that we all built together, through our familial ties, our ancestral ties, and our community ties. And that's why we work together to make decisions for ourselves as a community for our spaces."

That's not an answer to what to do about the remains unearthed in the storm; nor does it specify how many people would constitute a quorum when that decision is made. But if a "new day" is going to dawn over East End and Evergreen, especially after Enrichmond's collapse, Peighton offers rich ideas about where to start: a definition of descendant community that reflects a sense of place, the complexities of African American history, and the community built around the cemeteries as people engage in care for them. Historical rigor and new creative energies can coexist in this approach. In contrast to Mitchell's "start from scratch" ethos, the Descendants Council embraces an inheritance of ideas from other people who have fought against the erasure of Black spaces, and a network of mutual support with other burial grounds.

De-Centering the Dead

The Enrichmond Foundation failed even those descendants who became its allies and defenders, feeding off their concern for the cemeteries without really sharing power.[74] It made use of these people's connections to the dead while disrespecting the actual remains that emerged from the soil. Nearly all of Enrichmond's discourse perpetuated a sense that East End and Evergreen's population of the dead was "lost and forgotten in time," as Enrichmond's tree expert put it, not complex participants in a cemetery revision.[75]

This pattern was also evident in the foundation's long-term plans for the cemetery. The plans consistently invoked the "hallowed" ancestors in broad, reverent tones without preparing for the historic research and preservation that would seek out, dignify, and contextualize all the dead in East End and Evergreen.[76] In fact, in a graphic that John Sydnor shared in 2019, "The cemeteries and land around them were labeled simply 'Green,' as if they were meadows or parks, not long-abused, historic Black burial grounds."[77]

Enrichmond's record of chaos and neglect in East End and Evergreen is shocking, but it also helps illuminate something central about what other groups are doing *right* in marginalized cemeteries. It leaves us not only with a cautionary tale but also a richer picture of an ethic of revision.

Cemetery citizens not only care for burial grounds as places; they also create and articulate forms of belonging with the dead. Revising a cemetery can become part of "trying to find your own identity and your name," as Debra Taylor Gonzalez-Garcia puts it, via these relationships. Whether they are mourners or descendants, or crafting other connections based on shared stories or chosen lineages, cemetery citizens keep the dead at the center of the concentric circles. They explore "How the living go on living/And how the dead go on living with them," in poet Laura Gilpin's words.[78]

A cemetery is not a scarcity economy, where investing in relationships with the living detracts from attending to the dead. In marginalized cemeteries, attention builds on attention. The cemetery citizens most attuned to their relationships with each other also seem to pay the closest and most multifaceted attention to the ancestors in the soil. They treat the dead as complex individuals, and as participants in revision. "Look around as though they were here," is how disability historian Alex Green put it, reflecting on a place where people were buried under numbers, then left to the weeds for decades. Start with their presence, then see what flows from there.

Plant, Animal, Citizen

Revisions to a cemetery expose, and even reshape, the relationships that living humans have with each other and with the dead. But nonhuman life is part of the process too.[79] Chronicling the history of an African American cemetery in Oxford, Georgia, Mark Auslander writes:

> [I]n 1990, an unscrupulous, politically well-connected pulpwood merchant
> clear cut the oldest part of the black cemetery, taking out hundreds of pines
> and destroying scores of gravesites dating back to slavery times and Recon-
> struction. With the trees went much of the community's capacity to locate
> and recall the resting places of the dead. The town matriarch, Miss Sarah,
> recalled a decade later, as she tried to find her way across the meadow, "I
> used to be going by the trees. I was going by the trees."[80]

The destruction of nonhuman life—of these trees—became its own violence against the living and the dead. Cutting trees was an unmapping, a book-burning.

The English ivy, privet, wild grape vine, Japanese knotweed, greenbrier, wisteria, pokeweed, and other plants that grow over graves and cover cemeteries are key players in their daily drama. Weeds cover up histories and create obstacles for people wishing to locate and care for their dead. Initially, they seem to play an opposite role to that of the trees in Oxford. The main "work that plants do" in these cemeteries is the work of erasure and forgetting: an inexorable force, enveloping, destroying, and returning to wildness a site that people had intentionally carved out from nature to bury their dead.[81]

But certain types of plants were also used by enslaved people and their descendants to mark burial sites. Periwinkle and yucca can be signs leading to hidden burials, hidden ancestors.[82] The writer Alice Walker, reaching the end of a quest to find the grave of her literary hero, the novelist and anthropologist Zora Neale Hurston, describes a feeling beyond "normal responses of grief, horror, and so on" when she sees "the field full of weeds where Zora is."[83] Yet even in this anguished essay, Walker finds ambivalent beauty when she "plunge[s] into the weeds": "Some of them are quite pretty, with tiny yellow flowers. They are thick and healthy, but dead weeds under them have formed a thick gray carpet on the ground," she writes.[84] It's an image of life and flourishing creativity supported from underneath by the hidden dead: an echo of the connection linking Walker to her chosen ancestor Hurston.

For groups of cemetery citizens, plants have also been a call to action. When a neighboring property owner cut down a tree in Geer Cemetery, letting it slam down on top of graves, it was a desecration that also galvanized the resurgent Friends of Geer Cemetery organization. The Friends of East End logo, a stylized rendering of curling vines, elegantly speaks to the presence and importance of plants. Without weeds to clear from plots and grave markers, cemetery work would largely consist of more specialized and less accessible tasks. Unless you know how to wash and clean a headstone properly, you risk damaging it. Research about the people buried in the cemeteries also requires specialized training, as well as access to the internet and relevant databases. By contrast, weeding and clearing brush are tasks that almost anyone can jump right into, on almost any day. They are the most immediate ways for new people to "physically feel themselves reclaiming," as Friends of East End volunteer Melissa Pocock describes it.[85]

Plant life, and the different procedures for removing or taming it, comes to seem like part of the identity of a cemetery. I associate Geer and East End with long, stringy vines of English ivy and the ever-present danger of poison ivy, which leaves itchy souvenirs of workdays on my body. When I went to work with the Lane Street Project in Wilson, North Carolina, I had to get used to the thick strands of wisteria growing like baskets around the graves, a "lattice" of coiled tension that Lisa Y. Henderson described vividly:

> That wisteria, especially—I don't think I've ever . . . I mean, I grew up sort of rambling through those woods and swinging on those vines, but I never particularly paid attention to the way that it grows, and just this lattice of runners underground. I was trying to describe to somebody: I'm like, it's— it's a *thunnkk*. I mean, the tension is so incredible in these vines, the release of energy when you cut this thing is pretty amazing.[86]

The wisteria was far more daunting than the weeds I was used to pulling, but perhaps even more mesmerizing once I began to get into the flow. I could get my hands around the vines, making them into piles that helped me measure my progress.

Working in a cemetery also offers encounters with nonhuman animals. Sometimes these are planned: Brian and Erin's dog, Teacake, goes to East End nearly every day, sometimes playing with Mark Schmieder's dog, Willow. She circulates with her ball, look-

FIGURE 5.2. Black-and-white sketch of a volunteer leaning back as they pull long vines from the ground at Geer Cemetery. They wear a bandanna, glasses, gardening gloves, and a plaid shirt. Drawing by the author, November 13, 2022.

ing for someone to toss it for her while making people laugh. Unbeknownst to her, she's doing important work: for students and others visiting the cemetery for the first time, she breaks the ice, easing them into spending time in a place they may initially find sad or morbid.

Deer, insects, birds of prey—encounters with all of them are reminders that living and dead humans are not the only cemetery citizens, not the only beings with a stake in what happens in burial grounds. We must widen the circle of belonging in cemeteries to include the nonhuman.

In July 2022, Lisa Y. Henderson posted a new update to the *Black Wide-Awake* blog. The City of Wilson had agreed to sponsor the use of ground-penetrating radar to analyze Vick Cemetery, a public African American burial ground founded in 1913 and active until the 1960s. No existing records of the burials at Vick have survived. In 1995, a contractor for the city removed all the grave markers from the cemetery for a "cleanup." City employees kept the headstones in storage and subsequently destroyed them; they also lost the key to a map that had been made recording the information found on those headstones. It was now impossible to reestablish people's burial locations; Vick became a field of erasure. "Five decades of people caring for the dead, leaving names and key details carved into headstones, eliminated," is how Lisa described it.[87]

As Lisa expected, ground-penetrating radar was revealing Vick to be an orderly and "well-populated" cemetery (countering a common misimpression that overgrown cemeteries were always unplanned and disordered spaces). But before the technical analysis was complete, the plants were already saying things. Lisa wrote that photographer George Edward Freeney Jr. had just flown a drone over Vick Cemetery to photograph it from above. Wilson County was in a drought, and Freeney's aerial images revealed a formerly hidden green grid of places where the grass was still growing: "row after row" of nearly perfect rectangles.

Those little lozenges where the grass is growing greener and lusher? These are the ancestors revealed in plain sight. **These are the graves of our people.**

Last month, when I spoke at a Wilson City Council meeting to give thanks to all who made radar survey of Vick Cemetery possible, I stated as one reason the work is important is that the dead cannot speak.

I was wrong.

Row after row. Side by side. Despite decades in which its stewards allowed a forest to spring up over it, and tires to pile high in its weeds, and power poles to punch through its sacred soil, and its headstones to be ripped up and cast away, Vick Cemetery's dead—my father's baby brother, my cousins, your grandmothers and grandfathers, aunts and uncles—are speaking loudly and clearly: WE ARE NOT LOST. WE ARE HERE. . . .[88]

To Lisa, it seemed the ancestors were reasserting their presence, revealing their power to speak through patterns in the grass. In her description, she moves seamlessly from "my father's baby brother, my cousins" to "your grandmothers and grandfathers, aunts and uncles." Finally, at the end of her post, the "I" and the "you" blend into a "we": "We rejoice, we give thanks, we renew our vows to restore recognition and dignity to our dead." *Our* dead. A song of belonging, passing from the dead into the grass, then from Lisa to her city and her people.

SIX

Revising Public Space

When I go out to the cemetery now
even with all that summer growth which is, you know,
getting a little out of control
I can still feel that power that, yes—
all of these records, all of these plots, all of these stones
are still here and if we can't
clear them today, we'll do it tomorrow,

or next week

or next month

But we'll be back
to that clearing.

BRIAN PALMER[1]

In February 2022, North Carolina Central University history professor Charles Johnson and I joined a group of local activists at the Johnson Historic Slave Cemetery in a wooded subdivision near Durham.[2] Descendants of enslaved people and of their enslavers are now working together to preserve the cemetery. As we walked up and down the rows of the cemetery and inspected its boundaries, our conversation moved between archaeological, historical, legal, and political questions. Charles reflected, "We're becoming experts at so many different things, slowly."[3]

Yet there are questions that no amount of expertise, self-taught or otherwise, can prepare cemetery citizens to answer definitively. What should a reclaimed cemetery look like at the end of a year's work, ten years', or into the distant future? When are those revisions enough?

Cemetery citizens navigate a common set of dilemmas as they transform marginalized cemeteries into (in some cases, *back* into) vibrant public spaces. They struggle to balance the relationship between the human culture that is inscribed on a cemetery—its boundaries, plots, headstones, and other artifacts—and its other natural features. They must plan for the future of the work in these spaces: whether it can be maintained over the long haul, and what it might look like when the revisions are finished. When the urgency around reclaiming a precarious cemetery has passed, when cemetery citizens have "done their job," does that mean all of the energies they harnessed will also dissipate? As they craft new public spaces for the living and the dead, cemetery citizens also trouble and intensify the relationships between cemeteries, surrounding neighborhoods, and entire cities. They ask who the cemetery serves, and grapple with the vulnerabilities that come with inviting people in.

For the most part, cemetery citizens seem to deal with these daunting questions decision by decision—or, in bad times: crisis by crisis. Though there are burgeoning efforts to create better networks, for the most part they have rarely had the space, time, or resources to come together from their disparate sites, reflect, or share their innovations and problem-solving. This book, and especially this chapter, seeks to foster some of those connections, that reflective space.

"I Want to See Wild Here"

Consider whether or not the large trees may remain even though they may be on top of graves.

> R. KELLY BRYANT JR., letter to "Those Interested
> in Geer Cemetery," February 1, 1990[4]

[The cemetery founders] didn't necessarily keep everything manicured . . . there were things growing. I want to see wild here.

> JENN O'DONNELL, at Mount Moriah Cemetery, July 24, 2021

I spoke to Cathy McBride-Schmehl and her son John Schmehl Jr. by videoconference from their home in New Jersey one Sunday afternoon. Their speech was comfortingly familiar to me, bringing back memories of visits to the suburb of Fair Lawn, where my parents grew up. Cathy and her husband, John Sr., have "people in the ground" at Mount Moriah—in fact, John Sr.'s grandfather worked as the cemetery's caretaker. Their family now volunteers in the cemetery together, tending their own plots as well as many others they have "adopted." They respond to requests for help from other families that come in via social media, clearing pathways, resetting heavy headstones with a crane setup they call "the Beast," and making friends in the process.[5]

But Cathy and John Jr. sounded a bitter note when they talked about how some other volunteers had responded to their work. "When people see that you're cutting trees down, they're like . . . 'Leave the trees!'" Cathy said. "No! It's a cemetery. It's not a park."[6] Left to grow, she said, trees would eventually knock headstones off their bases. John chimed in:

> I get the idea of leaving the trees. I think it's a really good idea if they're not in the wrong spot. And I think if they *are* in the wrong spot, then . . . it's got to go. I mean, how would you like it if, you know, your family member's grave and there was a tree a foot over and, you know, just kind of . . . think of where those roots are, is the best way I can describe it.

The idea of roots going through bodies in the ground was so unacceptable that John wouldn't even name it.

Two years later, I brought students to Geer Cemetery for a tour with the Friends of Geer Cemetery's volunteer coordinator, Carissa Trotta. Carissa described the exact same phenomenon, pointing out to students that somewhere under the ground a network of roots was connecting all the trees in the cemetery to each other and passing in and out of the remains of the dead. But her interpretation was the inverse of John's: "These *are* the ancestors," she said, placing her hand on a tree. "We have to protect them."[7]

Jo Cosgrove, the head of the Friends of Mount Moriah's Green Committee, spoke appreciatively about the Schmehls' deep ties to the cemetery and hard work. But she offered a very different perspective on the landscape. Jo is a professional horticulturist who had been volunteering for about a year when I met her at a workday in April 2021. She first visited the cemetery in summer 2019 when she was selling her hand-crafted leather goods at the Darksome Art & Craft Market, an arts event that Mount Moriah hosts. Her knowledge and warmth quickly turned her into the unofficial leader of the small group of volunteers I joined.

I followed up with a Zoom interview, just before she was elected to the

Friends of Mount Moriah board. Jo reminded me that Paulette Rhone, the trans-formative leader the Friends had recently lost, was "passionate about ecology" and dedicated to making Mount Moriah a nature preserve.[8] In 2016, under Pau-lette's leadership, the Friends got the cemetery accredited as an arboretum.

Like Paulette before her, Jo thought a greener future for Mount Moriah was compatible with respect for the dead: "It's a cemetery first, and an arbore-tum second," she told me on another occasion.[9] She envisions planting micro-meadows of native plants and wildflowers within the coping walls around some of Mount Moriah's graves; the plants would be chosen not to grow too high or cover over any grave inscriptions. We also talked about social and en-vironmental justice, and Mount Moriah's place in the community surrounding it. Jo suggested that the cemetery had room for orchards of fruit trees—a food forest—where neighbors and visitors could harvest their own fresh produce.

Jo saw the need for a "paradigm shift" to a "restorative forestry perspec-tive" in the cemetery.[10] "Sometimes it's not realistic to work around things, but sometimes it *is*. . . . There's a native plant community that if you don't have the eye that's trained to identify plants, then you're not going to say, 'Wow, that's a really great mass of golden ragwort,' or like some other species that is worth salvaging."[11]

In some cases, cemetery citizens can go back to an original plan for the cem-etery and try to discern what the layout was, where there were trees, paths, and landscaping. The Schmehls say they have looked at the deeds for the plots where their family members are buried in Mount Moriah, which specify that nothing should be planted in the cemetery without the authorization of the cemetery association. The trees and shrubs that now grow wild through the cemetery, they point out, are not on earlier maps.[12]

In other cemeteries with fewer records, such as Geer, there is more guess-work to do. Visitors to the burial ground may be inclined to compare it to the newer cemeteries they are more familiar with, such as Beechwood, the public African American cemetery established nearly fifty years after Geer. We know from aerial photographs and historical research that Geer Cemetery was origi-nally on farmland, and not as densely wooded as it is today. But this does not tell us its original design, or what plans its founders had for how it would look over the long term. Many older cemeteries were never envisioned as long expanses of manicured lawn. They were places of wooded seclusion, where the boundaries between the tended and untended were closer and less stark than at a modern cemetery. In these spaces, cemetery citizens must nevertheless make decisions about where trees are a threat to grave markers (and potentially to living humans when their dead branches fall), and where they are an indispensable part of the beauty and sacredness of a place.

The Schmehls have an "originalist" perspective on Mount Moriah, seeking to restore the cemetery as much as possible to whatever vision its founders had, based on whatever records they can find. But cemetery citizens often face new realities that did not exist at the time, from climate change to the way once-rural cemeteries have been absorbed into growing cities.

In historic African American cemeteries, there may even be value in having the space continue to make visible the structural violence inflicted on it, rather than erasing it entirely. Azzurra Cox, a landscape architect involved in long-term planning for Greenwood Cemetery in St. Louis, Missouri, says, "Restoration is not about going back to what the cemetery looked like in 1874. It's about seeing what's happened since then and working with that, and trying to have the site speak to its many legacies."[13] Like Jo Cosgrove, she imagines wild places, orchards and fields for growing food, existing within a more traditional cemetery landscape.

Cemetery citizens want to do right by the dead humans in a cemetery, making headstones visible to descendants and the public, clearing graves and the spaces around them from weeds, crafting beauty. In this sense, many of them follow a longstanding impulse in historic preservation efforts: separating out elements of human culture from the natural world.[14] But many of them also want to be good stewards of the land. They think about the larger systems, including systems of environmental racism, in which these cemeteries are embedded. Dignifying a degraded landscape, they hope, can be consistent with care for all the living things inside and around it.

Sometimes there are tradeoffs. When I spoke with Lisa Y. Henderson about the Lane Street Project's work in African American cemeteries in Wilson, North Carolina, she asked whether the Friends of Geer Cemetery had ever used herbicide. We ourselves had not, but a City of Durham crew had done a round of spraying. The effects on Geer's vine-engulfed trees were dramatic, making it easier to walk around and spot graves. Lisa was thinking about her own relationship with the land and waterways around her, and struggling with whether to resort to the same methods:

> This is a wetland, you know, in the back. Introducing Roundup into the city water system is just not really something that I'm . . . It's already in some way such a degraded landscape. . . .
>
> I grew up about, as a crow flies, maybe a quarter mile from the cemetery, and Sandy Creek ran past the end of our neighborhood. . . . As I was walking through there two weeks ago, I just was like, *This is disgusting, like, where did this trash come from?* It floods all the time, and that trash, that plastic just gets caught up in these woods, and it's—you know, it's terrible. I'm really conscious of what for me was this really idyllic playground, and now, I think, if I were a child I would be repelled at what it looks like. So I don't want to add anything to further degrade that landscape.[15]

A few weeks after our interview, Lisa posted that on an upcoming workday at Odd Fellows Cemetery, Lane Street Project volunteers, working with a professional, would spray defoliant on sections of the cemetery they had previously cleared. She wrote, "We have made amazing progress clearing the growth strangling the cemetery, but without treatment much of our effort could be undone in the course of a single hot, humid growing season."[16]

"Not for a Year, or a Decade, or a Generation—But Forever"

Jarene Fleming's hopes for the future of Richmond's East End and Evergreen—where so many of her ancestors are buried—are tinged with the knowledge that they have already been through many cycles of "rejuvenation and return" to an overgrown state.[17] There is no point at which a cemetery is fully restored or reclaimed; and the process can easily go back in the other direction.

In its advice about cemetery preservation work, South Carolina's Chicora Foundation warns:

> There are some community groups that want to do the "right thing" and begin to "restore" a cemetery. People band together for a short period of cemetery cleaning, but fail to follow through—the work is never completed, or

is completed but nothing is put in place to maintain the cemetery after this one effort. It does NO good to clean up a cemetery, only to walk away and allow it to return to its original condition. If you take on a cemetery cleaning project you MUST make provisions to keep the cemetery maintained not for a year, or a decade, or a generation—but forever.[18]

How does anyone plan to care forever? The processes that make cemeteries into marginalized landscapes are multifaceted, and they take place over decades. We need an equally long, complex view of how revisions unfold—and how they can fail.

As new energy builds in places of the marginalized dead it can also, in Ryan K. Smith's words, have "the effect of fracturing community interest."[19] Cemetery citizens' time and interests are spread thin between multiple sites, each with urgent needs and their own complex politics. Angela Thorpe, the executive director of Durham's Pauli Murray Center for History and Social Justice, has urged people caring for African American cemeteries to embrace a "spirit of abundance, not deficit."[20] But Smith is also right that when a wave of new people start attending to marginalized histories and degraded landscapes, some sites and organizations will harness that energy better or sustain it for longer. Others will, as the Chicora Foundation warns, clear a space that soon becomes overgrown again.

Working in marginalized cemeteries immerses you in painful histories, and it can cause new pain. Cemetery citizens shared with me how much they have gained from working in cemeteries: community, sense of meaning, a new understanding of history in the place where they live. But the threat of burnout is always around the corner; there are costs to the constant exposure to people's stories of loss and

FIGURE 6.1. Black-and-white sketch of Erin Hollaway Palmer during a workday at Geer Cemetery, May 6, 2020. Her hair is tied in a ponytail, and she wears a hooded sweatshirt, face mask, and sneakers. She is leaning toward the ground, using a small spade to expose a hidden grave marker. Drawing by the author, March 2022.

trauma, or their anguished search for graves they may never find. Jenn O'Donnell vividly recalls "standing in the cemetery, crying with a stranger" on multiple occasions.[21]

In Geer, East End, or Mount Moriah, there are ambivalent moments when you look up from work in a particular section—a place where you and your companions are making good progress, perhaps—to the acres of overgrowth and hidden graves. I wrote in my field notes while working at East End in March of 2019: "The thick, endless vegetation can lead you to a sense of meditative flow, you lose your sense of time. But also, when you step back, to a kind of despair." While the words were delivered matter-of-factly, I heard a similar ambivalence, thicker with grief and exhaustion, from Naji Muhammad: "Springtime come again, I'll be right at it again."

Cemetery citizens go to great lengths to make cemeteries into places where people can gather, mourn, and learn. But I have also noticed how important silence and solitude are for many of these volunteers. Revising cemeteries is both a very public act—a form of politics—and a private meditation.

I have arrived at Geer Cemetery on multiple occasions to find Eddie Davis, a longtime advocate for the cemetery, working there alone. Brian Palmer's photographs from East End tend to capture the public nature of the revision process: volunteers in action and the transformations they make to a cemetery. Meanwhile, Erin Hollaway Palmer trains her gaze on insects, toads, and flowers. They're the kinds of things you only notice when you are bent down to the earth, focused, and very quiet. When revising a cemetery is not a means to an end, but an end in itself.

"A Nice Inviting Place"

How much of a public space should a cemetery be? This is an old debate, with its roots in the rural cemeteries' original status as the nation's first public parks. Though the landscape at Cambridge, Massachusetts' Mount Auburn Cemetery was originally thought to promote solemn reflection, landscape designer Andrew Jackson Downing soon complained that "people seem to go there to enjoy themselves, and not to indulge in any serious recollections or regrets."[22] For a while, the cemetery issued limited tickets for admission and even policed speeding carriages.[23] When a railroad station was built nearby, the trustees worried about "crowds of persons who [would] make it a resort for pleasure and amusement and thus disturb the sacred quiet of the place."[24] Only the grim realities of the American Civil War and all its dead, along with the opening of alternative urban parks, could disrupt this tense back-and-forth.[25]

The Enrichmond Foundation's plans for Evergreen Cemetery envisioned the space transcending these old debates. The cemetery could honor the dead, teach history lessons to the living, and provide them with what the Mount Auburn trustees called "pleasure and amusement."

> The cemetery is a memorial first, but also functions as an outdoor museum and educational space, as well as a green space for the public. Historic Evergreen offers opportunities to learn about ecology, enjoy nature, learn history, and spend recreation time. Visitors are encouraged to explore and experience the cemetery, even if they are not related to those interred. This open invitation builds community ownership and draws more people onto the site, which therefore increases safety.[26]

Once people looked at the details, though, they saw millions of dollars earmarked for a visitor center, bus parking, a memorial garden, and "the areas where the most famous people are buried"—with little in the way of a plan for the thousands of graves still swallowed in the weeds (which, according to some archaeologists, would be disturbed or even "obliterate[d]" by the water, sewer, and electricity lines for the visitors center and other amenities).[27] Descendant Jarene Fleming responded: "I don't feel the need for Wi-Fi. . . . I mean, it is an outdoor university, it is a wonderful place to go and learn about history. But I don't see it as a 'green space' to go and have coffee. It's a sacred place. It's important to tell the stories. I don't think you need a multimillion-dollar visitor center in order to do that."[28] Urban planning scholars Gough, Howell, and Cameron, echoing Fleming, say that Enrichmond "offer[ed] a vision of the cemetery as an open space that happens to be sacred, rather than a sacred space that is open to all."[29]

The 2018 strategic plan for Mount Moriah Cemetery also tilts hard in the "open space" direction. It suggests renaming the cemetery "Mount Moriah Cemetery & Nature Sanctuary," and "repositioning" the burial ground as both a historic cemetery and a "green space amenity."[30] Part of the cemetery's educational mission would be to teach about "the value of nature and conservation in an urban environment."[31] Dante Leonard, who grew up near the cemetery and spoke at the 2017 community meeting about burying his young friends there, also imagines it as a "teachable" space. However, he invests it with a different set of potential lessons, closer in many ways to the kinds of spiritual reflection that rural cemeteries were first meant to prompt in their visitors:

> [I]f we were to actually . . . you know, fifteen years from now, be able to see this cemetery actually be a beautiful place in the neighborhood, it'll beautify the neighborhood, but it'll also give the neighborhood a different understanding of what life and death is. . . . You know, this is a teachable thing . . . to honor this. And it's really something that is of our culture, but we've gotten so far away from it. . . . This is like sacred ground, you know, but if we don't honor it, then how can we expect anybody else to come in and honor it?[32]

Jenn O'Donnell of the Friends of Mount Moriah told me the group was still struggling with what the cemetery could offer to the community around it. Most of the organization's die-hard volunteers drive in from other parts of the Philadelphia area or New Jersey; many are older, and most are White. The death of the Friends' longtime leader Paulette Rhone, who grew up near the cemetery and was the Friends' closest connection to it, seemed like another setback. Jenn said:

> I get the sense that there's an interest from the local community in keeping the cemetery looking nice. You know, grass cut and just looking like a nice inviting place. But there are many people in that neighborhood who don't have a large interest in using the space themselves. So we do see a lot of people coming to walk, take photos, walk their dog, ride their bikes. But it's normally not Southwest Philadelphia residents. It's normally West Philly residents and suburban folks and people who are coming in from a couple miles away to do that. And so we talk a lot about how can we engage the local community—the truly local neighborhood community—and I don't think we have figured out exactly how to do that.[33]

Southwest Philadelphia, West Philly, the suburbs: anyone who knows the city can recognize how Jenn is mapping both race and class in her remarks. Southwest Philadelphia—especially the "truly local neighborhood community" around Mount Moriah—is predominantly Black. West Philadelphia, just north of it, includes historically African American areas where longstanding residents

are rapidly being pushed out by soaring housing costs.[34] While there are suburbs in many directions, one of the easiest routes into Mount Moriah is from the
much more affluent, predominantly White suburbs to the west. It's the route I
used to take from Haverford, where I lived and taught, watching upscale shop-
ping plazas and private schools give way to fast food restaurants and discount
sneaker stores.

As the new strategic plan for Mount Moriah explains, only seven percent of
Lower Southwest Philadelphia is park land.[35] Opening up more access to Mount
Moriah would nearly double the green space available to its neighbors, most of
whom live more than a half mile from any accessible park or open land.[36] Subur-
banites on bicycles—and groups of predominantly White cemetery volunteers
gathering in the cemetery—may exacerbate the sense that Mount Moriah now
belongs to someone else. Jo Cosgrove wondered, "[W]here is the line between
gentrification and community improvement? I would like there to be some
agency for the surrounding community. They're the ones who are going to be
looking at [the cemetery] all the time."[37] After years of removing trash from the
cemetery, she said, some longtime Friends of Mount Moriah volunteers had developed "a lot of ownership of the space" and resentment toward neighbors they
held responsible for the dumping. She was frank about "a schism between the
demographics of people who are involved with the Friends of Mount Moriah and
the surrounding community." Her hopes for a different future for the Friends
and for the cemetery were bound up with getting local schools involved, bringing in young people and new volunteers to mix with the ones who had been
around longer.[38]

On a visit to Mount Moriah in November 2022, I stood with Jenn and Jo at
a table at the cemetery's main entrance, awaiting guests from Interfaith Philadelphia who were coming for a tour. Three lanky Black teens from the neighborhood, holding drinks in an array of vibrant colors, saw that the cemetery gates
were open and stopped in front of them. "What is this?" one of them asked. "Is
it just old people?" (I wasn't immediately sure if the "old people" were the dead
buried in the cemetery, or my middle-aged friends and me chatting at the entrance.) Jo offered a very brief explanation of the cemetery's history, and welcomed the group to come in. "I might come here sometime," said the same teen,
dubiously, and they all walked on.

Ten minutes later they were back. They asked about one of the mausoleums near the entrance, and whether it had any bodies inside. Then they walked off into the cemetery together, holding their sweet chemical concoctions, talking quietly, poking around.

Along with dilemmas about who is "the public" and how to reach them, cemetery citizens must also confront the vulnerabilities that come with drawing attention to the marginalized dead. In August 2020, amid the ongoing Black Lives Matter protests that were transforming Richmond's landscape, vandals defaced the entrance to Evergreen Cemetery and Maggie Walker's gravesite. They sprayed graves at East End and the historic African American cemeteries in Barton Heights, as well as the nearby Jewish cemetery, Sir Moses Montefiore, with the same neon green graffiti. It mostly featured the number "777" in various configurations.[39]

It was a sign both muddled and clear. Brian, Erin, and I, texting each other, recognized that some variety of neo-Nazis were likely responsible. But it took us a while to understand the roots of the "777" symbol, called the triskele, which was used in early Nazi iconography and later appropriated by White supremacists in South Africa and the United States.

As we searched on websites and texted each other information, the irony caught up with me. The people who had vandalized the cemeteries likely still knew next to nothing about who was buried there or the lives they lived: about the streetcar boycotts or the *Richmond Planet* or all of Maggie Walker's achievements. And yet here we were, our researcher hats on, learning all about their bullshit: the defunct militant groups and recycled symbols. They had succeeded in forcing us to know them—making *themselves* public—even as they had moved through these cemeteries ignorant of the landscape and the people they were wounding. They saw Black, and they saw Jewish. No history, no other meaning.

In December 2020, Nicholas Levy of the Friends of Geer Cemetery emailed the board to share some bad news. Someone had placed a small, pathetic-looking Confederate flag at the entrance to the cemetery, just under the stone marker that welcomes visitors. Nicholas promptly removed it, then reached out to the board to tell us what had happened.

In the discussion that followed, we agreed that the flag had likely appeared because our work was going *well*. In recent memory, Geer Cemetery had been a patch of woods you could drive past without even recognizing it as a cemetery. Now it was a place that mattered in conversations about memory, race, and public space in Durham—mattered enough to become a target.

The board made a collective decision not to respond—not to give the flag an audience. Friends of Geer Cemetery vice president DD Barnes wrote, "Those buried in Geer Cemetery endured much more and persevered. I would like to think that they have now overcome the indignities made against them. The work that the [Friends of Geer are] doing honors them and continues their resolve to fight against those indignities. Best to rise above it and not call attention to what was done. As my adopted grandmother would say, 'put it under our feet and keep on walking.'"[40]

YOU PLAN TO STICK AROUND? YES, VERY MUCH SO.
(Melissa Pocock, Friends of East End, March 30, 2019)

I love seeing the little kids out [at East End Cemetery].
Once you find a stone—if we're probing
and we hear that *tink tink* of a gravestone
I'll put the trowel in just to make sure it is one,
and then we go get one of the kids to come over.

Get two or three and they will spend time,
they are looking for that next stone,
they are looking to read the name.
They tell their mom to come over
and look at what they just did:
that's how you really get them hooked.

Once you pique that interest, then you can start filling in
the gaps that they didn't know about it.
You can start telling them more information
and they really seem to want to know more about it.
Because they helped, they had their hand in claiming the site.

I think that's important, for a lot of people, that they can
actually
      physically
            feel themselves reclaiming.

But afterwards, they all leave,
and you look around. You do
have a sense of a job well done that day.
It was a good day; it was a good morning.
But you know, you look still
at all the work that has to be done
and it will never end.
It will never end,
that work.

At least to have the work done right, in my mind.

Fields of Weeds, Fields of Care

I DON'T KNOW IF THERE IS A FIX
(Jenn O'Donnell, Friends of Mount Moriah, January 19, 2020)

I. A lot of work
I don't have any family buried there. And in fact,
I think many of the volunteers don't actually have family
buried there.

A lot of feelings about a cemetery that size being abandoned,
having whoever was running it walk away,
leaving so many families
grieving families
just dangling.

There are still people that I hear from regularly
that don't understand what happened at Mount Moriah
and are looking for answers.
They're upset, they're angry,
and I get it.

This is a place that had burials
up until the week that they closed.
So this was not a forgotten space,
and it just seems so wrong to me.

I don't have the answers.
I don't know if I can fix this.
I don't know if there is a fix
or what the fix would be.

But I felt compelled to do something
even if that was just a little something
because I really do feel pretty strongly that

a lot of people all doing a little bit
is a lot of work.

II. Anybody's research

A lot of people email the Friends of Mount Moriah and say,
"Can you tell me where this person is buried?"
So that's one of the things I started doing
because I like research
I like anybody's research.

I have to pay attention to just how much of myself
I'm investing in the work that we're doing.

I'd say at least fifty percent of the time I find myself
standing in the cemetery, crying with a stranger,
holding their hands,
or whatever it is.

I think it's really easy to burn out
and find yourself running the other direction
because you just cannot do this work
anymore.

III. A fair bit of my grieving

After working with Mount Moriah for about a year,
I experienced my own loss.
One of my brothers died.
He's buried about two and a half hours away
from where I live. And I very quickly found
that spending time at cemeteries,
Mount Moriah and other places,
just made me feel some sort of
connection.

I couldn't always visit his burial site,
but I could visit a cemetery.
And to me a cemetery is a cemetery.

So I did a fair bit of my grieving for my brother
at Mount Moriah.

I've had somebody say to me, "What's new? How are you doing?"
And I said, "Well, my father passed away a few weeks ago,

and so that's really been in the forefront of my mind."
And I've actually had people say things to me like,
"Well, that's a conversation killer."

Sometimes I think you get more caring and compassion
from a complete stranger. And I found a number of people—
that's one of the reasons they're drawn to cemeteries.

There are a million things I could put my energy toward.
I think that cemeteries are far more about the living
than they are the dead. There's a lot of people
who don't see it that way.
But I think that cemeteries
are about life.

In April 2023, as I was wrapping up revisions on this book, I drove from Durham to Philadelphia, stopping off in Richmond. The night before I departed, my students and I hosted the opening of the *In Plain Sight* exhibit about Geer Cemetery—installed outdoors on Duke's campus this time, not at the cemetery. A clear forecast changed to rain at the last minute, far too late to make another plan. At the opening, we took turns standing under the open sky and welcoming our intrepid guests. The rest of the time, we mostly huddled inside near the foil trays of catered food. My students lingered with each other and with Friends of Geer members, holding paper plates. Everyone looked waterlogged, tired, and happy.

The next day I arrived in Richmond during a pause in the rain. I had just enough time to put my bag down in the guest room before Brian drove me out to the cemeteries. Over the past few months, the neighboring industrial recycling company had removed all the trees between it and the cemetery. A flat dirt expanse, with a few construction vehicles parked on it, made up the new view from the front section of East End.

But the place was still green and quiet, somehow both ramshackle and full of grace. Brian and I disappeared into it. Teacake followed us, a bit older, content to carry a ball around in her mouth without having it thrown to her every few minutes.

Enrichmond was gone, leaving new picnic tables scattered around, chipped headstones, and a van they had purchased new and then abandoned. We found a collapsed tent and food wrappers; someone had camped out in Evergreen, taking refuge among the dead. Brian told me that Erin, who was away for the weekend, was still looking for the graves of Thomas Taylor's grandparents in a sloping section of the cemetery, deep in the wisteria, pokeweed, and ivy. She had started drawing a map by hand as she worked her way into the thickets.

Brian was in the last few months of a stint in New York as a visiting professor, preparing for his relocation back to Richmond. We talked about the ways in which the past year had pushed us both to the brink: a dangerous place, and a place where new things become possible. As we circled back into East End at the end of our walk, Brian pointed out the areas where he and a small crew of Friends of East End members had been clearing, the pile of branches he had made on a recent workday. His tall body seemed at ease in a place he knows as well as anyone. Brian was home.

The next day I woke up early and drove to Philadelphia for Paulette Rhone Community Day, held at Mount Moriah to honor the legacy of the Friends of Mount Moriah's late president and further her vision of making the cemetery a green space that would welcome the local community into its gates. The program included a tree giveaway, a herd of goats, and a "Raptor Jawns" booth featuring a red-tailed hawk and Eastern screech owl. In case anyone was in danger of forgetting we were in Philadelphia, soft pretzels and water ice were being handed out with semi-aggressive pride. (When I tried to take only a pretzel, I got the hard sell on the free water ice. It was delicious.)

The rain was light but steady, and it looked like the community day might not get much of a crowd. My former student Kate Weiler and I walked down to the Springfield Avenue section. It was impossible to be here in spring and not think of Naji Muhammad saying, "Springtime come again, I'll be right at it again."

When Kate and I got back to the main event, everyone had crowded around Paulette's grave. Her children and grandchildren were there. Along with some longtime Friends of Mount Moriah members, they shared memories of this tough, visionary woman who loved flowers. We stuck around after most of the crowd had gone, watching a few volunteers plant a magnolia tree and a pair of hydrangeas next to the grave.

Everyone was watching the rain, and the spring unfurling itself around us. Volunteers shook their heads, quipping about how the growth was about to out-

FIGURE CONCL.1.   The grave of Paulette Rhone, late president of the Friends of Mount Moriah Cemetery, and her husband, Gilbert. The red-tinged marble headstone has their names and the dates of their births and deaths (Gilbert Rhone, 1946–1993; Paulette Rhone, 1954–2019). The inscription "loving parents" is in smaller letters at its base. Pink and white flowers surround the headstone, and a basket of pink hydrangeas sits in the foreground of the photograph. The grassy landscape of Mount Moriah in spring, and rows of headstones, are in the background. Photograph by the author, April 29, 2023.

pace all their mowing and clearing, the hours and hours of care. At East End it was the same. At Geer, where volunteers had been finding graves that were lost for decades, green tendrils were snaking up again. This yearly cycle doesn't necessarily undo all the efforts and revisions in a cemetery, but it humbles them.

The juicy and maddening spring, with its vines and fronds and pollen, can't erase everything. Some changes last, even while cemetery citizens must perform the same tasks, and maintain the same sections, over and over.

My students meet DD Barnes and other Geer descendants; the reverence they cultivated while reading for my class, pondering ethical duties to both ancestors and descendants, turns into small talk, laughter. A group of students goes out in the evening to take time-lapse videos in the cemetery, draw its trees and headstones, compose music and write poems to capture their experiences. They learn about Mary Sparkman, Rubby G. Farrow, P. W. Dawkins, Susan Richardson. It changes them.

Brian and I stand in front of the great banker and civil rights activist Maggie L. Walker's grave in Evergreen, in the shadow of a stone cross she installed at her family plot. I'm sure she wished it would be a gathering place for more people, for a longer time, than has turned out to be the case.[1] But here we are: gathered, changed, our lives both completely revised by these cemeteries.

The next day, I leave Mount Moriah as the community day is winding down. People are still milling around, eating hot dogs. It was a decent crowd, in the end. I'm tired, but I feel pressure to stay longer. What if something else happens, or there's an interesting conversation, and I'm not there with my notebook?

But things are happening all the time in these cemeteries, and I'm not there with my notebook. My book revisions have met their deadline; the revisions in the cemeteries keep going. They're all "nice inviting places" in ways they weren't just a few years ago. They're also outdoor archives, sacred spaces, fields of struggle, painful and powerful places to mourn.

You should see for yourself. Remember them so you can.

ACKNOWLEDGMENTS

FOR CEMETERY CITIZENS
I was looking for a place

You taught me how places are made
from layers of the dead

I was looking for how to live, write, teach
and make new things
without always trying to be an expert

You taught me how to assemble expertise
and spread it around a community, a cemetery—
that you can become an expert slowly,
but hold it briefly
and then let it go,

> like a vine that's in your way
> when you're searching for a headstone
> not like something you cling to
> for your life

I was looking for lost names in my family
You taught me the names of plants, people, ways of taking care
of all the things that grow
in spaces that loss and forgetting
are making so sacred

The following people named in this book died during the period of my research (2017–2023): David Eustice, Naji Muhammad, and Paulette Rhone. I am grateful to have met them all and wish their loved ones comfort.

During the research I began in the U.S.-Mexico borderlands, which was cut short, I stayed in the home of Gayle and Don Weyers along with a pack of college students from the Midwest. Gayle was a member of the Ajo Samaritans who regularly left water and food in the desert for living migrants, and crosses to mark where they had died. While I was at her house, I wrote in my notebook: "She puts ABBA on the record player and merrily crushes us at Scrabble. A prayer before dinner. Watching how Gayle's hospitality changes the students . . . Gayle is literally the most joyful person I've ever met." Amid all her hosting duties, she made time to show me her garden—a hilltop in Ajo, humble and sacred. It, and she, quietly altered my sense of how I wanted to live. Gayle died in 2021; I knew her briefly but remember her as a blessing.

I am also thankful to Alvaro Enciso, Judy Bourg, and everyone who welcomed me in Tucson, Ajo, and the Sonoran Desert. My understanding of that place and the work of honoring migrants who lose their lives there—what it means, and how it differs from cemetery revisions—continues to be shaped by the brilliance of Robin Reineke and Barbara Sostaita.

MetFern Cemetery appears on only a few pages, but this book was indelibly influenced by years of conversations with Alex Green about that burial ground, mass institutionalization, and the work of revising the stories and spaces of disability history.

Thank you to my writing buddy Collie Fulford, whose encouragement, wisdom, humor, and index card drawings have been a constant source of joy and connection. I am also deeply indebted to Jennifer Ahern-Dodson, Monique Dufour, Michelle Gregersen, Cecilia Márquez, Karin Shapiro, Melissa Simmermeyer, and everyone who organizes and participates in the Faculty Write Program at Duke. Much of the most significant and most pleasurable writing for this book was done in their company, following their advice, and drinking coffee brought by Barbara Dickinson.

Erin Hollaway Palmer and Brian Palmer have left countless marks on this book, and on me, as my readers, coauthors, companions in research, teachers, and friends. Erin was also my copy editor, showing once again just how many things she knows how to fix. Teacake always made me feel welcome upon arrival in Richmond by wagging not just her tail, but the entire back half of her body when she saw me.

Thank you to Michelle Smallwood-Kassab and Keisha L. Phillips for allowing me to share their expressions of grief and love.

The Friends of Geer Cemetery are my most constant and beloved community in Durham. The transformations they have made in the cemetery, and our city, are not adequately captured in these pages. Nicholas Levy, Jessica Eustice, and Carissa Trotta shared additional archival materials about Geer Cemetery and preservation efforts there, and Nicholas has gone extra lengths as a thoughtful editor, questioner, and fact-checker for my writing about Geer.

My colleagues in the Durham Black Burial Grounds Collaboratory—Alicia Jiménez, Charles Johnson, Khadija McNair, and Jenna Smith—have consistently inspired me to be a better scholar and cemetery citizen.

DD Barnes, Elizabeth Baughan, Jo Cosgrove, Jeannine Keefer, Jaymelee Kim, Alicia Jiménez, Amanda Levinson, Nicholas Levy, Jenn O'Donnell, Yamona Pierce, Melissa Pocock, Robin Reineke, Debra Taylor Gonzalez-Garcia, Carissa Trotta, and anonymous reviewers from Stanford University Press read all or parts of this manuscript, or of my book proposal before that. I am grateful for the suggestions they made and for asking of me the best I could give. Dylan Kyung-lim White has been a thoughtful, supportive editor.

My research for this book started with an Amtrak ticket to Richmond purchased for me by Haverford College's Center for Peace and Global Citizenship. At some of the hardest moments in the journey, Ryan Smith spent time on the phone with me offering both warm encouragement and keen suggestions. I had many conversations with Jaymelee Kim about anthropology, structural violence, and the dead—and left all of them with my horizons expanded. My work has benefited from ongoing conversations with the Collective for Radical Death Studies, at the Fall 2020 "Mourning on the Margins" workshop, organized by Kami Fletcher and Jenny Woodley, and at the "Excesses of Death" workshop at Duke, convened by my generous colleague Anne Allison and Hannah Gould, with assistance from artist, knitter, and death studies scholar Ben Sperber. Alexa Hagerty wrote and gifted me a copy of *Still Life with Bones*, which reminded me, just when it counted most, what I wanted my own writing to do. Zach Oberfield asked, in slightly different words, whether the dead are an emergency, and gave me a chance to think hard about the answer. Colin Cheney was always there with voice memos and synthesizers. Chris Burner has helped me see things with more clarity and far more gentleness than I would have found on my own.

I have been energized, inspired, and challenged as I taught and worked alongside students from my "Death, Burial, and Justice in the Americas" seminar in 2020 and 2023, and a summer 2021 Story+ team at Duke, on projects related to Geer and other cemeteries. The Duke Endowment, Duke Service-Learning, the Duke Human Rights Center, John Hope Franklin Humanities Center, International Comparative Studies, and the Duke Forum for Scholars and Publics have all supported those collaborations. One of my former students, Molly Mendoza, worked as a research assistant at a key stage, helping me manage sources, citations, and formatting with care and patience. I also benefit, in all my work on this book and at Duke, from Briani Meyers and Denecia Miller's warm, skilled administrative help.

Lynda Barry, Andrew Causey, Peter Elbow, William Germano, Elizabeth Gilbert, and Tom Hart all wrote, drew, and/or podcasted things that sustained me and gave me courage to incorporate drawings and poems in these pages. I am grateful for sketchbooks in different shapes and sizes: each one a little golden promise.

Above all, I thank my family—Amanda, Leo, Sal, and Matzo—for accompanying me to more cemeteries than they would ever have wished, for every day, for this life we revise together.

Permissions acknowledgments: The epigraph from Stephen J. Jackson's "Rethinking Repair" was originally published in Gillespie, Tarleton, Pablo J. Boczkowski & Kirsten A. Foot (eds.), *Media Technologies: Essays on Communication, Materiality, and Society*, ©2014 Massachusetts Institute of Technology, Cambridge, MA: The MIT Press, (p. 223). Additional permissions include *The Buried Giant: A Novel* by Kazuo Ishiguro, copyright © 2015 by Kazuo Ishiguro. Used by permission of Alfred A. Knopf, an imprint of the Knopf Doubleday Publishing Group, a division of Penguin Random House LLC. All rights reserved.

NOTES

Beauty in Dirt

1. The title of this section comes from Modest Mouse, "So Much Beauty in Dirt," track 6 on *Everywhere and His Nasty Parlor Tricks*, Epic Records, 2001.

Introduction

1. On the terminology of headstones versus gravestones (or tombstones), see Lynn Rainville, *Hidden History: African American Cemeteries in Central Virginia* (Charlottesville: University of Virginia Press, 2014), 23.

2. Rainville, *Hidden History*.

3. See Ryan M. Seidemann and Christine L. Halling, "Landscape Structural Violence: A View from New Orleans's Cemeteries," *American Antiquity* 84, no. 4 (2019): 669–683, https://doi.org/10.1017/aaq.2019.49.

4. For influential definitions and discussions of structural violence, see Paul Farmer, "An Anthropology of Structural Violence," *Current Anthropology* 45, no. 3 (2004): 305–325, https://doi.org/10.1086/382250; Johan Galtung, "Violence, Peace, and Peace Research," *Journal of Peace Research* 6, no. 3 (1969): 167–191, https://doi.org/10.1177/002234336900600301.

5. In his well-known essay "The Case for Reparations," Ta-Nehisi Coates writes, "When we think of white supremacy, we picture COLORED ONLY signs, but we should picture pirate flags." *The Atlantic*, June 2014, https://www.theatlantic.com/magazine/archive/2014/06/the-case-for-reparations/361631/.

6. See Mindy Thompson Fullilove, *Root Shock: How Tearing Up City Neighborhoods Hurts America, And What We Can Do About It* (New York: NYU Press, 2016).

7. "Historically deep and geographically broad" is from Farmer, "An Anthropology of Structural Violence," 309.

8. Sociologist Loïc Wacquant worries that the notion of structural violence "threatens to stop inquiry just where it should begin, that is, with distinguishing various species of violence and different structures of domination. . . ." Wacquant response essay in Farmer, "An Anthropology of Structural Violence," 322. Any attempt to distinguish between types of violence must also confront the fact that they tend to accompany and

flow into one another: as anthropologist Alexa Hagerty says, "The marks of structural violence often accompany the marks of apocalyptic violence." Alexa Hagerty, *Still Life with Bones: Genocide, Forensics, and What Remains* (New York: Crown, 2023), 29.

9. For example, in an open letter to residents of Durham that they disseminated widely, scholar Kim Smith and descendant Stephanie Davis offer a granular account of how "a network of historical preservation entities, city planners, civil engineers, and the real property industry" have each played a part in the overgrowth and indignities inflicted on two of Durham's historic African American cemeteries. See Kim Smith and Stephanie Davis, "An Open Letter: The Fitzgerald Family Cemetery and Henderson Cemetery," November 4, 2021, updated January 27, 2022, https://drive.google.com/file/d/149knrJL_lRDxyNsBv3KKdiuOulqeNTqQ/view.

10. By "memory landscape," I mean how the natural and built environments around us, from individual structures to entire cities, tell stories about our past and present. Tim Cole, describing Holocaust survivors' visits to Auschwitz in similar terms, writes that the former concentration camp "is an active landscape in memory making. It is a place that 'solicits and provokes, initiates and connects . . . [and] engenders its own effects and affects.'" Tim Cole, "Crematoria, Barracks, Gateway: Survivors' Return Visits to the Memory Landscapes of Auschwitz," *History and Memory* 25, no. 2 (2013): 102–31, https://doi.org/10.2979/histmemo.25.2.102. The phrase "landscapes of memory" appears throughout Blanche Linden-Ward's history of Mount Auburn Cemetery, *Silent City on a Hill: Landscapes of Memory and Boston's Mount Auburn Cemetery* (Columbus: Ohio State University Press, 1989).

11. Caitlin DeSilvey writes, "It may be that in some circumstances a state of gradual decay provides more opportunities for memory making, and more potential points of engagement and interpretation, than the alternative." *Curated Decay: Heritage Beyond Saving* (Minneapolis: University of Minnesota Press, 2017), 14–15.

12. Architecture historian Max Page offers a vision of historic preservation that is not "fetishistic" about the past but rather explicitly oriented toward social justice in the present and future. *Why Preservation Matters* (New Haven, CT: Yale University Press, 2016). "Almost all of the terms that are used to describe attitudes of care, toward both cultural artifacts and natural environments, assume the desirability of a return to a prior state," geographer Caitlin DeSilvey writes. Her work explores an emerging alternative to traditional preservation frameworks—a "postpreservation" paradigm that accepts, and makes meaning out of, inevitable decay and the blurring of boundaries between nature and culture. *Curated Decay*, 20.

13. See Alexis Pauline Gumbs, "Even in the Grave, Black People Can't Rest in Durham," *INDY Week*, February 25, 2020, https://indyweek.com/news/voices/even-in-the-grave-black-people-cant-rest-in-durham/.

14. Jill Stauffer, *Ethical Loneliness: The Injustice of Not Being Heard* (New York: Columbia University Press, 2015), 112–13. Stauffer gets the term "revisionary practices"

from Meir Dan-Cohen, "Revising the Past: On the Metaphysics of Repentance, Forgiveness, and Pardon," in *Forgiveness, Mercy, and Clemency*, ed. Austin Sarat and Nasser Hussain (Stanford, CA: Stanford University Press, 2007), 117–37.

15. In Jewish thought, especially post-Holocaust, the idea of *tikkun olam* is often used to capture a similar notion: the necessity of working to repair a world that is beautiful, sacred, and damaged. See Jonathan Krasner, "The Place of Tikkun Olam in American Jewish Life," *Jewish Political Studies Review* 25, no. 3–4 (November 1, 2014), https:// jcpa.org/article/place-tikkun-olam-american-jewish-life1/.

16. See Adam Richard Rosenblatt, "Engraved: A Family Forensics," *Fieldsights*, Society for Cultural Anthropology, February 9, 2023, https://culanth.org/fieldsights/ engraved-a-family-forensics.

17. In an interview my grandmother, Jean Bialer, gave my sister in the late 1980s, she said, "It's like unreal. I can't believe that I actually went through all of that, that I could withstand all the pain and all the suffering and be able still to give love to others. It's so unbelievable what you could endure. It's just not real. I sit often and I think about it."

The testimony where she discusses hunger with such great frequency is in the archives of the Polish Research Institute at the University of Lund, Sweden, where it is tagged with keywords such as:

Deportations	Manufactory work (Textile)
Jews	Trade
Children	Sabotage
Humiliation	Sexual abuse
Ghetto	Supervisors (German)
Round up	Weapons industry
Authorities	Psychological abuse
Guards (Ukrainian)	

See Genia Rotman [later Jean Bialer], Record of Witness Testimony 194, interview by Luba Melchior, March 2, 1946, The Polish Research Institute, http://www.alvin -portal.org/alvin/view.jsf?pid=alvin-record%3A102719&dswid=-8778.

18. "Folks with people in the ground" is from Brian Palmer, "Friends of East End Cemetery," interview by Bret Payne, *Burning Bright*, July 2020, audio, 41:29, https:// open.spotify.com/episode/1wMTOoJW11ayBXDyzA6Jpk.

For canonical statements on descendant authority over burial grounds and sites of enslavement, see Michael L. Blakey, "African Burial Ground Project: Paradigm for Cooperation?" *Museum International* 62, no. 1/2 (May 2010): 61–68, https://doi.org/10.1111/j.14 68-0033.2010.01716.x; National Trust for Historic Preservation and African American Cultural Heritage Action Fund, *Engaging Descendant Communities in the Interpretation of Slavery at Museums and Historic Sites*, Version 1.0 (Montpelier Station, VA: Montpelier Descendants Committee, 2018), https://montpelierdescendants.org/rubric/.

19. Rosenblatt, "Engraved: A Family Forensics."

20. Menachem Kaiser, *Plunder: A Memoir of Family Property and Nazi Treasure* (Boston: Houghton Mifflin Harcourt), 2021, 194.

21. See Thomas W. Laqueur, *The Work of the Dead: A Cultural History of Mortal Remains* (Princeton, NJ: Princeton University Press, 2015); Hagerty, *Still Life with Bones*, 159; *Death, Mourning, and Burial: A Cross-Cultural Reader*, ed. Antonius C. G. M. Robben (Hoboken, NJ: John Wiley & Sons, 2017).

22. Graham Fairclough, "Conservation and the British," 158, quoted in DeSilvey, *Curated Decay*, 4. See also DeSilvey on how dominant preservation paradigms ignore or exclude cultural traditions that embrace "intangible and transient" relationships with the past. Ibid., 8.

23. "I learned, you don't lose a cemetery. A state hospital cemetery has to be disappeared." Patricia E. Deegan, "Remember My Name: Reflections on Spirituality in Individual and Collective Recovery," shared via email to the author, April 16, 2021, 1.

24. I capitalize both Black and White throughout *Cemetery Citizens* when they are used as racial identifications. "Blackness and many other cultural identities are labels bestowed upon us and carried from birth. It is an indicator of personhood, culture, and history. The lower case 'b' fails to honor the weight of this identity appropriately. . . . Choosing to not capitalize White while capitalizing other racial and ethnic identifiers would implicitly affirm Whiteness as the standard and norm. Keeping White lowercase ignores the way Whiteness functions in institutions and communities." Kristen Mack and John Palfrey, "Capitalizing Black and White: Grammatical Justice and Equity," MacArthur Foundation, August 26, 2020, https://www.macfound.org/press/perspectives/capitalizing-black-and-white-grammatical-justice-and-equity.

25. For over two decades, a Gloucester man living close to the cemetery, Walter McGrath, mowed its grasses and tended its graves. He has only recently given up the work due to his age.

26. On death as "the great leveler," see Robert Kastenbaum and Christopher Moreman, *Death, Society, and Human Experience*, 12th ed. (Routledge, 2018), 60–62. On Evergreen Cemetery in Richmond as a site where African Americans were striving for posthumous parity, see Ray Bonis and Selden Richardson, "The Shame of Evergreen Cemetery—What Do You Think?" *The Shockoe Examiner: Blogging the History of Richmond, Virginia*, August 10, 2015, https://theshockoeexaminer.blogspot.com/2015/08/the-shame-of-evergreen-cemetery-what-do.html.

27. Linden-Ward, *Silent City on a Hill*, 295, 301, 310.

28. Gary Laderman, *The Sacred Remains: American Attitudes Toward Death, 1799–1883* (New Haven, CT: Yale University Press, 1999), 44; First Baptist Church (Philadelphia), "Lists of burials for removal to Mount Moriah Cemetery, 1860," *Philadelphia Congregations Early Records*, https://philadelphiacongregations.org/records/item/ABHS.FBCGravesForRemovalToMtMoriah1860.

29. Laderman, *The Sacred Remains*, 81–85.

30. Greg Melville, *Over My Dead Body: Unearthing the Hidden History of America's Cemeteries* (New York: Abrams, 2022), 65; see also Linden-Ward, *Silent City on a Hill*, 341.

31. Keith Eggener, "Our First Public Parks: The Forgotten History of Cemeteries," interview by Rebecca Greenfield, *The Atlantic,* March 16, 2011, https://www.theatlantic .com/national/archive/2011/03/our-first-public-parks-the-forgotten-history-of-ceme teries/71818/. See also Laderman, *The Sacred Remains*, 69; Linden-Ward, *Silent City on a Hill*, 295–320.

32. Melville, *Over My Dead Body*, 5.

33. Ibid., 107–112.

34. See Louise Harmon, "Honoring Our Silent Neighbors to the South: The Problem of Abandoned or Forgotten Asylum Cemeteries," *Touro Law Review* 34, no. 4 (2018): 901–82; Jonathan Kendall, "Remembering When Americans Picnicked in Cemeteries," Atlas Obscura, October 18, 2021, https://www.atlasobscura.com/articles/picnic-in -cemeteries-america; Linden-Ward, *Silent City on a Hill*, 319.

35. Judaic Studies scholar Allan Amanik captures this complexity in his analysis of New York's Jewish rural cemeteries: "The city and the nation's first Jewish rural cemeteries therefore embodied an important duality. On the one hand, Jews touted them as symbols of mobility and integration, marking their embrace of American material culture and religiosity in death. Lush Jewish landscapes that neighbored Protestant cemeteries stood as testaments to Jewish inclusion, nearly unprecedented on either side of the Atlantic. On the other hand, Jewish New Yorkers sought to temper that very integration into American life by doubling down on physical and ritual borders in death." Allan Amanik, "'A Beautiful Garden Consecrated to the Lord': Marriage, Death, and Local Constructions of Citizenship in New York's Nineteenth-Century Jewish Rural Cemeteries," in *Till Death Do Us Part*, ed. Allan Amanik and Kami Fletcher (Jackson: University Press of Mississippi, 2020), 16.

36. On the naming conventions of rural cemeteries, see James J. Farrell, *Inventing the American Way of Death, 1830–1920* (Philadelphia: Temple University Press, 1980), 111.

37. See Violet Park Cemetery Correspondence (NCC.0250), North Carolina Collection, Durham County Library, NC, donated by R. Kelly Bryant, https://archive. durhamcountylibrary.org/repositories/2/resources/54.

38. Farrell, *Inventing the American Way of Death*, 118–20.

39. On the number of cemeteries in the U.S. compared to chain restaurants, see Melville, *Over My Dead Body*, 5.

40. See Sandee LaMotte, "Cremation Has Replaced Traditional Burials in Popularity in America and People Are Getting Creative with Those Ashes," CNN, January 23, 2020, https://www.cnn.com/2020/01/22/health/cremation-trends-wellness/index .html.

41. For accounts of American death as an event increasingly managed by paid professionals and removed from the visible urban landscape, see Philippe Ariès, *The Hour*

of Our Death, trans. Helen Weaver (New York: Alfred A. Knopf, 1981); Joseph Bottum, "Death & Politics," *First Things*, June 2007, https://www.firstthings.com/article/2007/06/001-death-politics; Jessica Mitford, *The American Way of Death* (New York: Simon & Schuster, 1963).

42. Suzanne E. Smith, *To Serve the Living: Funeral Directors and the African American Way of Death* (Cambridge, MA: Harvard University Press, 2010), 17–18, 85–86.

43. Kami Fletcher, "Race and the Funeral Profession: What Jessica Mitford Missed," *TalkDeath*, December 2, 2018, https://www.talkdeath.com/race-funeral-profession-what-jessica-mitford-missed/.

44. It turns out that Americans have long debated the appropriateness of eating in cemeteries. See Kendall, "Remembering When Americans Picnicked in Cemeteries."

45. Lauret Edith Savoy, *Trace: Memory, History, Race, and the American Landscape* (Berkeley, CA: Counterpoint Press, 2015), 180.

46. In Louisiana, a "petrochemical corridor" of oil and plastics companies, occupying land that once housed plantations where enslaved people harvested sugarcane, has destroyed many Black burial grounds and constitutes an ongoing threat to others. See Forensic Architecture and RISE St. James, "Environmental Racism in Death Alley, Louisiana," Forensic Architecture, June 28, 2021, https://forensic-architecture.org/investigation/environmental-racism-in-death-alley-louisiana.

47. See Amanik and Fletcher, *Till Death Do Us Part.*

48. In 1993, swastikas and Nazi slogans were painted on ninety-eight headstones in a Workmen's Circle Cemetery in Saddle Brook, New Jersey. My biological grandfather, Arthur Rosenblatt, is buried there. He survived the Holocaust, though his early death from heart failure, at age forty-eight, was likely the result of the conditions he endured as a concentration camp prisoner. See Robert Hanley, "Tombstones Defaced with Pro-Nazi Slogans in North Jersey Jewish Cemetery," *The New York Times*, September 22, 1993, https://www.nytimes.com/1993/09/22/nyregion/tombstones-defaced-with-pro-nazi-slogans-in-north-jersey-jewish-cemetery.html.

49. Harmon, "Honoring Our Silent Neighbors to the South," 959.

50. Ryan M. Seidemann and Christine L. Halling argue that whenever cemeteries are damaged and destroyed in ways that "reinforce . . . preexisting social prejudices," we should think of it as "landscape structural violence." Seidemann and Halling, "Landscape Structural Violence," 669–83, 670.

51. , Chris Suarez, "Maggie L. Walker's Grave Site Among Those Vandalized at Historic Cemeteries," *Richmond Times-Dispatch*, August 3, 2020, https://richmond.com/news/local/maggie-l-walkers-grave-site-among-those-vandalized-at-historic-cemeteries/article_aef50403-bc87-5c77-b1db-7095db70c896.html.

52. Vanessa Harding, "Whose Body? A Study of Attitudes Towards the Dead Body in Early Modern Paris," in *The Place of the Dead: Death and Remembrance in Late Medieval and Early Modern Europe*, ed. Bruce Gordon and Peter Marshall (Cambridge: Cambridge University Press, 2000), 172.

53. "A government that cannot maintain its cemeteries has failed as a government," Joseph Bottum argues. Joseph Bottum, "The Unhaunted Graveyard," review of *The Work of the Dead: A Cultural History of Mortal Remains*, by Thomas W. Laqueur, The Washington Free Beacon, January 2, 2016, https://freebeacon.com/culture/the-unhaunted-graveyard/. Anthropologist Jason De León, in his study of migrant deaths on the U.S.-Mexico border, writes, "Looking at the bodies left in the desert reveals what the physical boundary of sovereignty and the symbolic edge of humanity look like." Jason De León, *The Land of Open Graves: Living and Dying on the Migrant Trail* (Berkeley: University of California Press, 2015), 84.

54. For a variety of perspectives on structural violence and the dead, see Jennifer F. Byrnes and Iván Sandoval-Cervantes, eds., *The Marginalized in Death: A Forensic Anthropology of Intersectional Identity in the Modern Era* (Lanham, MD: Lexington Books, 2022).

55. In an essay on racially segregated cemeteries, David Sherman writes, "To conjugate the idea of whiteness with a fetus or corpse—let alone with a zygote or cremains—is to reveal it for what it is, a desperate and incoherent claim for an exclusive social prestige that can be passed down through generational lineage, from one mortal body to another." David Sherman, "Grave Matters: Segregation and Racism in U.S. Cemeteries," The Order of the Good Death, April 20, 2020, https://www.orderofthegooddeath.com/article/grave-matters-segregation-and-racism-in-u-s-cemeteries/.

56. Jill Lepore, "When Black History Is Unearthed, Who Gets to Speak for the Dead?" *The New Yorker*, September 27, 2021, https://www.newyorker.com/magazine/2021/10/04/when-black-history-is-unearthed-who-gets-to-speak-for-the-dead.

57. Ryan K. Smith, *Death and Rebirth in a Southern City: Richmond's Historic Cemeteries* (Baltimore: Johns Hopkins University Press, 2020), 3.

58. Seth Freed Wessler, "Developers Found Graves in the Virginia Woods. Authorities Then Helped Erase the Historic Black Cemetery," ProPublica, December 16, 2022, https://www.propublica.org/article/how-authorities-erased-historic-black-cemetery-virginia.

59. Friends of Geer Cemetery, Facebook post, October 10, 2022, https://www.facebook.com/friendsofgeer/posts/pfbid0CngkNMRxNSiyJ2FtrZXgTXSFDCZn6eXSpS6NnwrBtBrxkkBvq6YvxKT7aqyDQ7W2l.

60. Jarene Fleming, interview with the author, January 24, 2021; see also Daniel Figueroa IV, "Abandoned Cemeteries Task Force Adds 'Teeth' and New Category to Policy Framework," Florida Politics, November 30, 2021, https://floridapolitics.com/archives/476555-abandoned-cemeteries-task-force-adds-teeth-and-new-category-to-policy-framework/.

61. "Neglect," Online Etymology Dictionary, https://www.etymonline.com/search?q=neglect.

62. Angela Thorpe, interview with the author, July 6, 2023.

63. See Elizabeth Williamson, "America's Black Cemeteries and Three Women

Trying to Save Them," *The New York Times*, September 27, 2023, https://www.nytimes
.com/2023/09/27/us/black-cemeteries.html.

64. Thanks to Maurice Hamington for suggesting I investigate this distinction. Maintenance can, in fact, be care*less*. When activists pushed for the State of Massachusetts to take responsibility for maintaining the burial grounds at a former state mental hospital in Danvers, "[t]he contractor simply ran a bobcat type bulldozer through the cemetery to clear out the brush," reports the Danvers State Memorial Committee. "When we went out to see the work, members of our committee wept. It was an awful sight: some markers were pulled out, tractor tire marks marred the hillside, and roots and stumps remained two inches above the ground making it difficult to walk about." Danvers State Memorial Committee, "History of Our Work" (November 4, 1998 entry), 2001, http://dsmc.info/work.shtml.

65. See Gravetender, "Perpetual Care Isn't What You Think It Is," *Gravewords*, January 31, 2021, https://gravewords.wordpress.com/2012/01/31/perpetual-care-isnt-what-you-think-it-is/.

66. On care ethics, feminist theories of care, and caring for the dead, see Adam Richard Rosenblatt, *Digging for the Disappeared: Forensic Science after Atrocity*, Stanford Studies in Human Rights (Stanford, CA: Stanford University Press, 2015), 167–198.

67. See Rainville, *Hidden History*, 61.

68. "Tender," Online Etymology Dictionary, accessed May 31, 2023, https://www.etymonline.com/search?q=tender.

69. Lisa Y. Henderson, interview with the author, February 9, 2021.

70. "Degrade," Online Etymology Dictionary, accessed May 31, 2023, https://www.etymonline.com/search?q=degrade.

71. "Margin," Online Etymology Dictionary, accessed May 31, 2023, https://www.etymonline.com/search?q=margin.

72. Margaret Jones's story appears in chapter 2 of this book. On Mount Moriah's inclusive, "democratic" spirit, see Christopher Doherty, "Confederates, Catholics, Muslims and Masons: The Mount Moriah Cemetery Tour," *The Necessity for Ruins*, December 1, 2007, https://ruins.wordpress.com/2007/12/01/mount-moriah-cemetery/.

73. See Chad Pradelli, Cheryl Mettendorf, and Maia Rosenfeld, "Data Investigation: Philadelphia Metro Area Among Most Racially Segregated in Country," 6abc Philadelphia, July 22, 2021, https://6abc.com/philadelphia-metro-housing-equality-segregation-census-bureau-data/10901948/.

74. See Sammy Caiola, "57 Blocks in Philly Are Prone to Shootings. Community Groups Are Mobilizing to Curb the Gun Violence," *The Philadelphia Tribune*, December 23, 2022, https://www.phillytrib.com/news/local_news/57-blocks-in-philly-are-prone-to-shootings-community-groups-are-mobilizing-to-curb-the/article_c50ef3a5-2967-50f9-838c-9c9dc725bef9.html; on incarceration rates in Philadelphia neighborhoods, see "Philadelphia Prison Population Report: July 2015-July 2023," Prison Policy Institute, https://www.phila.gov/media/20230811114011/July-2023-Full-Public-Prison

-Report.pdf; on police violence in Philadelphia, see George Fachner and Steven Carter, *An Assessment of Deadly Force in the Philadelphia Police Department*, Collaborative Reform Initiative (Washington, DC: Office of Community Oriented Policing Services, 2015), https://www.phillypolice.com/assets/directives/cops-w0753-pub.pdf.

75. See Liat Ben-Moshe, *Decarcerating Disability: Deinstitutionalization and Prison Abolition* (Minneapolis: University of Minnesota Press, 2020); Laura I. Appleman, "Deviancy, Dependency, and Disability: The Forgotten History of Eugenics and Mass Incarceration," *Duke Law Journal* 68, no. 3 (December 2018): 417–78, https://dlj.law.duke.edu/article/deviancy-dependency-and-disability-appleman-vol68-iss3/.

76. For more on MetFern Cemetery, see Jaymelee Kim and Adam Richard Rosenblatt, "Whose Humanitarianism? Whose Forensic Anthropology?" in *Anthropology of Violent Death: Theoretical Foundations for Forensic Humanitarian Action*, ed. Roberto C. Parra and Douglas H. Ubelaker (Hoboken, NJ: John Wiley & Sons, 2023), 153–176.

77. Alex Green et al., "The MetFern Cemetery," 2017, MetFern Cemetery, accessed September 29, 2023, http://www.metfern.org; Asia London Palomba and Szu Yu Chen, "Below the Surface: A Special Report," accessed May 31, 2023, https://below-the-surface.github.io/main.html.

78. Ibid.

79. See Jennifer Natalya Fink, *All Our Families: Disability Lineage and the Future of Kinship* (Boston: Beacon Press, 2022).

80. See Susan Burch, *Committed: Remembering Native Kinship in and Beyond Institutions* (Chapel Hill: University of North Carolina Press), 2021; Danvers State Memorial Committee, "History of Our Work"; Patricia E. Deegan, *From Numbers to Names*, coproduced by Laurie Block and Bestor Cram, Northern Light Productions, 2010, video, 13:52, https://www.commongroundprogram.com/blog/from-numbers-to-names; Green et al.,"The MetFern Cemetery"; Nathan Flis and David Wright. "'A Grave Injustice': The Mental Hospital and Shifting Sites of Memory," in *Exhibiting Madness in Museums*, ed. Catharine Coleborne and Dolly MacKinnon (London: Routledge, 2011), 101–15; David Mack-Hardiman, *Of Grave Importance: The Restoration of Institutional Cemeteries* (Buffalo, NY: Museum of disABILITY History and People Ink Press, 2014); Asia Palomba, "The Quest to Honor Disabled Patients Buried in Anonymous Graves," Atlas Obscura, July 1, 2021, https://www.atlasobscura.com/articles/metfern-cemetery; Pemina Yellow Bird, "Wild Indians: Native Perspectives on the Hiawatha Asylum for Insane Indians," National Empowerment Center, https://power2u.org/wild-indians-native-perspectives-on-the-hiawatha-asylum-for-insane-indians-by-pemima-yellow-bird/.

81. Andrés J. Gallegos, "NCD Letter to NGA Re: Vaccine Allocation," Letter to Andrew Cuomo, National Council on Disability, February 9, 2021, https://ncd.gov/publications/2021/ncd-letter-nga-re-vaccine-allocation.

82. On using the term "inmates" for people held in state hospitals and disability institutions, see Alex Green, "Process: Editor's Note," 2017, MetFern Cemetery, accessed September 29, 2023, http://metfern.org/process.

83. See Susan Burch and Hannah Joyner, *Unspeakable: The Story of Junius Wilson* (Chapel Hill: University of North Carolina Press, 2007), 38–50; Jim Downs, *Sick from Freedom: African-American Illness and Suffering during the Civil War and Reconstruction* (Oxford: Oxford University Press, 2015); Caitlin Doucette Foltz, "Race and Mental Illness at a Virginia Hospital: A Case Study of Central Lunatic Asylum for the Colored Insane, 1869–1885" (master's thesis, Virginia Commonwealth University, 2015), 4–44, https://doi.org/10.25772/RRJX-NN19.

84. King Davis, who leads a research project on the archives of Central State Hospital in Petersburg, says: "Poverty was a key factor in admissions then [from the hospital's founding in 1868 until it was integrated in the mid-1960s] and now and blacks were more likely to have been involuntarily admitted through the court system." "A Treasure Trove of Historical Data on the History of Mental Illness Among African Americans," *The Journal of Blacks in Higher Education*, February 6, 2014, https://www.jbhe.com/2014/02/treasure-trove-of-historical-data-on-the-history-of-mental-illness-among-african-americans/.

85. Burch and Joyner, *Unspeakable*, 49–50.

86. On sterilization at these two institutions, see Burch and Joyner, *Unspeakable*, 44–50; Grace M. Gordon, "'For the Best Interest of the Patient and of Society'; Sterilization in Virginia's Mental Institutions in the 20th Century" (Senior Honors Projects, James Madison University, May 13, 2022), https://commons.lib.jmu.edu/cgi/viewcontent.cgi?article=1159&context=honors202029.

87. Information on the Bass siblings from Friends of Geer Cemetery, Instagram post, January 16, 2023 (research by Tim Foley), https://www.instagram.com/p/Cnep9dMrjcr; Henrietta Bass entry on Find a Grave (research by Suzannah McCuen), https://www.findagrave.com/memorial/117859535/henrietta-bass.

88. "Best known" for now, that is. As anthropologist Sally Raudon points out, "Reiterations of public exposure, shock, disquiet and forgetting have marked New Yorkers' relationships with Hart Island since the cemetery opened in 1869." Sally Raudon, "Huddled Masses: The Shock of Hart Island, New York," *Human Remains and Violence: An Interdisciplinary Journal* 8, no. 1 (2022): 87, https://doi.org/10.7227/hrv.8.1.6.

89. Ryan Grim, "Rikers Island Prisoners Are Being Offered PPE and $6 an Hour to Dig Mass Graves," The Intercept, March 31, 2020, https://theintercept.com/2020/03/31/rikers-island-coronavirus-mass-graves/.

90. Corey Kilgannon, "Dead of AIDS and Forgotten in Potter's Field," *The New York Times*, July 3, 2018, https://www.nytimes.com/2018/07/03/nyregion/hart-island-aids-new-york.html.

91. In April 2020, drone footage from the island showed workers in protective gear stacking simple wooden coffins into trenches. Many reacted with horror. But as Jody Rosen wrote in the *New York Times*, "The deeper shock of the Hart Island videos may be the realization that they reveal a workaday event. A mass burial on Hart Island is business as usual, a thing that happens all the time, every week. . . . Hart Island is the

domain of the dispossessed, where the poorest and most marginalized citizens are laid to rest in unmarked graves by a work force drawn from the country's second-oldest prison system." Jody Rosen, "How Covid-19 Has Forced Us to Look at the Unthinkable," *The New York Times*, April 29, 2020, https://www.nytimes.com/2020/04/29/magazine/covid-hart-island.html. See also Raudon, "Huddled Masses."

92. "About the Hart Island Project," Hart Island Project, accessed May 31, 2023, https://www.hartisland.net/about; Raudon, "Huddled Masses," 97.

93. See Corey Kilgannon, "A Million Bodies Are Buried Here. Now It's Becoming a Park," *The New York Times*, March 24, 2023, https://www.nytimes.com/2023/03/24/nyregion/hart-island-cemetery-park.html.

94. See "When Remains Unclaimed, NC's Dead Scattered at Sea," WRAL News, August 8, 2014, https://www.wral.com/story/when-remains-unclaimed-nc-s-dead-scattered-at-sea/13876971/.

95. Chip Colwell, "How the Archaeological Review Behind the Dakota Access Pipeline Went Wrong," The Conversation, November 20, 2016, https://theconversation.com/how-the-archaeological-review-behind-the-dakota-access-pipeline-went-wrong-67815.

96. Christine Hauser and Isabella Grullón Paz, "U.S. to Search Former Native American Schools for Children's Remains," *The New York Times*, June 23, 2021, https://www.nytimes.com/2021/06/23/us/indigenous-children-indian-civilization-act-1819.html.

97. "Department of the Interior Releases Investigative Report, Outlines Next Steps in Federal Indian Boarding School Initiative," U.S. Department of the Interior, May 11, 2022, https://www.doi.gov/pressreleases/department-interior-releases-investigative-report-outlines-next-steps-federal-indian.

98. See Yellow Bird, "Wild Indians"; Burch, *Committed*.

99. Burch, *Committed*, 16.

100. Burch, *Committed*, 17, 102–3; Yellow Bird, "Wild Indians," 7; Tim Giago, "Paying Tribute to Harold Iron Shield," Indianz.Com, February 27, 2008, https://www.indianz.com/News/2008/007334.asp; Steve Young, "S.D. Revisits Past at Native American Insane Asylum," *USA Today*, May 5, 2013, https://www.usatoday.com/story/news/nation/2013/05/05/sd-native-american-insane-asylum/2137011/.

101. On Alvaro Enciso's work, see Barbara Sostaita, "Making Crosses, Crossing Borders: The Performance of Mourning, the Power of Ghosts, and the Politics of Counter-memory in the U.S.-Mexico Borderlands," *Conversations: An Online Journal of the Center for the Study of Material and Visual Cultures of Religion*, August 18, 2016, https://doi.org/10.22332/con.med.2016.3. On immigration policy, the weaponization of the Sonoran Desert, and the border as a "killing field," see De León, *The Land of Open Graves*; Robin Reineke and Bruce E. Anderson, "Missing in the US-Mexico Borderlands," in *Missing Persons: Multidisciplinary Perspectives on the Disappeared*, ed. Derek Congram (Toronto: Canadian Scholars' Press, 2016), 249–68.

102. While researching this book I also visited the Har Hasetim Cemetery in Glad-

wyne, Pennsylvania, used by Jewish burial societies from 1890 to 1945 and just barely saved from destruction. The Friends of the Gladwyne Jewish Memorial Cemetery now tend the site and mobilize local congregations, schools, and other volunteers. See Paul Jablow, "After Decades of Neglect, Volunteers Work to Save a Historic Main Line Jewish Cemetery," *The Inquirer*, December 28, 2022, https://www.inquirer.com/real-estate/gladwyne-jewish-memorial-cemetery-har-hasetim-beth-david-20221228.html.

103. On the perils of "damage-centered research" on people and places, see Eve Tuck, "Suspending Damage: A Letter to Communities," *Harvard Educational Review* 79, no. 3 (October 6, 2009): 409–28, https://doi.org/10.17763/haer.79.3.n0016675661t3n15.

104. See, e.g., Char Adams, "The Growing Movement to Save Black Cemeteries," NBC News, February 10, 2022, https://www.nbcnews.com/news/nbcblk/growing-movement-black-cemeteries-rcna15566.

105. See Matt Blitz, "'The Second Desecration of Our Ancestors': Activists Fight Construction Near Historic Cemetery in Bethesda," DCist, July 8, 2020, https://dcist.com/story/20/07/08/moses-african-cemetery-bethesda-preservation-protests/; Forensic Architecture and RISE St. James, "Environmental Racism in Death Alley, Louisiana."

106. See William Sturkey, "The Geer Cemetery: A Lesson in Black History," *The Herald Sun*, February 5, 2019, https://www.heraldsun.com/opinion/article225427335.html.

107. Angela Thorpe, interview with the author, July 6, 2023.

108. Ibid.

109. See Williamson, "America's Black Cemeteries and Three Women Trying to Save Them"; "Support Preservation of African American Burial Grounds," National Trust for Historic Preservation, June 16, 2023, https://savingplaces.org/african-american-cultural-heritage/updates/support-preservation-of-african-american-burial-grounds.

110. Consolidated Appropriations Act, 2023, Pub. L. No. 117-328 (2022). http://www.congress.gov/bill/117th-congress/house-bill/2617. On the language of the African American Burial Grounds Preservation Act, see Brian Palmer, "Historic Black Cemeteries Need Substance from Lawmakers, Not Symbolism," Medium, July 15, 2022, https://medium.com/@bxpnyc/historic-black-cemeteries-need-substance-from-lawmakers-not-symbolism-aab2bfb93826.

111. Justin Dunnavant, Delande Justinvil, and Chip Colwell, "Craft an African American Graves Protection and Repatriation Act," *Nature* 593, no. 7859 (May 2021): 337–40, https://www.nature.com/articles/d41586-021-01320-4.

112. One exception is Simon Romero's article about the Indigenous burial ground under the contemporary tourist site at the Alamo, in San Antonio, Texas. Tāp Pīlam elder Raymond Hernandez compares his people's desire to protect these graves to reclamation efforts in Sugar Land, Texas, where African Americans who had been worked to death via the system of convict leasing were buried in anonymous graves. Simon Romero, "Burial Ground Under the Alamo Stirs a Texas Feud," *The New York Times*,

November 25, 2021, https://www.nytimes.com/2021/11/25/us/alamo-burial-native-americans.html.

113. Benjamin R. Barber, "The Art of Public Space," *The Nation*, August 12, 2009, https://www.thenation.com/article/archive/art-public-space/.

114. See Eric Chaplin and Sarah Holding, "Addressing the Post-Urban: Los Angeles, Las Vegas, New York," in *The Hieroglyphics of Space: Reading and Experiencing the Modern Metropolis*, ed. Neil Leach (London: Routledge, 2001), 185–200; Jenny Odell, *How to Do Nothing: Resisting the Attention Economy* (Brooklyn, NY: Melville House, 2019).

115. Odell, *How to Do Nothing*.

116. Rosenblatt, *Digging for the Disappeared*, 153–54.

117. Jarene Fleming, interview with the author, January 24, 2021.

118. See Katrina Spade, "Death Is Not an Emergency: How Recompose Is Redesigning the End of Life," interview by Michael Zakaras, *Forbes*, October 18, 2019, https://www.forbes.com/sites/ashoka/2018/10/19/death-is-not-an-emergency-how-recompose-is-redesigning-the-end-of-life/.

119. Carol J. Adams, "The War on Compassion," *Antennae: The Journal of Nature in Visual Culture* (Autumn 2010): 5–11.

120. Judith Butler, *Frames of War: When Is Life Grievable?* (London: Verso, 2009).

121. There are burial grounds called "Citizens Cemetery" located in North Carolina, Virginia, Arizona, Oklahoma, and many other states.

122. See Arely Cruz-Santiago, "Lists, Maps, and Bones: The Untold Journeys of Citizen-Led Forensics in Mexico," *Victims & Offenders* 15, no. 3 (April 2, 2020): 350–69, https://doi.org/10.1080/15564886.2020.1718046; Robin C. Reineke, "Forensic Citizenship Among Families of Missing Migrants Along the U.S.-Mexico Border," *Citizenship Studies* 26, no. 1 (January 2, 2022): 21–37, https://doi.org/10.1080/13621025.2021.2018675.

123. In "Forensic Citizenship Among Families of Missing Migrants Along the U.S.-Mexico Border," Reineke surveys alternative definitions of citizenship, describing how undocumented migrants often engage deeply in practices of citizenship even as they lack access to its legal dimension.

124. Sprackland, *These Silent Mansions*, 28.

125. Geographer Doreen Massey tries to describe a sense of place that is "progressive"—awakened to how political struggle often centers on claims to physical space—while also avoiding making a fetish of rootedness. "A Global Sense of Place," in *The Cultural Geography Reader*, ed. Timothy S. Oakes and Patricia L. Price (London: Routledge, 2008), 152.

126. Steven J. Jackson, "Rethinking Repair," in *Media Technologies: Essays on Communication, Materiality, and Society*, ed. Tarleton Gillespie, Pablo J. Boczkowski, and Kirsten A. Foot (Cambridge, MA: MIT Press, 2014), 221–40.

127. Donna J. Haraway, *Staying with the Trouble: Making Kin in the Chthulucene* (Durham, NC: Duke University Press, 2016), 56.

128. See Lynn Butler-Kisber, *Qualitative Inquiry: Thematic, Narrative and Arts-Informed Perspectives*, 2nd ed. (Los Angeles: Sage, 2018), 95–113.

129. Lauren Rosenberg adopts a similar strategy: "This book features the participants speaking for themselves, often without my intrusion. Understanding their accounts relies on readers to interpret their words not simply as uncomplicated stories . . . but as narratives that carry a significance that I did not wish to appropriate." Lauren Rosenberg, *The Desire for Literacy: Writing in the Lives of Adult Learners* (Urbana, IL: Conference on College Composition and Communication/National Council of Teachers of English, 2015), 12.

130. Marilyn Nelson, "Communal Pondering in a Noisy World," interview by Krista Tippet, *On Being*, February 23, 2017, audio, 51:02, https://onbeing.org/programs/marilyn-nelson-communal-pondering-in-a-noisy-world/.

131. I was inspired by Peter Elbow's case for "Poetry as No Big Deal," in *Writing with Power: Techniques for Mastering the Writing Process* (New York: Oxford University Press, 1998), 101–119, and Verlyn Klinkenborg, *Several Short Sentences About Writing* (New York: Vintage Books, 2013).

132. Andrew Causey, *Drawn to See: Drawing as an Ethnographic Method* (North York, Ontario: University of Toronto Press, 2017), 122.

Chapter 1: "When Summer Comes Again, the Cemetery Disappears"

1. Jessica T. Eustice, "The Geer Cemetery" (master's thesis, North Carolina Central University, June 8, 2002), courtesy of the Friends of Geer Cemetery.

2. See Tia Hall et al., "Uneven Ground: Dismantling Hayti," Bull City 150, 2017, accessed May 29, 2023, https://www.bullcity150.org/uneven_ground/dismantling_hayti /; Mark Robinson, "Battered by Demolition and Displacement, Jackson Ward Stands Strong at 150th Anniversary," *Richmond Times-Dispatch*, April 17, 2021, https://richmond.com/news/local/battered-by-demolition-and-displacement-jackson-ward -stands-strong-at-150th-anniversary/article_4d064300-4d2c-56cf-b73d-4956b43b26 ea.html; Drew Sisk, "Jackson Ward: Displacement and Buried History," GDES Workshop, September 12, 2016, https://drewsisk.com/workshop/jackson-ward-displacement -and-buried-history/.

3. It is possible that, as has been the case at East End Cemetery, continuing archaeological work at Geer will reveal a more grid-like and planned layout of burials. See "East End Cemetery Map," East End Cemetery Collaboratory, accessed May 26, 2023, https://cemeterycollaboratory.org/east-end-cemetery-map/.

4. Thanks to Alicia Jiménez for suggesting I situate Geer historically in terms of the timeline of Emancipation, Reconstruction, Jim Crow, and beyond.

5. Smith and Davis, "The Fitzgerald Family Cemetery and Henderson Cemetery."

6. See Pauli Murray, *Proud Shoes: The Story of an American Family* (Boston: Beacon Press, 1999), 27–32, 274–76; Smith and Davis, "The Fitzgerald Family Cemetery and Henderson Cemetery."

7. These pending and unfinished projects always exceed the capacities of the small, often all-volunteer (or understaffed) organizations that bring cemetery citizens together. Thanks to Nicholas Levy for making this point.

8. See Amanda Levinson, "Reckoning with the Legacy of Jewish Enslavement of African Americans in the South," Medium, October 3, 2022, https://medium.com/@amanda_levinson/beyond-solidarity-reckoning-with-the-legacy-of-jewish-enslavement-of-african-americans-in-the-861da4860d44.

9. Brian Palmer, "Confederate Monuments Topple in Richmond, Virginia," Reveal, August 17, 2020, http://revealnews.org/article/confederate-monuments-topple-in-richmond-virginia/.

10. Robin Kirk, "Reflections on a Silent Soldier," *The American Scholar*, September 3, 2019, https://theamericanscholar.org/reflections-on-a-silent-soldier/.

11. Charles Johnson, "Historic Fayetteville St.: The Fifth Avenue of Black Durham," Durham County Library/Digital NC, https://deegsnccu.maps.arcgis.com/apps/Cascade/index.html?appid=75566fb038b24ebc90b2b51f72fb5c74. On gender oppression and early Black Durham, see Leslie Brown, *Upbuilding Black Durham: Gender, Class, and Black Community Development in the Jim Crow South* (Chapel Hill: University of North Carolina Press, 2008).

12. W. E. B. Du Bois, "The Upbuilding of Black Durham. The Success of the Negroes and Their Value to a Tolerant and Helpful Southern City," *The World's Work*, January 1912, Documenting the American South, The North Carolina Experience, https://docsouth.unc.edu/nc/dubois/dubois.html#p335.

13. Thomasi McDonald, "Durham's Hayti District Receives $10 Million in Newly Adopted Budget for Rebuilding," *INDY Week*, June 28, 2023, http://indyweek.com/news/durham/durhams-newly-adopted-budget-includes-10-million-to-rebuild-hayti/.

14. Sarah Kreuger, "'Black Wall Street' Icon NC Mutual Life Insurance Company Begins Liquidation Process," *WRAL*, October 11, 2022, https://www.wral.com/story/black-wall-street-icon-nc-mutual-life-insurance-company-begins-liquidation-process/20517940/; "Investment Advisor Sentenced in Fraud That Added to NC Mutual's Troubles," *Insurance Journal*, October 31, 2022, https://www.insurancejournal.com/news/southeast/2022/10/31/692364.htm. Mechanics and Farmers Bank, still in existence today, was also important in fostering Black entrepreneurship and wealth-building in the region.

15. Walter B. Weare, *Black Business in the New South: A Social History of the NC Mutual Life Insurance Company* (Durham, NC: Duke University Press, 1993), viii.

16. Weare, *Black Business in the New South*, 31, 43.

17. Though based on multiple sources, this section and the one that follows owe an outsize debt to the archival research for the Friends of Geer Cemetery's *In Plain Sight* outdoor exhibit that was on display from January to April 2021 at the cemetery. Nicholas Levy led those research efforts, with an array of other volunteers including Kaylee Alexander, Vera Cecelski, Tim Foley, Pat Graham, Courtney McGuire, Madge McKei-

then, Molly Mendoza, Jason Norris, Ashley Parker, Marsha Shearin, Lewis Shiner, Debra Taylor Gonzalez-Garcia, Carissa Trotta, Adrian Tucker, James Wahlberg, and Vera Whisenton.

18. "Geer Cemetery—in Plain Sight," November 25, 2020, https://durhaminplainsight .com/about/.

19. Ibid.

20. Denise Rowson and Durham Service Corps, *Reclaiming Yesterday: The Geer Cemetery Project* (Durham, NC: Durham Service Corps, 1992), courtesy of the Friends of Geer Cemetery, 16; Deidre Barnes, interview with the author, June 22, 2021.

21. Rowson and Durham Service Corps, *Reclaiming Yesterday*, 16.

22. Kaylee P. Alexander, "Reclaiming Marginalized Deaths Through Data Analysis: The Case of Geer Cemetery," *Friends of Geer Cemetery*, February 26, 2021, https:// friendsofgeercemetery.org/index.php/2023/06/16/reclaiming-marginalized-deaths/.

23. Nicholas Levy, email message to the author, May 23, 2023.

24. "Geer Cemetery—in Plain Sight."

25. "Geer Cemetery—in Plain Sight."

26. vMLK Project Team, "A Creative Protest ["Fill Up the Jails"]," Virtual Martin Luther King, Jr. Project, November 27, 2018, https://vmlk.chass.ncsu.edu/experience/ historical/a-creative-protest/.

27. Research on Augustus Shepard in Beechwood Cemetery records by Debra Taylor Gonzalez-Garcia.

28. See André D. Vann, "From a Dream to New Horizons," North Carolina Central University News, April 22, 2020, https://www.nccu.edu/news/dream-new-horizons.

29. "Geer Cemetery—in Plain Sight."

30. David Eustice, "Geer #2," February 22, 2012, YouTube video, https://www. youtube.com/watch?v=akHaj9n_CIE&t=3s, 6:47.

31. See, e.g., Megan Carroll, "Brambles Choke a Cemetery," *News and Observer*, July 1, 2003.

32. Another of Frederick and Priscilla's children, Ritta (or Retta) Geer, was buried in Maplewood, possibly the only Black person buried within its boundaries during the Jim Crow era. Her headstone, next to members of the household where she was employed after Emancipation, follows a common trope of remembering her as a "good and faithful servant," and nothing else. See "Ritta Geer (1860–1932)—Find a Grave Memorial," Find a Grave, accessed May 30, 2023, https://www.findagrave.com/memorial/11 6784232/ritta-geer.

33. Deidre Barnes, interview with the author, June 22, 2021.

34. "Died: To the Durham, N.C. Herald," *Durham Morning Herald* (published as *The Morning Herald*), September 26, 1909, provided to the author by Deidre Barnes and the Friends of Geer Cemetery.

35. Rowson and Durham Service Corps, *Reclaiming Yesterday*, 18.

36. Quoted in Gary Kueber, "Geer Cemetery," Open Durham, last modified August 20, 2011, https://www.opendurham.org/buildings/geer-cemetery.

37. "Geer Cemetery—in Plain Sight."

38. Ibid.

39. Ibid.

40. Ibid.

41. Gumbs, "Even in the Grave, Black People Can't Rest in Durham."

42. "Violet Park Cemetery Correspondence."

43. Rowson and Durham Service Corps, *Reclaiming Yesterday*, 16.

44. Letter from Caleb W. Morgan to the Hon. Mayor and Members of the City Council. Document provided by the Friends of Geer Cemetery.

45. DD Barnes in "In Plain Sight—Geer Cemetery Exhibit Opening," Friends of Geer Cemetery, January 23, 2021, YouTube video, 6:22, https://www.youtube.com/watch?v=6BZPlb92DlQ.

46. "Several Cases Were Tried During the Day—Negro Preacher Was Tried for an Affray," *Durham Morning Herald*, September 1, 1922, courtesy of the Friends of Geer Cemetery.

47. "Doris Belk Tilley Obituary (1924–2017)," *The Herald Sun*, December 29, 2017, Legacy.com, https://www.legacy.com/us/obituaries/heraldsun/name/doris-tilley-obituary?id=11788555; Eustice, "Geer #2," 2:11.

48. "Geer Cemetery—in Plain Sight,"

49. Rowson and Durham Service Corps, *Reclaiming Yesterday*, 3.

50. Eustice, "Geer #2," 4:00.

51. Jessica Eustice, interview with the author, June 28, 2021.

52. Ibid.

53. Ibid.

54. Ben Evans, "Geer Cemetery Cleanup on the Way," *The Herald-Sun*, January 20, 2004. Access World News—Historical and Current.

55. Minutes of the Friends of Geer Cemetery, July 11, 2005. Courtesy of the Friends of Geer Cemetery.

56. Eustice, "Geer #2," 5:00.

57. See Jessica T. Eustice, "Geer Cemetery Emerges as a Historic Cemetery," *The Herald Sun*, June 28, 2015, Allen Dew Genealogy, http://www.apdew.com/FOGC/2015-06-28-news.pdf.

58. "Millie Markham," Federal Writers' Project: Slave Narrative Project, Vol. 11, North Carolina, Part 2, Jackson-Yellerday, 1936, Manuscript/Mixed Material, https://www.loc.gov/item/mesn112/.

59. Laqueur, *The Work of the Dead*, 9.

60. Laderman, *The Sacred Remains*, 6; Melville, *Over My Dead Body*, 23–35.

61. See Charlotte Sussman et al., "Small Boy," Remembering the Middle Passage: A

Duke Bass Connections Project, 2022, accessed May 31, 2023, http://rememberingthe middlepassage.com/#small_boy; Saidiya Hartman, "Venus in Two Acts," *Small Axe* 12, no. 2 (2008): 1–14, https://doi.org/10.1215/-12-2-1.

62. See Jelani Cobb, "Would Showing Graphic Images of Mass Shootings Spur Action to Stop Them?" *The New Yorker*, June 4, 2022, https://www.newyorker.com/news /daily-comment/would-showing-graphic-images-of-mass-shootings-spur-action-to -stop-them; Karla FC Holloway, *Passed On: African American Mourning Stories, A Memorial* (Durham, NC: Duke University Press, 2003), 60.

63. Ross W. Jamieson, "Material Culture and Social Death: African-American Burial Practices," *Historical Archaeology* 29, no. 4 (1995): 39–58, https://doi.org/10.1007/bf0337 4216.

64. Smith, *To Serve the Living*, 27.

65. Holloway, *Passed On*, 136. *Jet* is an African American magazine that began publication in 1951.

66. Claudia Rankine, "'The Condition of Black Life Is One of Mourning,'" *The New York Times*, June 22, 2015, https://www.nytimes.com/2015/06/22/magazine/the-con dition-of-black-life-is-one-of-mourning.html. On the "politically charged" 21st-century funerals of Rosa Parks and Coretta Scott King, see Smith, *To Serve the Living*, 194–202.

67. See "List of Unarmed African Americans Killed by Law Enforcement Officers in the United States," Wikipedia, September 4, 2021, accessed May 31, 2023. https://en. wikipedia.org/wiki/List_of_unarmed_African_Americans_killed_by_law_enforce ment_officers_in_the_United_States.

68. Nicholas Bogel-Burroughs, "At Daunte Wright Funeral, Minneapolis Mourns the 'Prince of Brooklyn Center,'" *The New York Times*, April 22, 2021, https://www. nytimes.com/2021/04/22/us/daunte-wright-funeral.html.

69. Anthropologist Jason De León defines necroviolence as "violence performed and produced through the specific treatment of corpses that is perceived to be offensive, sacrilegious, or inhumane by the perpetrator, the victim (and [their] cultural group), or both." De León, *The Land of Open Graves*, 69.

70. On the concept of care disruption, see Adam Richard Rosenblatt, Erin Hollaway Palmer, and Brian Palmer, "Permanent Reconstruction in Richmond's Black Cemeteries," in *Grave History: Death, Race, and Gender in Southern Cemeteries* (Athens: University of Georgia, 2023), 253–282.

71. Anjelyque Easley-DeLuca, "Cemeteries, Construction, and Complicity: Tyler's Universe Cemetery as a Black Burial Site Under Distress" (master's thesis, University of Texas Arlington, 2022), 48, https://rc.library.uta.edu/uta-ir/handle/10106/30242.

72. Morgan Jerkins, "Black Cemetery Loss Is a National Crisis," ZORA, July 15, 2020, https://zora.medium.com/black-cemetery-loss-is-a-national-crisis-875adf6b7448.

73. Ibid. Also see Leanna First-Arai, "Even in Death, Black Bodies Face Environ-

mental Racism," Truthout, July 10, 2020, https://truthout.org/articles/even-in-death-black-bodies-face-environmental-racism/.

74. Lenora McQueen, "Re: AA Cemetery Coalition," email message to the author, March 10, 2022. For more on the Shockoe Hill African Burying Ground, see Jeremy M. Lazarus, "History Marker to Be Placed at Shockoe Hill African Burying Ground," *Richmond Free Press*, June 24, 2021, http://richmondfreepress.com/news/2021/jun/24/history-marker-be-placed-shockoe-hill-african-bury/; Ryan K. Smith, "Shockoe Hill African Burying Ground," *Richmond Cemeteries*, accessed May 18, 2023, https://www.richmondcemeteries.org/potters-field/.

75. Jerrel Floyd, "I Went in Search of Abandoned African-American Cemeteries," ProPublica, June 29, 2018, https://www.propublica.org/article/abandoned-african-american-cemeteries-illinois-jerrel-floyd?token=xbvF5KLcDIV6vr6B2AF9DoLlUK_IwLni.

76. The linguistic roots of "neglect" associate it with unspoken, unaccounted for phenomena. See Online Etymology Dictionary, "Neglect."

77. "Respect for Our Dead," *The Carolina Times*, August 2, 1941, courtesy of Carissa Trotta.

78. Veronica A. Davis, *Here I Lay My Burdens Down: A History of the Black Cemeteries of Richmond, Virginia* (Richmond, VA: Dietz Press, 2003), ix.

79. Brian Palmer, "For the Forgotten African-American Dead," *The New York Times*, January 7, 2017, https://www.nytimes.com/2017/01/07/opinion/sunday/for-the-forgotten-african-american-dead.html.

80. See Brian Palmer and Seth Freed Wessler, "The Costs of the Confederacy," *Smithsonian Magazine*, December 2018, https://www.smithsonianmag.com/history/costs-confederacy-special-report-180970731/.

81. Smith, *Death and Rebirth in a Southern City*, 226. See also Zach Mortice, "Perpetual Neglect: The Preservation Crisis of African-American Cemeteries," *Places Journal*, May 30, 2017, https://doi.org/10.22269/170530.

82. "East End Oral History Project: Thomas A. Taylor, Extended Interview," Friends of East End Cemetery, July 7, 2020, YouTube video, https://www.youtube.com/watch?v=Icu2kmP5gNo.

83. Melville, *Over My Dead Body*, 93.

84. Smith, *Death and Rebirth in a Southern City*, 226.

85. Joanne Abel. "Persistence and Sacrifice: Durham County's African American Community and Durham's Jeanes Teachers Build Community and Schools, 1900–1930" (master's thesis, Duke University, 2009), 48.

86. See Leoneda Inge, "Blacks on the Move, Back to the South," *News & Notes*, North Carolina Public Radio, April 20, 2006, audio, 5:57, https://www.npr.org/templates/story/story.php?storyId=5353041.

87. "Geer Cemetery: Labor, Dignity, and Practices of Freedom in an African Ameri-

can Burial Ground," John Hope Franklin Humanities Institute, 2021, https://fhi.duke
.edu/story-plus-project/geer-cemetery-labor-dignity-and-practices-freedom-african
-american-burial-ground.

88. DD Barnes, *Cemetery Citizens* book chapter workshop, May 4, 2023.

Chapter 2: "The Contrast in the Care and Keeping of Our Cemeteries"

1. "Body of Woman Identified Here," *Richmond Times-Dispatch*, September 6, 1956,
Newspapers.com.

2. "Woman's Death Called Accident, Due to Fall," *Richmond Times-Dispatch*, September 7, 1956, Newspapers.com.

3. Estelle Jackson, "Cemeteries Fight Losing Battle," *Richmond Times-Dispatch*, July
22, 1981, sec. C, 1–2, courtesy of John Shuck.

4. See Rainville, *Hidden History*, 25. I was introduced to the term "courtesy marker"
by Erin Hollaway Palmer.

5. Sprackland, *These Silent Mansions*, 189.

6. Avery F. Gordon, *Ghostly Matters: Haunting and the Sociological Imagination*
(Minneapolis: University of Minnesota Press, 2008), 163.

7. Michel Foucault, "Lives of Infamous Men," in *The Essential Foucault: Selections
from Essential Works of Foucault, 1954–1984*, ed. Paul Rabinow and Nikolas Rose (New
York: New Press, 2003), 284; quoted in Hartman, "Venus in Two Acts," 2.

8. Hartman, "Venus in Two Acts," 5.

9. Ibid., 8.

10. Ibid., 8, 11.

11. Saidiya Hartman, *Wayward Lives, Beautiful Experiments: Intimate Histories of
Social Upheaval* (New York: W. W. Norton, 2019), 34.

12. On plot markers, see Rainville, *Hidden History*, 24.

13. Erin Hollaway Palmer, telephone conversation with the author, September 1,
2023.

14. Daina Ramey Berry, *The Price for Their Pound of Flesh: The Value of the Enslaved,
from Womb to Grave, in the Building of a Nation* (Boston: Beacon Press, 2017).

15. See Eve Tuck's call for resisting "one-dimensional narratives of damage" with
"desire-based research" focused on "the hope, the visions, the wisdom of lived lives and
communities." Tuck, "Suspending Damage," 417.

16. Portions of this section are adapted from Rosenblatt, Hollaway Palmer, and
Palmer, "Permanent Reconstruction in Richmond's Black Cemeteries."

17. Smith, *Death and Rebirth in a Southern City*, 217.

18. Greg Melville found, similarly, that Google Maps provided detailed street-view
images of the northern, historically White section of Laurel Grove cemetery in Savannah, Georgia, while at the time those images did not exist for Laurel Grove South. The
latter is home to the graves of enslaved people and generations of Savannah's post-
Emancipation Black community. Greg Melville, *Over My Dead Body*, 88. The "unmap-

ping" of some people's dead occurred long before digital technologies, however. Kim Smith and Stephanie Davis's open letter about the Fitzgerald and Henderson cemeteries in Durham is, among other things, a heartbreaking study of how two Black burial grounds were un-mapped and un-named by a constellation of actors, using technologies that long predate Google and smartphones. See Smith and Davis, "The Fitzgerald Family Cemetery and Henderson Cemetery." Beyond the context of historic African American cemeteries, Sally Raudon writes, "The inability of many New Yorkers to locate Hart Island," a longstanding site of mass burials for the city's poor and marginalized people, "is perhaps unsurprising, when its cultural invisibility is officially reified by omission from famous City maps. Arguably, the map New Yorkers see most often is the New York City Subway Map, published by the Metropolitan Transportation Authority and available in all subway stations and many subway cars. Yet, it omits Hart Island from its graphical representation of public transport routes, though it includes other islands without subway access." Raudon, "Huddled Masses," 96.

19. Smith, *Death and Rebirth in a Southern City*, 65.

20. "Shockoe Bottom," Venture Richmond, accessed May 16, 2023, https://venture richmond.com/live-downtown/historic-neighborhoods/shockoe-bottom/.

21. See Smith, *Death and Rebirth in a Southern City*, 43–68.

22. See Ibid., 57–69.

23. Ibid., 117–8.

24. Ibid., 215–16.

25. Ibid., 217.

26. Ibid., 216–7.

27. Ibid., 217.

28. Smith, *Death and Rebirth in a Southern City*, 217–218; Davis, *Here I Lay My Burdens Down*, 31–4.

29. Bonis and Richardson, "The Shame of Evergreen Cemetery."

30. "Notice!!!" *The Richmond Planet*, page 8, February 8, 1902, Chronicling America: Historic American Newspapers, https://chroniclingamerica.loc.gov/lccn/sn84025841/1902-02-08/ed-1/seq-8/.

31. "East End Oral History Project."

32. See also Smith, *Death and Rebirth in a Southern City*, 214–15.

33. Kiki Petrosino and Brian Palmer. "The Lives of East End: Recovering African American Burial Grounds." *The Virginia Quarterly Review* 96, no. 4 (Winter 2020): 60–83, 66.

34. Amanik and Fletcher, *Till Death Do Us Part*, 143. See also Holloway, *Passed On*, 33–34.

35. Smith, *Death and Rebirth in a Southern City*, 208.

36. Thanks to Ryan K. Smith for emphasizing this point in a conversation with me. On the ideology of racial uplift, see Gaines, *Uplifting the Race*; Weare, *Black Business in the New South*, 3–28.

37. The term "freedom's first generation," from historian Robert F. Engs's book of the same name, is one that Brian Palmer and Erin Hollaway Palmer often use when educating people about East End Cemetery. On the challenges faced by African American cemetery founders, see Smith, *Death and Rebirth in a Southern City*, 211.

38. "Should Have Better Cemeteries: The Forum Passes Resolution in Regard to Our Cemeteries." The resolution passed on June 29, 1915, and was published on the *Planet*'s front page on July 10. Smith notes that the "former cemeteries" referred to in the resolution are likely the ones in Barton Heights. Its authors leave the cause of the cemeteries' condition unstated, when in fact White neighbors had waged a targeted campaign against these burial grounds. Ryan K. Smith, telephone conversation with the author, June 9, 2022; see Smith, *Death and Rebirth in a Southern City*, 117–19.

39. Smith, *Death and Rebirth in a Southern City*, 227.

40. Ibid.

41. Jackson, "Cemeteries Fight Losing Battle."

42. Ibid.

43. Smith, *Death and Rebirth in a Southern City*, 228.

44. Ibid., 228.

45. Ibid., 234–35.

46. John Shuck, interview with the author, October 15, 2017.

47. Smith, *Death and Rebirth in a Southern City*, 238–39.

48. Brian Palmer, "Into the Woods," Wok Docs, December 22, 2014, http://www.wokdocs.com/blog.

49. Ibid.

50. Anne McCrery, Erol Somay, and the Dictionary of Virginia Biography, "Mitchell, John Jr. (1863–1929)," Encyclopedia Virginia. Virginia Humanities, February 12, 2021, https://encyclopediavirginia.org/entries/mitchell-john-jr-1863-1929/; See also Smith, *Death and Rebirth in a Southern City*, 219.

51. The cemetery was already overgrown and frequently used for dumping by the time of Ashe's death, leading to public outcry about such an important historical figure being buried in such an undignified place. See Mike Holtzclaw, "Rest in Peace? Ashe's Grave Sparks Controversy," *Daily Press*, June 13, 1993, https://www.dailypress.com/news/dp-xpm-19930613-1993-06-13-9306130080-story.html.

52. Caroline Mamajane Jones quoted in Jeremy M. Lazarus, "Woodland Cemetery Sale Completed to Nonprofit Evergreen Restoration Foundation," *Richmond Free Press*, August 6, 2020. http://richmondfreepress.com/news/2020/aug/06/woodland-cemetery-sale-completed-nonprofit-evergre/.

53. See Michael Levenson, "Protesters Topple Statue of Jefferson Davis on Richmond's Monument Avenue." *The New York Times*, June 11, 2020, https://www.nytimes.com/2020/06/11/us/Jefferson-Davis-Statue-Richmond.html. Eventually city authorities removed most of Richmond's Confederate monuments. See Gregory S. Schneider,

"Two Years after Protests, Some of Richmond's Confederate Statues Remain," *The Washington Post*, July 26, 2022, https://www.washingtonpost.com/dc-md-va/2022/07/23/richmond-confederate-statues-stonewall-hill/.

54. Questions of scientific objectivity, activism, and solidarity with one's interlocutors are hotly contested in anthropology. See Nancy Scheper-Hughes, "The Primacy of the Ethical: Propositions for a Militant Anthropology," *Current Anthropology* 36, no. 3 (1995): 409–40; Setha M. Low and Sally Engle Merry, "Engaged Anthropology: Diversity and Dilemmas," *Current Anthropology* 51, no. S2 (2010): S203–226, https://doi.org/10.1086/653837. The best term I have found for thinking about my obligations to the cemeteries and cemetery citizens at the center of this book is a Spanish-language one, used by some Latin American anthropologists: *antropología comprometida*—literally, anthropology that makes promises. See Greta Friedemann-Sanchez, "Antropología pública y comprometida: el legado de Nina S. de Friedemann," *Revista Antípoda*, no. 46 (January 1, 2022): 23–51, https://doi.org/10.7440/antipoda46.2022.02.

55. Adam Richard Rosenblatt, "Wider Concerns About Cemetery Reclamation Lacking in Article," *Richmond Free Press*, December 31, 2020, http://richmondfreepress.com/news/2020/dec/31/wider-concerns-about-cemetery-reclamation-lacking-/; Adam Richard Rosenblatt, "Cemetery Credibility and What It Means to Be a Descendant," Radical Death Studies, June 14, 2021 (page no longer available), https://radicaldeathstudies.com/2021/06/14/cemetery-credibility/; Adam Richard Rosenblatt and Ryan K. Smith, "Letter to the Editor: Enrichmond Took Credit for the Work of Others," *Richmond Times-Dispatch*, March 4, 2020, https://richmond.com/opinion/letters-to-editor/letter-to-the-editor-march-3-2020-enrichmond-took-credit-for-the-work-of-others/article_8428233b-a84c-5252-8d8d-809e965aea05.html.

56. Quoted in David Streever, "Keeping the Faith," *Style Weekly*, March 12, 2019, https://www.styleweekly.com/richmond/keeping-the-faith/Content?oid=14132112.

57. John Mitchell, interview with the author, March 5, 2021. Mitchell is describing one of the most entrenched racial power dynamics in historic preservation and urban planning: "Because of the ongoing inequality of access to credit, philanthropic funding, wealth and political access rooted in white supremacy, white institutions are often well-positioned to engage in spaces where funding and embedded capacity are needed." Meghan Z. Gough, Kathryn Howell, and Hannah Cameron, "The Structural Challenge of Power and Whiteness in Planning: Evidence from Historic Black Cemetery Restoration," *Planning Theory & Practice* 23, no. 4 (2022): 536–55, https://doi.org/10.1080/14649357.2022.2113557, 537.

58. See Brian Palmer, "Enwhatnow?" Medium, December 23, 2022, https://medium.com/@bxpnyc/enwhatnow-312157ef4ca7; Brian Palmer, "The Enrichmond Files," Medium, May 26, 2023, https://medium.com/@bxpnyc/the-enrichmond-files-948eof bcd8af. Ryan K. Smith closely followed and analyzed Enrichmond's cemetery plans, and relationships with other stakeholders, in his *Richmond Cemeteries* blog. Three ex-

perts involved in Enrichmond's planning and descendant engagement processes for Evergreen and East End offer an insider's account in Gough, Howell, and Cameron's "The Structural Challenge of Power and Whiteness in Planning."

59. Description of the Virginia Outdoors Foundation from Gough, Howell, and Cameron, "The Structural Challenge of Power and Whiteness in Planning," 542.

60. Virginia Outdoors Foundation, "PTF Purchase Project with Public Access: Evergreen and East End Cemeteries."

61. Palmer, "The Enrichmond Files."

62. Chapman, January 24, 2019, online comment on Ryan K. Smith, "East End Goes the Way Things Go," *Richmond Cemeteries*, January 24, 2019, https://www.richmond cemeteries.org/2019/01/24/east-end-goes-the-way-things-go/.

63. The memo was obtained via a Freedom of Information Act request in May 2023. Palmer, "The Enrichmond Files."

64. Erin Jenkins, "Enrichmond Acquires Evergreen Cemetery," Enrichmond Foundation, May 24, 2017. Site inactive as of June 2022, accessed via Internet Archive May 31, 2023, https://web.archive.org/web/20221002042632/https://enrichmond.org/2017/05/enrichmond-evergreen/.

65. Ibid.

66. See Laura Kebeder, "Volunteers Rescue 4 Cemeteries," *Richmond Times-Dispatch*, February 16, 2014. NewsBank.

67. Palmer, "Enwhatnow?"

68. Palmer, "For the Forgotten African-American Dead."

69. See "HB 1547—Virginia House (2017)," Open States, https://openstates.org/va/bills/2017/HB1547/.

70. See "Virginia HB284," 2018, LegiScan, https://legiscan.com/VA/text/HB284/id/1786618. Italics in "owns" added by the author.

71. Michael Paul Williams. "Restoration of Black Cemeteries Can't Be Exclusive." *Richmond Times-Dispatch*. June 27, 2017.

72. Julie V. Langan, email to Brian Palmer, June 19, 2019.

73. John Sydnor, "Re: request for approval to operate at East End Cemetery," email to the Friends of East End, May 17, 2019.

74. Va. Code Ann. § 57-27.1 (2011), https://lis.virginia.gov/cgi-bin/legp604.exe?111+ful+CHAP0257&111+ful+CHAP0257.

75. Smith, "East End Goes the Way Things Go."

76. Adrienne Gray Rhone, "Re: Circuit Case CL17-5911-2," July 24, 2018. Provided by Erin Hollaway Palmer.

77. Stauffer, *Ethical Loneliness*, 112–13.

78. Cat Modlin-Jackson. "A New Funding Stream for Historic African American Cemeteries." Radio IQ, August 18, 2020, https://www.wvtf.org/post/new-funding-stream-historic-african-american-cemeteries#stream/0.

79. The original agreement that Enrichmond offered gave it exclusive rights to the likenesses, images, and voices of any volunteers working on the site. The foundation and any known descendants would control all images of burials or grave markers, and any fundraising by other organizations would require approval from Enrichmond. Otherwise, the foundation could deny access to the site. In my interview with him, Sydnor acknowledged that the initial agreement cast too wide a net over the activity and intellectual property of others. But he defended the clause about Enrichmond and descendants sharing control over any images of graves as an important protection for the community. Regardless, the scope of the initial agreement, and its very broad interpretation of what ownership of the cemeteries meant for Enrichmond, further accelerated the distrust stoked by how the foundation had gone about acquiring the cemeteries. Even the amended versions of the agreement still put many restrictions on the types of physical work volunteers could do. The Friends of East End were proud of having unearthed over three thousand hidden markers from the soil of East End. Their research agenda was often a result of following up on markers they had exposed, which had remained hidden under the earth, possibly for decades. According to Schmieder, while it might make sense to discourage other, more casual volunteers from handling grave markers, for the Friends it felt like being relegated to "a glorified weed-puller" (Mark Schmieder, interview with the author, April 28, 2021). In fact, crews hired by Enrichmond had damaged and misplaced markers, and left brush and clippings on the graves. The Friends felt they were the ones needing to worry about what was going to happen in the cemetery when they weren't watching.

80. Mark Schmieder, interview with the author, April 28, 2021.

81. See "Reclamation East End: Resisting the Recreation Plantation (Feat. Brian Palmer)," prod. Chelsea Higgs Wise, Naomi Isaac, Kalia Harris, *Race Capitol*, March 2021, audio, 1:26:55, https://soundcloud.com/user-461048344/reclamation-east-end -resisting-the-recreation-plantation-feat-brian-palmer.

82. See, e.g., "Enrichmond Foundation—Evergreen Cemetery Legacy #RVA #Enrichmond #History," Enrichmond Foundation, May 17, 2021, YouTube video, https:// www.youtube.com/watch?v=NYaBRWDmUaw.

83. Caitlin DeSilvey writes, "The act of extending care actually produces value, although it is often presented as a response to the inherent value of the threatened object or structure." *Curated Decay*, 178.

84. Anthropologists Ellen Moodie and Leigh Binford describe how a troubling "tourist economy of pain" can develop at sites of suffering and atrocity. El Mozote is a village where a counterinsurgency unit of the Salvadoran Army, trained at the U.S. Army's School of the Americas in Georgia, committed mass rape, torture, and murder of civilians in 1981. Survivors and their communities later found themselves repeating the same stories of horror for an audience of tourists eager to get an "authentic" account, and to feel a sense of having atoned for the U.S. role there. "Selling Affect, Seeing

Blood: The Economy of Pain at El Mozote, El Salvador," in *Detours: Travel and the Ethics of Research in the Global South*, ed. M. Bianet Castellanos, 122–46 (Tucson: University of Arizona Press, 2019).

85. Jordan Valinsky, "Walmart Apologizes for Selling Juneteenth Ice Cream," CNN Business, May 24, 2022, https://www.cnn.com/2022/05/24/business-food/walmart-juneteenth-ice-cream/index.html.

86. Kaitlyn Greenidge, "What Walmart Doesn't Get About Juneteenth," *The New York Times*, June 18, 2021, https://www.nytimes.com/2021/06/18/opinion/juneteenth-emancipation-walmart.html.

87. Berry, *The Price for Their Pound of Flesh*.

88. Peighton Young, interview with the author, June 30, 2022.

89. Alex Thorson and Amelia Heymann, "Cemetery Worker Discovers Exposed Human Bones Spilling from Embankment in Henrico," ABC 8 News, July 20, 2020, https://www.wric.com/news/local-news/henrico-county/bones-found-out-of-place-in-henrico-cemetery/.

90. "Enrichmond Foundation—Response to False Rumors (#RVA #Community-overcontest)," Enrichmond Foundation, May 3, 2021, YouTube video, https://www.youtube.com/watch?v=nb4eNFpgARU.

91. Berry, *The Price for Their Pound of Flesh*, 178–79; Paul R. Mullins, *Revolting Things: An Archaeology of Shameful Histories and Repulsive Realities* (Gainesville: University Press of Florida), 2021, 111–12.

92. Berry, *The Price for Their Pound of Flesh*; see also Smith, *Death and Rebirth in a Southern City*, 215–16.

93. Virtual public hearing on the discovery of human remains at East End Cemetery, October 23, 2020.

94. See "About | East Marshall Street Well Project," Virginia Commonwealth University, accessed May 30, 2023, https://emsw.vcu.edu/about/; Tina Griego, "Into the Light," *Richmond Magazine*, September 8, 2015, https://richmondmagazine.com/api/content/ebcbcf88-5658-11e5-8b3e-22000b078648/. For more on Ana Edwards and the group she cofounded, the Virginia Defenders for Freedom, Justice & Equality, see Smith, *Death and Rebirth in a Southern City*, 57–69.

95. A list of the recommendations of the Family Representative Council for the East Marshall Street Well Project can be found at "Recommendations," East Marshall Street Well Project, September 2021, https://emsw.vcu.edu/recommendations/.

96. Ryan K. Smith, "Three Minutes Each at the Horror Show," *Richmond Cemeteries*, October 26, 2020, https://www.richmondcemeteries.org/2020/10/26/three-minutes-each-at-the-horror-show/.

97. Ryan K. Smith, "Disappointing Preservation Plans," *Richmond Cemeteries*, July 6, 2021, https://www.richmondcemeteries.org/2021/07/06/disappointing-preservation-plans/.

98. "East End and Evergreen Preservation Plans Letter," July 6, 2021, https://acrobat

.adobe.com/link/track?uri=urn%3Aaaid%3Ascds%3AUS%3A52d8a359-d1d7-420c
-8e32-e83a0b078f9a#pageNum=1.

99. John Sydnor, interview with the author, June 17, 2021. A letter from the Friends of East End to Judge Gregory L. Rupe, sent just before the 2019 court hearing about the cemetery's ownership, disputes the language that Beth Weisbrod, an Enrichmond board member, had used in a statement submitted to the court. Weisbrod claimed that East End had "languished without any group raising the necessary resources to restore it and educate the community on its significance to Richmond's racial history." The Friends of East End sought to rebut this claim with evidence of their skills at mobilizing volunteers, raising funds, establishing collaborations with academic and other institutions, and publicizing stories from the cemetery across many media and platforms. "RE: Parity, LLC v. Trustees in Liquidation of East End Burial Association—Case No. CL17-5911-2," December 21, 2018, courtesy of Erin Hollaway Palmer.

100. John Sydnor, interview with the author, June 17, 2021.

101. Gough, Howell, and Cameron, "The Structural Challenge of Power and Whiteness in Planning," 551.

102. Palmer, "The Enrichmond Files."

103. Smith referred to Enrichmond's acquisition of East End as a "top-down solution from whites without buy-in from all segments of the community." Smith, "East End Goes the Way Things Go." On Richmond's long history of placing portions of African American history within a "palatable market narrative" and erasing the rest, see Mullins, *Revolting Things*, 109.

104. On "fields of care," see Kenneth E. Foote, *Shadowed Ground: America's Landscapes of Violence and Tragedy* (Austin: University of Texas Press, 2003), 7.

105. In February 2021, the East End Cemetery Collaboratory, a network of scholars collaborating with the Friends of East End, held a "community conversation" with descendants over Zoom. The event had no set agenda; older descendants, Thomas Taylor and Alice Wooldridge, simply reminisced about the cemetery, Richmond's past, and other things (Wooldridge's daughter, Alicia Aroche, served as moderator). It seemed to me that this warm and aimless conversation—so unlike the tightly controlled, hierarchical "public hearings" where Enrichmond representatives had appeared—was an example of care for the living and dead that went above and beyond the logics of "stewardship."

106. Erin Hollaway Palmer, text message to the author, July 14, 2021.

107. On "authentic caring" see Angela Valenzuela, *Subtractive Schooling: U.S.-Mexican Youth and the Politics of Caring*, The Social Context of Education (Albany, NY: SUNY Press, 1999).

108. "Our group, the Friends of East End, did our work with the understanding that the comprehensive reclamation and restoration of these sites, where tens of thousands of Black folk were buried during Jim Crow and after, would require significant government funding and assistance," Brian wrote later. Palmer, "The Enrichmond Files."

109. Maggie Nelson, "Let's Talk About the Anxiety Freedom Can Cause," interview by Ezra Klein, *The Ezra Klein Show*, October 8, 2021, transcript, https://www.nytimes.com/2021/10/08/podcasts/transcript-ezra-klein-interviews-maggie-nelson.html.

110. Lepore, "When Black History Is Unearthed, Who Gets to Speak for the Dead?"

111. Maggie Nelson, "Let's Talk About the Anxiety Freedom Can Cause."

112. Chris Suarez, "Enrichmond Foundation Executive Director Gone after Years of Tumult over Stewardship of Historic Black Cemeteries," *Richmond Times-Dispatch*, May 20, 2022, https://richmond.com/news/local/enrichmond-foundation-executive-director-gone-after-years-of-tumult-over-stewardship-of-historic-black-cemeteries/article_3bf061e1-05f0-5e6f-a6c3-c5f387bdd0f4.html.

113. Jeremy M. Lazarus, "Enrichmond Foundation's Status Is Unclear," *Richmond Free Press*, June 30, 2022, http://richmondfreepress.com/news/2022/jun/30/enrichmond-foundations-status-unclear/.

114. Jeremy M. Lazarus, "City Officials Debate How to Investigate Defunct Nonprofit," *Richmond Free Press*, July 28, 2022, http://richmondfreepress.com/news/2022/jul/28/city-officials-debate-how-investigate-defunct-nonp/; Palmer, "Enwhatnow?"; Chris Suarez, "Still No Answers for Missing $3 Million the Enrichmond Foundation Was Managing for Local Groups," *Richmond Times-Dispatch*, September 17, 2022, https://richmond.com/news/local/still-no-answers-for-missing-3-million-the-enrichmond-foundation-was-managing-for-local-groups/article_b8347d9c-d79a-5082-a713-4eebc4f12e25.html.

115. , Nicole Dantzler, "Richmond Nonprofits Hurt by Enrichmond's Breakup Could Receive Funds Through New Grant," WRIC, July 19, 2023, https://www.wric.com/news/local-news/richmond/richmond-nonprofits-hurt-by-enrichmonds-breakup-could-receive-funds-through-new-grant/; Henry Graff, "FBI, Attorney General Investigating Enrichmond Foundation Missing Money," NBC 12, April 5, 2023, https://www.nbc12.com/2023/04/05/fbi-virginia-attorney-general-investigating-enrichmond-foundation-missing-money/.

116. Ryan K. Smith, "Enrichmond's Collapse," *Richmond Cemeteries*, July 6, 2022, https://www.richmondcemeteries.org/2022/07/06/enrichmonds-collapse/.

117. Palmer, "The Enrichmond Files."

118. See, e.g., "Meet Our Board," National Association of Park Foundations, accessed September 21, 2023, https://www.the-napf.org/board. On suspicions of fraud and embezzlement, see Henry Graff, "New Documents Shed Light on Missing Money Following Enrichmond Foundation Collapse," NBC 12, April 6, 2023, https://www.nbc12.com/2023/04/06/new-documents-shed-light-missing-money-following-enrichmond-foundation-collapse/.

119. Erin Hollaway Palmer, note to the author, August 28, 2023.

120. Friends of East End (@friendsofeastend), Instagram post, July 2, 2022, https://www.instagram.com/p/Cfh2MI7FX82/.

Chapter 3: "The Largest, Most Beautiful, and Popular of All Our Cemeteries"

1. "Inquest Clears Mother in 'Pepper Death' of Son," *The Daily Intelligencer*, January 29, 1960, Newspapers.com.

2. Michelle Smallwood-Kassab, Facebook post, November 5, 2017, https://www.facebook.com/groups/Fommci/posts/1530848373646855.

3. Keneth J. Rabben, "Dead Tot's Mother Called Outstanding Parent by Pastor, Neighbors, Agency," *The Bristol Daily Courier*, January 13, 1960, Newspapers.com.

4. Michelle Smallwood-Kassab, Facebook post.

5. Rabben, "Dead Tot's Mother Called Outstanding Parent."

6. Michelle Smallwood-Kassab, interview with the author, July 19, 2021.

7. Ken Smith, Facebook post, November 5, 2017, https://www.facebook.com/groups/Fommci/posts/1530848373646855.

8. Michelle Smallwood-Kassab, interview with the author, July 19, 2021.

9. Al Wilson, Facebook post, November 5, 2017, https://www.facebook.com/groups/Fommci/posts/1530848373646855.

10. Michelle Smallwood-Kassab, interview with the author, July 19, 2021.

11. Community Meeting about Mount Moriah Cemetery, November 4, 2017.

12. I encountered many different numbers for Mount Moriah's acreage. Historian Thomas H. Keels says that Mount Moriah started at fifty-four acres and eventually grew to two hundred twenty-seven. Thomas H. Keels, *Philadelphia Graveyards and Cemeteries*, Images of America: Pennsylvania (Mount Pleasant, SC: Arcadia Publishing, 2003), 50. The strategic plan for Mount Moriah says that at one point it was as large as three hundred eighty acres, and currently occupies one hundred forty-two. Fairmount Ventures, *Strategic Plan for Mount Moriah Cemetery*, November 2018, 1, 105. Jo Cosgrove of the Friends of Mount Moriah estimates it is between two hundred and two hundred twenty acres (Jo Cosgrove, conversation with the author, April 30, 2023).

13. Gritty, introduced as the new "wild-eyed, Muppet-looking mascot" for the Philadelphia Flyers hockey team in 2018, quickly became both a symbol of Philadelphia's "fighting spirit" as an "underdog city" and an anti-Donald Trump, left-wing icon. Kelly Weill, "Gritty Is Antifa Now," The Daily Beast, October 3, 2018, https://www.thedailybeast.com/gritty-the-philadelphia-flyers-bizarre-new-mascot-is-antifa-now.

14. Benjamin Gilbert Buckley, "Perpetual Care: A Sustainable Approach to Restoring the Lost Landscapes of America's Rural Cemeteries" (master's thesis, University of Pennsylvania, 2013), 1, https://repository.upenn.edu/cgi/viewcontent.cgi?article=1548&context=hp_theses; Farrell, *Inventing the American Way of Death*, 99–112.

15. Fairmount Ventures, *Strategic Plan for Mount Moriah Cemetery*, 33.

16. Mount Moriah Cemetery Association of Philadelphia, "Mount Moriah Cemetery," Cooperative Printing Co., 1871, courtesy of the Friends of Mount Moriah; Christopher Doherty, in "Confederates, Catholics, Muslims and Masons," refers to the cemetery as "arguably Philadelphia's most democratic burial ground."

17. Buckley, "Perpetual Care," 1–2.

18. Mount Moriah Cemetery Association, "Mount Moriah Cemetery."

19. The cemetery's new strategic plan offers a demographic snapshot. It says that more than 90 percent of residents in the neighborhoods around Mount Moriah are Black, 23 percent are foreign born (many of them West African), and both income and educational attainment levels are low. Fairmount Ventures, *Strategic Plan for Mount Moriah Cemetery*, 6.

20. Fairmount Ventures, *Strategic Plan for Mount Moriah Cemetery*, 1.

21. Pamela J. Forsythe, "The Long Road Ahead to Resurrect Mount Moriah," WHYY, December 3, 2014, https://whyy.org/articles/the-long-road-ahead-to-resurrect-mount -moriah/.

22. Quoted in Michael Z. Muhammad, "Philadelphia Muslim Tends to Burial Ground for Believers," *The Final Call*, August 4, 2018. According to Jenn O'Donnell, Muslim burials at Mount Moriah seem to have peaked in the early 2000s. Jenn O'Donnell, interview with the author, July 24, 2021.

23. Abigail Hauslohner, "'Muslim Town': A Look Inside Philadelphia's Thriving Muslim Culture," *The Washington Post*, July 21, 2017, https://www.washingtonpost.com /news/post-nation/wp/2017/07/21/muslim-town-how-one-american-city-embraced-a -muslim-community-in-decline/.

24. Sammy Caiola, "Philly Faith Leaders Try to Create Safe Havens from Gun Violence during Ramadan and Beyond," WHYY, April 18, 2023, https://whyy.org/articles/ philly-ramadan-baitul-aafiyat-mosque-iftar-gun-violence-prevention/.

25. Farrell, *Inventing the American Way of Death*, 110–11.

26. Lori Wysong, "Cemeteries, Segregation, and the Funerals of Henry Jones," Hidden City Philadelphia, October 9, 2020, https://hiddencityphila.org/2020/10/ceme teries-segregation-and-the-funerals-of-henry-jones/.

27. Weekly Notes of Cases Argued and Determined in the Supreme Court of Pennsylvania, the County Courts of Philadelphia, and the United States District and Circuit Courts for the Eastern District of Pennsylvania, Vol. 2. Google Books (Philadelphia: Kay & Brother, 1876), 244–47.

28. Wysong, "Cemeteries, Segregation, and the Funerals of Henry Jones."

29. Weekly Notes of Cases Argued and Determined in the Supreme Court of Pennsylvania, 245.

30. Pennsylvania Supreme Court, Pennsylvania State Reports (West Publishing Company, 1877), Google Books, 241.

31. Wysong, "Cemeteries, Segregation, and the Funerals of Henry Jones."

32. "There are people at the cemetery who threaten to tear down the flowers I have planted in the lot and to injure the grave should my husband be buried there. I have suffered so long already that I feel I cannot bury him there and live in suspense," Jones wrote in an 1876 letter to the *Philadelphia Inquirer*. Quoted in Wysong, "Cemeteries, Segregation, and the Funerals of Henry Jones."

33. Community Meeting about Mount Moriah Cemetery, November 4, 2017.

34. Michaela Winberg, "Racism and Deadly Traffic on Cobbs Creek Parkway," WHYY, September 8, 2020. https://whyy.org/episodes/how-racism-fueled/.

35. "About | Friends of Mount Moriah Cemetery," accessed May 31, 2023, https://friendsofmountmoriahcemetery.org/about/.

36. Fairmount Ventures, *Strategic Plan for Mount Moriah Cemetery*, 44.

37. David Murrell, "What Happens When a Cemetery Dies?" *Philadelphia Magazine*, July 30, 2016, https://www.phillymag.com/news/2016/07/30/mount-moriah-cemetery-friends/.

38. Ken Smith, interview with the author, May 27, 2021.

39. "Naji Muhammad: The Passing of a Soldier's Soldier Who Was 'a Gift from God,'" *The Final Call*, June 7, 2022, https://new.finalcall.com/2022/06/07/naji-muhammad-the-passing-of-a-soldiers-soldier-who-was-a-gift-from-god/.

40. "Louis Farrakhan," Southern Poverty Law Center, accessed October 24, 2022, https://www.splcenter.org/fighting-hate/extremist-files/individual/louis-farrakhan.

41. Friends of Mount Moriah meeting, January 27, 2018.

42. Community Meeting about Mount Moriah Cemetery, November 4, 2017.

43. Ibid.

44. Rumors of illegal burials in Mount Moriah are very persistent; Dante Leonard repeated multiple times that criminals used the cemetery "to dispose of stuff," and not only bodies. Dante Leonard, interview with the author, May 30, 2023. Jenn O'Donnell says that the Friends of Mount Moriah have never seen any disturbed ground or other real evidence of such burials. Jenn O'Donnell, interview with the author, July 14, 2021.

45. Fairmount Ventures, *Strategic Plan for Mount Moriah Cemetery*, 16, 124–27.

46. Ibid., 125–26.

47. Rosalyn McPherson, interview with the author, June 4, 2021.

48. Letter to Governor Tom Wolf from Naji Muhammad, July 9, 2018, posted on "The People of Mt. Moriah" Facebook page, page subsequently removed.

49. Jenn O'Donnell, interview with the author, July 24, 2021.

50. Fairmount Ventures, *Strategic Plan for Mount Moriah Cemetery*, 125.

51. Naji Muhammad, interview with the author, January 20, 2020.

52. Friends of Mount Moriah Cemetery, Facebook post, April 3, 2021, https://www.facebook.com/groups/Fommci/permalink/3850330078365328/

53. Al Wilson, Facebook post on the Friends of Mount Moriah Cemetery page, April 12, 2021, https://www.facebook.com/groups/Fommci/permalink/3876346515763684.

54. A few months later, McPherson told me that she had tried and failed to encourage more dialogue between Paulette and Naji Muhammad. "I would've liked to have seen somebody who was more diplomatic take Naji on and take him under his wing, so that they could form a more harmonious alliance." Rosalyn McPherson, interview with the author, June 4, 2021.

55. Fairmount Ventures, *Strategic Plan for Mount Moriah Cemetery*, 126.

56. Ken Smith, interview with the author, May 27, 2021.

57. Naji Muhammad, Facebook post, "People of Mount Moriah Cemetery" page, March 15, 2022, page subsequently removed.

58. "Naji Muhammad, the Passing of a Soldier's Soldier."

A House That's Gone Now

1. See Jackson, "Rethinking Repair."

Chapter 4: Pathways to Revision

1. Smith, *Death and Rebirth in a Southern City*, 7.

2. Ibid., 7–8.

3. Ibid., 8.

4. Ibid. Smith does make note of the fact that many African Americans do not have a clear answer as to where their ancestors may be buried, and thus feel a stake in the fate of all African American burial grounds as members of a larger "descendant community"—a term used by the anthropologist Michael Blakey and discussed in the next chapter.

5. China Miéville, *The City & The City* (New York: Del Rey Ballantine Books, 2009).

6. The Friends of Geer did eventually share a post with members and on Facebook. The text, composed by Nicholas Levy, concluded, "A space to grieve is also a space to remember and recommit to resistance. And so we add George Floyd, Breonna Taylor, Ahmaud Arbery, and others to a list of far too many names. We mourn their loss even as we demand gains in the provision of justice to black and brown Americans that come too late for them. As at Geer Cemetery, may they rest in dignity and in power. And may we keep learning to live—never resting—with dignity, empowered." Friends of Geer Cemetery, Facebook post, June 3, 2020, https://www.facebook.com/friendsof geer/posts/pfbid0ezzTgzJXQqFH3yMkeRT2RnM1tDwLEiUPs4wMbu2YzrL1VTX8fQt VQArfk1EgAhcwl.

7. Anonymized interview with the author, January 26, 2021.

8. On racism and "colorblindness," see Eduardo Bonilla-Silva, *Racism without Racists: Color-Blind Racism and the Persistence of Racial Inequality in America*, 5th ed. (Lanham, MD: Rowman & Littlefield Publishers, 2017).

9. Anonymized interview with the author, May 19, 2021.

10. James Ferguson, *The Anti-Politics Machine: Development, Depoliticization, and Bureaucratic Power in Lesotho* (Minneapolis: University of Minnesota Press, 1994).

11. Debra Taylor Gonzalez-Garcia, interview with the author, March 5, 2021.

12. Ibid.

13. See Friends of Geer Cemetery, Facebook post, February 14, 2020, https://www.facebook.com/friendsofgeer/posts/february-is-a-month-of-love-with-valentines-day -in-the-middle-it-is-also-black-h/523539691610556.

14. "Outdoor archive" is from Brian Palmer, "These Abandoned Black Cemeteries Were Long Forgotten—Until Now," Economic Hardship Reporting Project, June 9,

2016, http://economichardship.org/archive//these-abandoned-black-cemeteries-were -long-forgotten-until-now. Palmer credits Lynn Rainville, who has called African American cemeteries "outdoor museums," with inspiring his own phrase. Quoted in Michael Paul Williams, "Uncovering Hidden Histories in Virginia's Black Cemeteries," *Richmond Times-Dispatch*, October 8, 2015, https://www.richmond.com/news/local/ michael-paul-williams/williams-uncovering-hidden-histories-in-virginia-s-black -cemeteries/article_2563311a-44a6-5b7e-88ff-fd9a8357d3e1.html.

15. Gerald Vizenor, *Manifest Manners: Post-Indian Warriors of Survivance* (Middleton, CT: Wesleyan University Press, 1994), 53, quoted in Tuck, "Suspending Damage," 422.

16. Lisa Y. Henderson, interview with the author, February 9, 2021.

17. See Beatrice Alvarez, "Black Quilters: Historians and Memory Keepers," PBS, accessed May 22, 2023, https://www.pbs.org/articles/black-quilters-historians-and -memory-keepers; Rankine, "The Condition of Black Life Is One of Mourning."

18. Brian Palmer, "It's the Looking That Matters: An Update on the Documentary," Wok Docs, September 13, 2016, http://www.wokdocs.com/blog.

19. Doris Francis, "Cemeteries as Cultural Landscapes," *Mortality* 8, no. 2 (2003): 222–27, 222.

20. Yoni Kadden, interview with the author, December 14, 2020.

21. Wendell Berry, "How to Be a Poet," *Poetry Magazine*, accessed October 29, 2020, https://www.poetryfoundation.org/poetrymagazine/poems/41087/how-to-be-a-poet.

22. Kimani S. K. Nehusi, *Libation: An Afrikan Ritual of Heritage in the Circle of Life* (Lanham, MD: University Press of America, 2015), 181–82.

23. Nehusi, *Libation*, 26–31.

24. According to one analysis, the Black Durhamites who buried their dead at Geer proclaimed their faith via headstone inscriptions more frequently than their White counterparts did at Maplewood. See Carter Cribbs in "Durham Cemetery Survey," Writing 101: The Archaeology of Durham, Duke University, taught by Andrew Tharler, ArcGIS StoryMaps, April 18, 2022, https://storymaps.arcgis.com/stories/883c26dcc202 489caea3e107e9830301.

25. The philosopher Tim Mulgan describes these as incompatible worldviews in which either the "Dead-Are-Gone" or the "Dead-Are-With-Us." This vocabulary is useful in clarifying the underpinnings of different cultural practices, though many people actually live in more complicated spaces than the stark philosophical binaries can capture. In fact, the popularity of libation rituals among observant Christians speaks to how they can hold two truths at once, adapting to different occasions and spaces. See Tim Mulgan, "The Place of the Dead in Liberal Political Philosophy," *Journal of Political Philosophy* 7, no. 1 (1999): 52–70, https://doi.org/10.1111/1467-9760.00065.

26. Kyrie Mason, "Things Which Don't Exist," *ROOM: A Sketchbook for Analytic Action*, March 9, 2021, https://analytic-room.com/essays/things-which-dont-exist-by -kyrie-mason/.

27. Lepore, "When Black History Is Unearthed, Who Gets to Speak for the Dead?"

28. Dr. E. Victor Maafo, libation ceremony at Geer Cemetery, December 4, 2021.

29. Virtual public hearing on the discovery of human remains at East End Cemetery, October 23, 2020.

30. "Unmarked," Reel South, Season 5, Episode 2, PBS, April 13, 2020, video, 26:34, https://www.pbs.org/video/unmarked-99cmss/.

31. All Jarene Fleming quotations in this section not otherwise cited are from an interview with the author, October 15, 2017.

32. Virtual public hearing on the discovery of human remains at East End Cemetery, October 23, 2020.

33. Melissa Pocock, interview with the author, March 30, 2019.

34. Ibid.

35. "Lemon Project Committee on Memorialization," The Lemon Project, William & Mary, accessed May 23, 2023, https://www.wm.edu/sites/lemonproject/memorialization%20/index.php.

36. Smith, *Death and Rebirth in a Southern City*, 111.

37. Alex Green, "A Holiday Light Show in Waltham Obscures a Devastating History," WBUR Cognoscenti, November 19, 2020, https://www.wbur.org/cognoscenti/2020/11/19/fernald-waltham-disability-rights-history-alex-green.

Chapter 5: Revising How We Belong

1. The first degree-granting historically Black university in the United States, located in Oxford, Pennsylvania.

2. Rainville, *Hidden History*, xii.

3. Ibid.

4. Ibid., xiii.

5. Ibid., 161.

6. Antoon De Baets, "A Declaration of the Responsibilities of Present Generations Toward Past Generations," *History and Theory* 43, no. 4 (2004): 130–64, later used as the basis for chapters in his book *Responsible History* (New York: Berghahn Books, 2008).

7. De Baets, "A Declaration of the Responsibilities of Present Generations Toward Past Generations," 134.

8. Itzél Delgado-Gonzalez, text message to the author, November 17, 2020.

9. See Williamson, "America's Black Cemeteries and Three Women Trying to Save Them."

10. See Annalisa Bolin and David Nkusi, "What Does It Mean to Decolonize Heritage?" Sapiens, October 6, 2021, https://www.sapiens.org/culture/decolonizing-heritage/; Chip Colwell, *Plundered Skulls and Stolen Spirits: Inside the Fight to Reclaim Native America's Culture* (Chicago: University of Chicago Press, 2019); Cheryl J. LaRoche and Michael L. Blakey, "Seizing Intellectual Power: The Dialogue at the New York

African Burial Ground," *Historical Archaeology* 31, no. 3 (September 1, 1997): 84–106, https://doi.org/10.1007/BF03374233; National Trust for Historic Preservation and African American Cultural Heritage Action Fund, *Engaging Descendant Communities*; Smith, *Death and Rebirth in a Southern City*, 7–8.

11. On concentric circles of care, see Maureen Sander-Staudt, "Care Ethics," Internet Encyclopedia of Philosophy, accessed May 24, 2023, https://iep.utm.edu/care-ethics/.

12. On philosophical debates about the interests of the dead, see Joan Callahan, "Harming the Dead," *Ethics* 97, no. 2 (1987): 341–52.

13. Palmer, "Friends of East End Cemetery." While the term "descendants" is often used to describe anyone with family members buried in a cemetery, I make a distinction between the descendants of generations long gone and mourners—people who have direct, living experience of their loved ones who are buried in the cemetery. At Mount Moriah, people such as Michelle Smallwood-Kassab and Keisha L. Phillips are still finding the graves of their children, siblings, and spouses. I refer to these people as mourners. It is, like all collective descriptions, an imperfect term. Some of these people may still be holding grief close, while others may not consider themselves to be in mourning anymore.

14. See "About Us," 2019, International Sites of Conscience, accessed May 31, 2023, http://www.sitesofconscience.org/en/who-we-are/about-us/.

15. See Green, "A Holiday Light Show in Waltham Obscures a Devastating History"; Tom Parry, "Preserve Indigenous Residential Schools as Sites of Conscience, MPs Urged," CBC, September 26, 2017, https://www.cbc.ca/news/politics/indigenous-resi dential-schools-sites-ry-moran-1.4306944; Linda Steele, "Sites of Conscience Redressing Disability Institutional Violence," *Incarceration* 3, no. 2 (July 1, 2022): 1–19, https://doi.org/10.1177/26326663221103435; Linda Steele, Bonney Djuric, Lily Hibberd, and Fiona Yeh, "Parramatta Female Factory Precinct as a Site of Conscience: Using Institutional Pasts to Shape Just Legal Futures," *University of New South Wales Law Journal* 43, no. 2 (2020): 521–51, https://doi.org/10.53637/gcar4734.

16. "Ascendant: The Power of Descendant Communities to Shape Our Stories, Places and Future," Thomas Jefferson's Monticello, June 18, 2022, https://www.monticello.org /exhibits-events/calendar-of-events/ascendant/.

17. National Trust for Historic Preservation and African American Cultural Heritage Fund, *Engaging Descendant Communities*.

18. "In Plain Sight—Geer Cemetery Exhibit Opening."

19. Deidre Barnes, interview with the author, June 22, 2021.

20. Ibid.

21. LaRoche and Blakey, "Seizing Intellectual Power," 84–86.

22. Michael L. Blakey, "Walking the Ancestors Home: On the Road to an Ethical Human Biology," *Anthropology Now* 14, no. 1-2 (2022), 9. At the time of this writing, Blakey was co-chairing the Commission for the Ethical Treatment of Human Remains

of the American Anthropological Association, which was further investigating how Indigenous repatriation programs might pave the way for a new framework for the handling of African American graves, remains, and cultural heritage.

23. Blakey, "African Burial Ground Project," 63. Some of the considerable complexities of NAGPRA are discussed in Kathleen S. Fine-Dare, *Grave Injustice: The American Indian Repatriation Movement and NAGPRA*, Fourth World Rising Series (Lincoln: University of Nebraska Press, 2002); Devon A. Mihesuah, *Repatriation Reader: Who Owns American Indian Remains?* (Lincoln: University of Nebraska Press, 2000). Blakey differentiates between "plural democracy" and "performative 'multiculturalism.'" In the former, arrangements such as those specified in NAGPRA put decision-making power in the hands of the most affected people. The latter usually winds up empowering "White-controlled institutions" that, due to structural racism, are de facto "majority stakeholders" in many settings. Blakey, "Walking the Ancestors Home," 12.

24. Blakey, "Walking the Ancestors Home," 9.

25. Ibid.

26. Ibid.; Michael L. Blakey lecture in "Principles of Archaeology" and "Death, Burial, and Justice in the Americas" classes, Duke University, April 4, 2023.

27. Blakey, "African Burial Ground Project," 62.

28. National Park Service, "Determining Cultural Affiliation Within NAGPRA." These determinations are quite complex and sometimes controversial. They can draw on evidence as diverse as linguistic patterns and folklore; but ultimately museums and federal agencies exert final determination over whether remains or objects are culturally affiliated with a contemporary group or not.

29. LaRoche and Blakey, "Seizing Intellectual Power," 100.

30. Blakey, "Walking the Ancestors Home," 13.

31. Ibid.

32. National Trust for Historic Preservation and African American Cultural Heritage Action Fund, *Engaging Descendant Communities*.

33. Ibid., 3.

34. Antoinette T. Jackson, *Speaking for the Enslaved: Heritage Interpretation at Antebellum Plantation Sites*, Heritage, Tourism, and Community (Walnut Creek, CA: Left Coast Press, 2012), 25. Thanks to Vera Cecelski and Khadija McNair for their extraordinarily moving and rich interpretation of the experiences of people enslaved at Stagville, shared on tours with my students and Durham Black Burial Grounds Collaboratory participants over the years.

35. National Trust for Historic Preservation and African American Cultural Heritage Action Fund, *Engaging Descendant Communities*, 1.

36. "Born of necessity, perhaps, the cultivation of extended kinfulness is also a source of black pride." Ruha Benjamin, "Black AfterLives Matter," *Boston Review*, July 11, 2018, https://bostonreview.net/articles/ruha-benjamin-black-afterlives-matter/.

37. See Jackson, *Speaking for the Enslaved*, 8.

38. Peighton Young, interview with the author, June 30, 2022.

39. See "Red Hill," Red Hill Patrick Henry Memorial Foundation, accessed May 31, 2023, https://www.redhill.org/red-hill/.

40. "Letter to the Honorable Ralph S. Northam," March 10, 2021, https://acrobat.adobe.com/link/track?uri=urn%3Aaaid%3Ascds%3AUS%3A592fa397-79df-4b02-b13f-e6ae5b0478b8#pageNum=1.

41. "Protect Richmond's African American Cemeteries," Change.org, accessed May 31, 2023, https://www.change.org/p/ralph-s-northam-protect-richmond-s-african-american-cemeteries.

42. Chris Suarez, "Richmond Withholding Money for Enrichmond Foundation after Concerns Raised about Management, Oversight of Historic Black Cemeteries," *Richmond Times-Dispatch*, May 16, 2021, https://richmond.com/news/local/govt-and-politics/richmond-withholding-money-for-enrichmond-foundation-after-concerns-raised-about-management-oversight-of-historic-black/article_bc8e54bc-7ffc-5282-a20c-04317313428a.html.

43. Ibid.

44. On the politics at James Madison's historic home at Montpelier, see Alana Wise, "Montpelier Says It's Open to Parity with Slave Descendants. Descendants Call Foul," NPR, April 20, 2022, https://www.npr.org/2022/04/20/1093673939/montpeliers-fight-with-descendants-of-the-enslaved-brings-employee-firings.

45. Peighton Young, interview with the author, June 30, 2022.

46. "Enrichmond Foundation—Evergreen Cemetery Legacy"; also Rosenblatt, "Cemetery Credibility and What It Means to Be a Descendant."

47. Peighton Young, interview with the author, June 30, 2022.

48. Ibid.

49. Brian Palmer, "Friends of East End Cemetery." On shame and African Americans' engagement with cemeteries and other historical sites, see also Smith, *Death and Rebirth in a Southern City*, 120–21.

50. In her ethnography *Exhuming Loss*, Layla Renshaw describes forensic exhumations of Civil War–era mass graves in Spain. She recounts that for some descendants, trying to recall long-dead relatives, whom in some cases they barely knew, provoked "shame and embarrassment." Similarly, it seems to me, assuming a deep interest and sacred bond between descendants and their ancestors buried in degraded cemeteries can be, to take another phrase from Renshaw, "a hard burden on those descendants who have not so much forgotten their dead, as never known them." Layla Renshaw, *Exhuming Loss: Memory, Materiality and Mass Graves of the Spanish Civil War* (Walnut Creek, CA: Taylor & Francis Group, 2011).

51. John Mitchell, speech at the Black History Museum and Cultural Center in Richmond, Virginia, February 24, 2019. Shared via email message to the author, February 24, 2019.

52. Jenn O'Donnell, interview with the author, January 19, 2020.

53. Famed civil rights activist Pauli Murray, who attended the West End Graded School, remembered it as follows: "I'll never forget West End School. It was a rickety old wooden built building with the paint peeling; I can see those scales now. You know how wood or shingles or paint blisters and I can see it. When there was a wind in a storm, you could just hear the wind blowing through that old building. I think that it was a two-story building, it might have been a three-story building, but anyway . . . And of course, the white kids' school, a nice brick school sitting in a lawn surrounded by a fence. West End was up on a sort of clay, barren ground. There was no lawn whatsoever. It just sat on clay. The fact that I can remember this today and I can see that old school building there, no swings, nothing to play with when you went out . . ." Pauli Murray, "Oral History Interview with Pauli Murray, February 13, 1976. Interview G-0044," interview by Genna Rae McNeil, Southern Oral History Program Collection (#4007), audio, 5:18:41, https://docsouth.unc.edu/sohp/playback.html?base_file=G-0044&duration=05:18:41.

54. Fink, *All Our Families*, x.

55. See Marty Fink, *Forget Burial: HIV Kinship, Disability, and Queer/Trans Narratives of Care* (New Brunswick, NJ: Rutgers University Press, 2021), 4–5, 77–104; Fink, *All Our Families*, 162, 165.

56. Deegan, "Remember My Name," 2.

57. On kin vs. population, see *Making Kin Not Population: Reconceiving Generations*, ed. Adele Clarke and Donna Haraway (Chicago: Prickly Paradigm Press, 2018). Fink, inspired by the writing of the late disability activist and author Stacey Milbern, champions a reclaiming of disability lineage: "By thinking of us as part of a larger web of disabled ancestors, their families, and caregivers, we share disability. Disability becomes woven into the fabric of the larger cultural story of what it is to be human. This also connects us to the vast universe of forgotten disabled people who died institutionalized, their names and lives unknown to their descendants, in a great unmarked grave. The concept of crip ancestry allows us to honor and imagine them." Fink, *All Our Families*, 165; see also Stacey Milbern, "On the Ancestral Plane: Crip Hand Me Downs and the Legacy of Our Movements," Disability Visibility Project, March 10, 2019, https://disabilityvisibilityproject.com/2019/03/10/on-the-ancestral-plane-crip-hand-me-downs-and-the-legacy-of-our-movements/.

58. Transcript, Enrichmond Zoom call for descendants, September 9, 2021. Shared by Brian Palmer via email message to the author, February 24, 2019.

59. Ibid.

60. Brian later summarized the process as "little more than a series of Zoom calls during which people on Enrichmond's payroll tried (unsuccessfully) to get whoever showed up to 'vote' on important matters." Palmer, "Enwhatnow?"

61. Jarene Fleming, interview with the author, January 24, 2021. Fleming also objected to a clause in the charter to form this committee, which stipulated that it served at the pleasure of Enrichmond and could be disbanded at any time: "I knew that we had no real power in the decision-making process or ownership or final say even," she said

in this interview. She proposed edits to the charter and was rebuffed, at which point she left the ExPRT Committee. See Palmer, "The Enrichmond Files."

62. See "The Cemeteries at Evergreen Family Council," The Cemeteries at Evergreen, accessed May 29, 2023 (page no longer available), https://cemeverstg.wpengine .com/. I am grateful to Michael Blakey for reminding me of this apt phrase in his lecture for Alicia Jiménez's "Principles of Archaeology" class and my "Death, Burial, and Justice in the Americas" class, Duke University, April 4, 2023.

63. "The Cemeteries at Evergreen Family Council."

64. Zoom meeting hosted by Enrichmond, September 9, 2021, transcript provided by Brian Palmer.

65. Ibid.

66. Palmer, "The Enrichmond Files."

67. Zoom meeting hosted by Virginia Outdoors Foundation, May 26, 2022, transcript provided by Brian Palmer.

68. Ibid.

69. Ibid.

70. LaRoche and Blakey, "Seizing Intellectual Power."

71. In a follow-up email, Mitchell said that his rejection of earlier models and sources such as the National Trust for Historic Preservation and African American Cultural Heritage Action Fund's *Engaging Descendant Communities* rubric was based on wanting to make a distinction between the burial grounds of enslaved people and post-Emancipation African American cemeteries. "The animosity towards ruthless slave owners is warranted. But African [American] Cemeteries have their own distinct issues," he said. When I asked him how he thought descendant voice and governance should differ at these two kinds of sites, he focused more on attitudes and immediate tasks than governance issues: "Building a cemetery community should start with the lowest common denominator. . . . Make the place safe and accessible for future work. Maybe that way direct descendants and community volunteers can interact. Exclusively cleaning the infrastructure. Build a new sense of camaraderie." After Enrichmond's collapse, he still maintained that they were "frustrated owners" not getting the public resources they needed, and that "[t]he system ended up pitting volunteers against those holding the deed." John Mitchell, email messages to the author, May 9, 2023, and May 10, 2023.

72. Zoom meeting hosted by Virginia Outdoors Foundation, May 26, 2022, transcript provided by Brian Palmer.

73. Peighton Young, email message to the author, May 15, 2023.

74. See Gough, Howell, and Cameron, "The Structural Challenge of Power and Whiteness in Planning."

75. On thinking about the dead as participants in transformative work around their graves, see Kim and Rosenblatt, "Whose Humanitarianism? Whose Forensic Anthropology?"

76. Smith, "Disappointing Preservation Plans."

77. Palmer, "The Enrichmond Files."

78. Laura Gilpin, *The Hocus-Pocus of the Universe* (Garden City, NY: Doubleday, 1977), 18.

79. See Jason De León's writing about the "hybrid system" of actors that influence whether, where, and in what state the remains of migrants are found, including U.S. border enforcement policy, desert landscapes and temperatures, vultures, coyotes, and migrants themselves. De León, *The Land of Open Graves*, 39–43.

80. Mark Auslander, "Saying Something Now: Documentary Work and the Voices of the Dead," *Michigan Quarterly Review* 44, no. 4 (Fall 2005): 685–86, ProQuest.

81. Thank you to Angela Naimou for the phrase "the work that plants do." Angela Naimou, conversation with the author, Rights at the Edge Conference, Haverford College, November 2–4, 2017.

82. See "Wilkins Cemetery," Wilkins Cemetery Committee, accessed May 25, 2023 (page no longer available), https://wilkinscemetery.com/the-enslaved.

83. Alice Walker, "Looking for Zora," *In Search of Our Mothers' Gardens: Womanist Prose* (New York: Harcourt Brace Jovanovich, 1983): 93–116, 115.

84. Ibid., 104.

85. Melissa Pocock, interview with the author, March 30, 2019.

86. Lisa Y. Henderson, interview with the author, February 9, 2021.

87. Lisa Y. Henderson, "Lane Street Project: Cemetery Records Request Update, No. 5, the City's Response," *Black Wide-Awake*, February 23, 2020, https://afamwilsonnc.com/2020/02/23/cemetery-records-request-update-no-5-the-citys-response/.

88. Lisa Y. Henderson, "Lane Street Project: Seek and Ye Shall Find," *Black Wide-Awake*, July 8, 2022. https://afamwilsonnc.com/2022/07/08/lane-street-project-seek-and-ye-shall-find/.

Chapter 6: Revising Public Space

1. Brian Palmer, "Friends of East End Cemetery."

2. See Thomasi McDonald, "Durham Residents Uncover Their Ancestral Legacies in the County's Old Black Cemeteries," *INDY Week*, September 1, 2021, http://indyweek.com/news/durham/durham-residents-are-uncovering-their-ancestral-legacies-in-countys-old-black-cemeteries/.

3. Charles Johnson, conversation with the author, February 7, 2022. Used with permission.

4. From the R. Kelly Bryant Papers, Wilson Library, University of North Carolina, retrieved June 2021 by Nicholas Levy and Kerry Rork.

5. By spring 2023, according to Cathy McBride-Schmehl, they had reset over three hundred stones in the cemetery. Email message to the author, May 31, 2023.

6. Cathy McBride-Schmehl and John Schmehl Jr., interview with the author, February 7, 2021.

7. Carissa Trotta, conversation with the author and students, Geer Cemetery, February 25, 2023. Not *all* of the trees at Geer can be protected, and Carissa's remark should not be misinterpreted as dogma. Some trees have already been removed from the cemetery for safety reasons; others are rotting and likely to fall, posing a risk to other trees, graves, and people. As DD Barnes put it, "Some of those trees have got to come down." Deidre Barnes, *Cemetery Citizens* book workshop, May 4, 2023.

8. Jo Cosgrove, interview with the author, April 11, 2021.

9. Jo Cosgrove, conversation with the author, November 6, 2022.

10. Greg Melville notes that recent changes in attitudes toward burial have brought us full circle. When Mount Auburn Cemetery in Massachusetts began allowing green burials in 2014, a cemetery "created two centuries ago because Bostonians specifically wanted to avoid ending up in shallow, unmarked graves" was now offering the same thing to enthusiastic customers. Melville, *Over My Dead Body*, 71.

11. Jo Cosgrove, interview with the author, April 11, 2021. In a follow-up email, Jo also pointed out that "historic, intentionally planted ornamental shrubs" around gravesites, as well as small trees, might be cut down if they are not recognized among the overgrowth. Jo Cosgrove, email message to the author, May 30, 2023.

12. Cathy McBride-Schmehl and John Schmehl Jr., interview with the author, February 7, 2021.

13. Quoted in Mortice, "Perpetual Neglect."

14. See DeSilvey, *Curated Decay*, 130–31.

15. Lisa Y. Henderson, interview with the author, February 9, 2021.

16. Lisa Y. Henderson, "Lane Street Project: March 27 Mini-Projects," *Black Wide-Awake*, March 24, 2021, https://afamwilsonnc.com/2021/03/24/lane-street-project-march-27-mini-projects/.

17. Jarene Fleming, interview with the author, January 24, 2021.

18. Chicora Foundation, Inc., "Frequently Asked Questions," accessed May 30, 2023, https://chicora.org/faqs.html.

19. Smith, *Death and Rebirth in a Southern City*, 122.

20. Angela Thorpe in "In Plain Sight—Reclaiming Hidden Histories," Friends of Geer Cemetery, February 20, 2021, YouTube video, https://www.youtube.com/watch?v=9HW_6xQ76uA.

21. Jenn O'Donnell, interview with the author, January 19, 2020.

22. Quoted in Linden-Ward, *Silent City on a Hill*, 308.

23. Ibid. 313.

24. Ibid. 315.

25. Ibid. 319–320.

26. See *Evergreen Cemetery Master Plan*, 23; on the concerns of archaeologists, see Palmer, "The Enrichmond Files."

27. Jeremy M. Lazarus, "Enrichmond Unveils $18.6M Master Plan for Evergreen Cemetery," *Richmond Free Press*, March 6, 2020, http://richmondfreepress.com/news/

2020/mar/06/enrichmond-unveils-186m-master-plan-evergreen-ceme/; Smith, "Disappointing Preservation Plans."

28. Jarene Fleming, interview with the author, January 24, 2021.

29. Gough, Howell, and Cameron, "The Structural Challenge of Power and Whiteness in Planning," 546.

30. Fairmount Ventures, *Strategic Plan for Mount Moriah Cemetery*, 2–3.

31. Ibid., 527.

32. Dante Leonard, interview with the author, May 30, 2023.

33. Jenn O'Donnell, interview with the author, January 19, 2020.

34. Taylor Allen, "Report: West Philadelphia Renters Face a Growing Risk of Displacement," WHYY, December 16, 2020. https://whyy.org/articles/west-philadelphia-renters-face-a-growing-risk-of-displacement/.

35. Fairmount Ventures, *Strategic Plan for Mount Moriah Cemetery*, 2.

36. Ibid. 2, 6.

37. The strategic plan for Mount Moriah echoes this sentiment, saying, "There is a cultural divide in terms of how the planners envision 'wonderful green space with leisure time potential' and how those who live in the neighborhood cope with day-to-day life and fears of gentrification. . . ." (133). Some of these tensions erupted when the Friends of Mount Moriah hosted another Halloween-themed arts and crafts market in the cemetery in October 2022. Neighbors, passing by in their cars, yelled that the event was disrespectful, and accused the attendees of partying on people's graves. This was not the case; the event had been carefully planned to keep traffic away from gravesites. It serves as an important fundraiser for the fuel and equipment costs the Friends incur in their work. But Jenn and others took the experience as an important sign that communication with the community around the cemetery still needed to improve. Jenn O'Donnell, interview with the author, November 6, 2022; see also K'Cee Horne, Facebook post on the Friends of Mount Moriah Cemetery page, October 10, 2022, https://www.facebook.com/groups/Fommci/posts/5502936159771370/.

38. Jo Cosgrove, interview with the author, April 11, 2021.

39. "Maggie L. Walker Historic Gravesite Spray-Painted," WWBT/NBC12, August 4, 2020, https://www.nbc12.com/2020/08/03/maggie-l-walker-historic-gravesite-spray-painted/.

40. Deidre Barnes, "Re: From Troubling News—to Renewed Resolve (FoGC board ONLY)," email message to Friends of Geer Cemetery board members, December 7, 2020. Used with permission.

Conclusion: Fields of Weeds, Fields of Care

1. Brian Palmer, conversation with the author, April 28, 2023.

BIBLIOGRAPHY

Abel, Joanne. "Persistence and Sacrifice: Durham County's African American Community and Durham's Jeanes Teachers Build Community and Schools, 1900–1930." Master's thesis, Duke University, 2009.

"About | East Marshall Street Well Project." Virginia Commonwealth University. Accessed May 30, 2023. https://emsw.vcu.edu/about/.

"About | Friends of Mount Moriah Cemetery." Accessed May 31, 2023. https://friendsof mountmoriahcemetery.org/about/.

"About the Hart Island Project." Hart Island Project. Accessed May 31, 2023. https:// www.hartisland.net/about.

"About Us." International Sites of Conscience. Accessed May 31, 2023. http://www. sitesofconscience.org/en/who-we-are/about-us/.

Adams, Carol J. "The War on Compassion." *Antennae: The Journal of Nature in Visual Culture* (Autumn 2010): 5–11.

Adams, Char. "The Growing Movement to Save Black Cemeteries." NBC News, February 10, 2022. https://www.nbcnews.com/news/nbcblk/growing-movement-black -cemeteries-rcna15566.

Alexander, Kaylee P. "Reclaiming Marginalized Deaths Through Data Analysis, The Case of Geer Cemetery." Friends of Geer Cemetery, May 1, 2023. https://friendsof geercemetery.org/index.php/2023/06/16/reclaiming-marginalized-deaths/.

Allen, Taylor. "Report: West Philadelphia Renters Face a Growing Risk of Displacement." WHYY, December 16, 2020. https://whyy.org/articles/west-philadelphia -renters-face-a-growing-risk-of-displacement/.

Alvarez, Beatrice. "Black Quilters: Historians and Memory Keepers." PBS. Accessed May 22, 2023. https://www.pbs.org/articles/black-quilters-historians-and-memory -keepers.

Amanik, Allan. "'A Beautiful Garden Consecrated to the Lord': Marriage, Death, and Local Constructions of Citizenship in New York's Nineteenth-Century Jewish Rural Cemeteries." In *Till Death Do Us Part*, edited by Allan Amanik and Kami Fletcher, 16–34. Jackson: University Press of Mississippi, 2020.

Amanik, Allan, and Kami Fletcher. *Till Death Do Us Part: American Ethnic Cemeteries as Borders Uncrossed.* Jackson: University Press of Mississippi, 2020.

Appleman, Laura I. "Deviancy, Dependency, and Disability: The Forgotten History of Eugenics and Mass Incarceration." *Duke Law Journal* 68, no. 3 (December 2018): 417–78. https://dlj.law.duke.edu/article/deviancy-dependency-and-disability-appleman-vol68-iss3/.

Ariès, Philippe. *The Hour of Our Death.* Translated by Helen Weaver. New York: Alfred A. Knopf, 1981.

"Ascendant: The Power of Descendant Communities to Shape Our Stories, Places and Future," Thomas Jefferson's Monticello. June 18, 2022. https://www.monticello.org/exhibits-events/calendar-of-events/ascendant/.

Auslander, Mark. "Saying Something Now: Documentary Work and the Voices of the Dead." *Michigan Quarterly Review* 44, no. 4 (Fall 2005): 685–703. ProQuest.

Barber, Benjamin R. "The Art of Public Space." *The Nation*, August 12, 2009. https://www.thenation.com/article/archive/art-public-space/.

Benjamin, Ruha. "Black AfterLives Matter." *Boston Review*, July 11, 2018. https://bostonreview.net/articles/ruha-benjamin-black-afterlives-matter/.

Ben-Moshe, Liat. *Decarcerating Disability: Deinstitutionalization and Prison Abolition.* Minneapolis: University of Minnesota Press, 2020.

Berry, Daina Ramey. *The Price for Their Pound of Flesh: The Value of the Enslaved, from Womb to Grave, in the Building of a Nation.* Boston: Beacon Press, 2017.

Berry, Wendell. "How to Be a Poet." *Poetry Magazine.* Accessed October 29, 2020. https://www.poetryfoundation.org/poetrymagazine/poems/41087/how-to-be-a-poet.

Blakey, Michael L. "African Burial Ground Project: Paradigm for Cooperation?" *Museum International* 62, no. 1/2 (May 2010): 61–68. https://doi.org/10.1111/j.1468-0033.2010.01716.x.

———. "Walking the Ancestors Home: On the Road to an Ethical Human Biology." *Anthropology Now* 14, no. 1-2 (2022): 1-20.

Blitz, Matt. "'The Second Desecration of Our Ancestors': Activists Fight Construction Near Historic Cemetery in Bethesda." DCist, July 8, 2020. https://dcist.com/story/20/07/08/moses-african-cemetery-bethesda-preservation-protests/.

"Body of Woman Identified Here." *Richmond Times-Dispatch,* September 6, 1956. Newspapers.com.

Bogel-Burroughs, Nicholas. "At Daunte Wright Funeral, Minneapolis Mourns the 'Prince of Brooklyn Center.'" *The New York Times*, April 22, 2021. https://www.nytimes.com/2021/04/22/us/daunte-wright-funeral.html.

Bolin, Annalisa, and David Nkusi. "What Does It Mean to Decolonize Heritage?" *Sapiens*, October 6, 2021. https://www.sapiens.org/culture/decolonizing-heritage/.

Bonilla-Silva, Eduardo. *Racism without Racists: Color-Blind Racism and the Persistence of Racial Inequality in America.* Fifth edition. Lanham, MD: Rowman & Littlefield Publishers, 2017.

Bonis, Ray, and Selden Richardson. "The Shame of Evergreen Cemetery—What Do You Think?" *The Shockoe Examiner: Blogging the History of Richmond, Virginia*, August 10, 2015. https://theshockoeexaminer.blogspot.com/2015/08/the-shame-of-ever green-cemetery-what-do.html.

Bottum, Joseph. "Death & Politics." *First Things*, June 2007. https://www.firstthings.com/article/2007/06/001-death-politics.

———. "The Unhaunted Graveyard." Review of *The Work of the Dead: A Cultural History of Mortal Remains*, by Thomas W. Laqueur. The Washington Free Beacon, January 2, 2016. https://freebeacon.com/culture/the-unhaunted-graveyard/.

Bowean, Lolly. "The Unspoken History Hidden Behind a Surname." *Chicago Tribune*, December 16, 2017. https://www.chicagotribune.com/opinion/commentary/ct-per spec-surname-names-history-heritage-1227-20171221-story.html.

Brown, Leslie. *Upbuilding Black Durham: Gender, Class, and Black Community Development in the Jim Crow South*. Chapel Hill: University of North Carolina Press, 2008.

Buckley, Benjamin Gilbert. "Perpetual Care: A Sustainable Approach to Restoring the Lost Landscapes of America's Rural Cemeteries." Master's thesis, University of Pennsylvania, 2013. https://repository.upenn.edu/cgi/viewcontent.cgi?article=15 48&context=hp_theses.

Burch, Susan. *Committed: Remembering Native Kinship in and Beyond Institutions*. Chapel Hill: University of North Carolina Press, 2021.

Burch, Susan, and Hannah Joyner. *Unspeakable: The Story of Junius Wilson*. Chapel Hill: University of North Carolina Press, 2007.

Butler, Judith. *Frames of War: When Is Life Grievable?* London: Verso, 2009.

Butler-Kisber, Lynn. *Qualitative Inquiry: Thematic, Narrative and Arts-Informed Perspectives*, 2nd ed. Los Angeles: Sage, 2018.

Byrnes, Jennifer F., and Iván Sandoval-Cervantes, eds. *The Marginalized in Death: A Forensic Anthropology of Intersectional Identity in the Modern Era*. Lanham, MD: Lexington Books, 2022.

Caiola, Sammy. "57 Blocks in Philly Are Prone to Shootings. Community Groups Are Mobilizing to Curb the Gun Violence." *The Philadelphia Tribune*, December 23, 2022. https://www.phillytrib.com/news/local_news/57-blocks-in-philly-are-prone -to-shootings-community-groups-are-mobilizing-to-curb-the/article_c50ef3a5 -2967-50f9-838c-9c9dc725bef9.html.

———. "Philly Faith Leaders Try to Create Safe Havens from Gun Violence during Ramadan and Beyond." WHYY, April 18, 2023. https://whyy.org/articles/philly-rama dan-baitul-aafiyat-mosque-iftar-gun-violence-prevention/.

Callahan, Joan. "Harming the Dead." *Ethics* 97, no. 2 (1987): 341–52.

Carroll, Megan. "Brambles Choke a Cemetery." *News and Observer*, July 1, 2003.

Causey, Andrew. *Drawn to See: Drawing as an Ethnographic Method*. North York, Ontario: University of Toronto Press, 2017.

"The Cemeteries at Evergreen Family Council." The Cemeteries at Evergreen. Accessed May 29, 2023 (page no longer available). https://cemeverstg.wpengine.com/.

Chaplin, Eric and Sarah Holding. "Addressing the Post-Urban: Los Angeles, Las Vegas, New York." In *The Hieroglyphics of Space: Reading and Experiencing the Modern Metropolis*, edited by Neil Leach, 185–200. London: Routledge, 2001.

Chicora Foundation, Inc. "Frequently Asked Questions." Accessed May 30, 2023. https://chicora.org/faqs.html.

Clarke, Adele, and Donna Haraway, eds. *Making Kin Not Population: Reconceiving Generations*. Chicago: Prickly Paradigm Press, 2018.

Coates, Ta-Nehisi. "The Case for Reparations." *The Atlantic*, June 2014. https://www.theatlantic.com/magazine/archive/2014/06/the-case-for-reparations/361631/.

Cobb, Jelani. "Would Showing Graphic Images of Mass Shootings Spur Action to Stop Them?" *The New Yorker*, June 4, 2022. https://www.newyorker.com/news/daily-comment/would-showing-graphic-images-of-mass-shootings-spur-action-to-stop-them.

Cole, Tim. "Crematoria, Barracks, Gateway: Survivors' Return Visits to the Memory Landscapes of Auschwitz." *History and Memory* 25, no. 2 (2013): 102–31. https://doi.org/10.2979/histmemo.25.2.102.

Colwell, Chip. "How the Archaeological Review Behind the Dakota Access Pipeline Went Wrong." The Conversation, November 20, 2016. https://theconversation.com/how-the-archaeological-review-behind-the-dakota-access-pipeline-went-wrong-67815.

Consolidated Appropriations Act, 2023. Pub. L. No. 117-328 (2022). http://www.congress.gov/bill/117th-congress/house-bill/2617.

Cruz-Santiago, Arely. "Lists, Maps, and Bones: The Untold Journeys of Citizen-Led Forensics in Mexico." *Victims & Offenders* 15, no. 3 (April 2, 2020): 350–69. https://doi.org/10.1080/15564886.2020.1718046.

Dan-Cohen, Meir. "Revising the Past: On the Metaphysics of Repentance, Forgiveness, and Pardon." In *Forgiveness, Mercy, and Clemency*, edited by Austin Sarat and Nasser Hussain, 117–37. Stanford, CA: Stanford University Press, 2007.

Dantzler, Nicole. "Richmond Nonprofits Hurt by Enrichmond's Breakup Could Receive Funds Through New Grant." WRIC, July 19, 2023. https://www.wric.com/news/local-news/richmond/richmond-nonprofits-hurt-by-enrichmonds-breakup-could-receive-funds-through-new-grant/.

Danvers State Memorial Committee. "History of Our Work." 2001. http://dsmc.info/work.shtml.

Davis, Veronica A. *Here I Lay My Burdens Down: A History of the Black Cemeteries of Richmond, Virginia*. Richmond, VA: Dietz Press, 2003.

De Baets, Antoon. "A Declaration of the Responsibilities of Present Generations Toward Past Generations." *History and Theory* 43, no. 4 (2004): 130–64.

———. *Responsible History*. New York: Berghahn Books, 2008.

Deegan, Patricia E. *From Numbers to Names.* Coproduced by Laurie Block and Bestor Cram. Northern Light Productions, 2010. Video, 13:52. https://www.common groundprogram.com/blog/from-numbers-to-names.

De León, Jason. *The Land of Open Graves: Living and Dying on the Migrant Trail.* Berkeley: University of California Press, 2015.

"Department of the Interior Releases Investigative Report, Outlines Next Steps in Federal Indian Boarding School Initiative." U.S. Department of the Interior. May 11, 2022. https://www.doi.gov/pressreleases/department-interior-releases-investiga tive-report-outlines-next-steps-federal-indian.

DeSilvey, Caitlin. *Curated Decay: Heritage Beyond Saving.* Minneapolis: University of Minnesota Press, 2017.

"Died: To the Durham, N.C. Herald." *Durham Morning Herald* (published as *The Morning Herald*). September 26, 1909. Provided to the author by Deidre Barnes and the Friends of Geer Cemetery.

Doherty, Christopher. "Confederates, Catholics, Muslims and Masons: The Mount Moriah Cemetery Tour." *The Necessity for Ruins*, December 1, 2007. https://ruins. wordpress.com/2007/12/01/mount-moriah-cemetery/.

"Doris Belk Tilley Obituary (1924–2017)." *The Herald Sun*, December 29, 2017. Legacy. com. https://www.legacy.com/us/obituaries/heraldsun/name/doris-tilley -obituary?id=11788555.

Downs, Jim. *Sick from Freedom: African-American Illness and Suffering during the Civil War and Reconstruction.* Oxford: Oxford University Press, 2015.

Du Bois, W. E. B. "The Upbuilding of Black Durham. The Success of the Negroes and Their Value to a Tolerant and Helpful Southern City." *The World's Work*, January 1912. Documenting the American South, The North Carolina Experience. https:// docsouth.unc.edu/nc/dubois/dubois.html#p335.

Dunnavant, Justin, Delande Justinvil, and Chip Colwell. "Craft an African American Graves Protection and Repatriation Act." *Nature* 593, no. 7859 (May 2021): 337–40. https://www.nature.com/articles/d41586-021-01320-4.

"Durham Cemetery Survey." Writing 101: The Archaeology of Durham, Duke University, taught by Andrew Tharler. ArcGIS StoryMaps, April 18, 2022. https://storymaps .arcgis.com/stories/883c26dcc202489caea3e107e9830301.

Easley-DeLuca, Anjelyque. "Cemeteries, Construction, and Complicity: Tyler's Universe Cemetery as a Black Burial Site Under Distress." Master's thesis, University of Texas Arlington, 2022. https://rc.library.uta.edu/uta-ir/handle/10106/30242.

"East End and Evergreen Preservation Plans Letter," July 6, 2021. https://acrobat.adobe .com/link/track?uri=urn%3Aaaid%3Ascds%3AUS%3A52d8a359-d1d7-420c-8e32 -e83a0b078f9a#pageNum=1.

"East End Cemetery Map." East End Cemetery Collaboratory. Accessed May 26, 2023. https://cemeterycollaboratory.org/east-end-cemetery-map/.

"East End Oral History Project: Thomas A. Taylor, Extended Interview." Friends of East

End Cemetery. July 7, 2020. YouTube video. https://www.youtube.com/watch?v=Icu2kmP5gN0.

Eggener, Keith. "Our First Public Parks: The Forgotten History of Cemeteries." Interview by Rebecca Greenfield. *The Atlantic*, March 16, 2011. https://www.theatlantic.com/national/archive/2011/03/our-first-public-parks-the-forgotten-history-of-cemeteries/71818/.

Elbow, Peter. *Writing with Power: Techniques for Mastering the Writing Process.* New York: Oxford University Press, 1998.

"Enrichmond Foundation—Evergreen Cemetery Legacy #RVA #Enrichmond #History." Enrichmond Foundation. May 17, 2021. YouTube video. https://www.youtube.com/watch?v=NYaBRWDmUaw.

"Enrichmond Foundation—Response to False Rumors (#RVA #Communityovercontest)." Enrichmond Foundation. May 3, 2021. YouTube video. https://www.youtube.com/watch?v=nb4eNFpgARU.

Eustice, David. "Geer #2." February 22, 2012. YouTube video. 9:14. https://www.youtube.com/watch?v=akHaj9n_CIE&t=3s.

Eustice, Jessica T. "The Geer Cemetery." Master's thesis, North Carolina Central University, June 8, 2002. Courtesy of the Friends of Geer Cemetery.

———. "Geer Cemetery Emerges as a Historic Cemetery." *The Herald Sun*, June 28, 2015. Allen Dew Genealogy. http://www.apdew.com/FOGC/2015-06-28-news.pdf.

Evans, Ben. "Geer Cemetery Cleanup on the Way." *The Herald-Sun*, January 20, 2004. Access World News—Historical and Current.

Fachner, George, and Steven Carter. *An Assessment of Deadly Force in the Philadelphia Police Department.* Collaborative Reform Initiative. Washington, DC: Office of Community Oriented Policing Services, 2015. https://www.phillypolice.com/assets/directives/cops-w0753-pub.pdf.

Fairmount Ventures. *Strategic Plan for Mount Moriah Cemetery.* November 2018.

Farmer, Paul. "An Anthropology of Structural Violence." *Current Anthropology* 45, no. 3 (2004): 305–25. https://doi.org/10.1086/382250.

Farrell, James J. *Inventing the American Way of Death, 1830–1920.* Philadelphia: Temple University Press, 1980.

Ferguson, James. *The Anti-Politics Machine: Development, Depoliticization, and Bureaucratic Power in Lesotho.* Minneapolis: University of Minnesota Press, 1994.

Figueroa IV, Daniel. "Abandoned Cemeteries Task Force Adds 'Teeth' and New Category to Policy Framework." *Florida Politics*, November 30, 2021. https://floridapolitics.com/archives/476555-abandoned-cemeteries-task-force-adds-teeth-and-new-category-to-policy-framework/.

Fine-Dare, Kathleen S. *Grave Injustice: The American Indian Repatriation Movement and NAGPRA.* Fourth World Rising Series. Lincoln: University of Nebraska Press, 2002.

Fink, Jennifer Natalya. *All Our Families: Disability Lineage and the Future of Kinship.* Boston: Beacon Press, 2022.

Fink, Marty. *Forget Burial: HIV Kinship, Disability, and Queer/Trans Narratives of Care.* New Brunswick, NJ: Rutgers University Press, 2021.

First-Arai, Leanna. "Even in Death, Black Bodies Face Environmental Racism." Truthout, July 10, 2020. https://truthout.org/articles/even-in-death-black-bodies-face-environmental-racism/.

First Baptist Church (Philadelphia), "Lists of burials for removal to Mount Moriah Cemetery, 1860," *Philadelphia Congregations Early Records.* https://philadelphiacongregations.org/records/item/ABHS.FBCGravesForRemovalToMtMoriah1860.

Fletcher, Kami. "Race and the Funeral Profession: What Jessica Mitford Missed." *TalkDeath*, December 2, 2018. https://www.talkdeath.com/race-funeral-profession-what-jessica-mitford-missed/.

Flis, Nathan, and David Wright. "'A Grave Injustice': The Mental Hospital and Shifting Sites of Memory." In *Exhibiting Madness in Museums*, edited by Catharine Coleborne and Dolly MacKinnon, 101–15. London: Routledge, 2011.

Floyd, Jerrel. "I Went in Search of Abandoned African-American Cemeteries." ProPublica, June 29, 2018. https://www.propublica.org/article/abandoned-african-american-cemeteries-illinois-jerrel-floyd?token=xbvF5KLcDIV6vr6B2AF9DoLlUK_IwLni.

Foltz, Caitlin Doucette. "Race and Mental Illness at a Virginia Hospital: A Case Study of Central Lunatic Asylum for the Colored Insane, 1869–1885," Master's thesis, Virginia Commonwealth University, 2015. https://doi.org/10.25772/RRJX-NN19.

Foote, Kenneth E. *Shadowed Ground: America's Landscapes of Violence and Tragedy.* Austin: University of Texas Press, 2003.

Forensic Architecture and RISE St. James. "Environmental Racism in Death Alley, Louisiana." Forensic Architecture, June 28, 2021. https://forensic-architecture.org/investigation/environmental-racism-in-death-alley-louisiana.

Forsythe, Pamela J. "The Long Road Ahead to Resurrect Mount Moriah." WHYY, December 3, 2014. https://whyy.org/articles/the-long-road-ahead-to-resurrect-mount-moriah/.

Foucault, Michel. "Lives of Infamous Men." In *The Essential Foucault: Selections from Essential Works of Foucault, 1954–1984*, edited by Paul Rabinow and Nikolas Rose. New York: New Press, 2003.

———. *Power/Knowledge: Selected Interviews and Other Writings, 1972–1977.* Edited by Colin Gordon. Translated by Colin Gordon, Leo Marshall, John Mepham, and Kate Soper. 1st American ed. New York: Pantheon Books, 1980.

Francis, Doris. "Cemeteries as Cultural Landscapes." *Mortality* 8, no. 2 (2003): 222–27.

Friedemann-Sanchez, Greta. "Antropología pública y comprometida: el legado de Nina

S. de Friedemann." *Revista Antípoda*, no. 46 (January 1, 2022): 23–51. https://doi.org
/10.7440/antipoda46.2022.02.

Fullilove, Mindy Thompson. *Root Shock: How Tearing Up City Neighborhoods Hurts
America, And What We Can Do About It.* New York: NYU Press, 2016.

Gallegos, Andrés J. "NCD Letter to NGA Re: Vaccine Allocation." Letter to Andrew
Cuomo. National Council on Disability. February 9, 2021. https://ncd.gov/publica
tions/2021/ncd-letter-nga-re-vaccine-allocation.

Galtung, Johan. "Violence, Peace, and Peace Research." *Journal of Peace Research* 6, no.
3 (1969): 167–91. https://doi.org/10.1177/002234336900600301.

"Geer Cemetery—in Plain Sight." November 25, 2020. https://durhaminplainsight.com
/about/.

"Geer Cemetery: Labor, Dignity, and Practices of Freedom in an African American
Burial Ground." John Hope Franklin Humanities Institute. 2021. https://fhi.duke.
edu/story-plus-project/geer-cemetery-labor-dignity-and-practices-freedom
-african-american-burial-ground.

Giago, Tim. "Paying Tribute to Harold Iron Shield." Indianz.Com, February 27, 2008.
https://www.indianz.com/News/2008/007334.asp.

Gilpin, Laura. *The Hocus-Pocus of the Universe.* Garden City, NY: Doubleday, 1977.

Gordon, Avery F. *Ghostly Matters: Haunting and the Sociological Imagination.* Minneapolis: University of Minnesota Press, 2008.

Gordon, Grace. "'For the Best Interest of the Patient and of Society'; Sterilization in
Virginia's Mental Institutions in the 20th Century." Senior Honors Projects, James
Madison University, May 13, 2022. https://commons.lib.jmu.edu/cgi/viewcontent
.cgi?article=1159&context=honors202029.

Gough, Meghan Z., Kathryn Howell, and Hannah Cameron. "The Structural Challenge
of Power and Whiteness in Planning: Evidence from Historic Black Cemetery Restoration." *Planning Theory & Practice* 23, no. 4 (2022): 536–55, https://doi.org/10
.1080/14649357.2022.2113557.

Graff, Henry. "FBI, Attorney General Investigating Enrichmond Foundation Missing
Money." NBC 12, April 5, 2023. https://www.nbc12.com/2023/04/05/fbi-virginia-at
torney-general-investigating-enrichmond-foundation-missing-money/.

———. "New Documents Shed Light on Missing Money Following Enrichmond Foundation Collapse." NBC 12, April 6, 2023. https://www.nbc12.com/2023/04/06/new
-documents-shed-light-missing-money-following-enrichmond-foundation-col
lapse/.

Gravetender. "Perpetual Care Isn't What You Think It Is." *Gravewords*, January 31, 2021.
https://gravewords.wordpress.com/2012/01/31/perpetual-care-isnt-what-you-think
-it-is/.

Green, Alex. "A Holiday Light Show in Waltham Obscures a Devastating History."
WBUR Cognoscenti, November 19, 2020. https://www.wbur.org/cognoscenti/2020/
11/19/fernald-waltham-disability-rights-history-alex-green.

————. "Process: Editor's Note." 2017. MetFern Cemetery. Accessed September 29, 2023. http://metfern.org/process.

Green, Alex, Yoni Kadden, Kevin Levin, Jacob Daitzman, Seth Battis, Susan Cheloff, Joshua Gutoff, Landa Ruen, and John Loeppky. "The MetFern Cemetery." 2017. MetFern Cemetery. Accessed September 29, 2023. http://metfern.org/.

Greenidge, Kaitlyn. "What Walmart Doesn't Get About Juneteenth." *The New York Times*, June 18, 2021. https://www.nytimes.com/2021/06/18/opinion/juneteenth-emancipation-walmart.html.

Griego, Tina. "Into the Light." *Richmond Magazine*, September 8, 2015. https://richmondmagazine.com/api/content/ebcbcf88-5658-11e5-8b3e-22000b078648/.

Grim, Ryan. "Rikers Island Prisoners Are Being Offered PPE and $6 an Hour to Dig Mass Graves." The Intercept, March 31, 2020. https://theintercept.com/2020/03/31/rikers-island-coronavirus-mass-graves/.

Gumbs, Alexis Pauline. "Even in the Grave, Black People Can't Rest in Durham." *INDY Week*, February 25, 2020. https://indyweek.com/news/voices/even-in-the-grave-black-people-cant-rest-in-durham/.

Hagerty, Alexa. *Still Life with Bones: Genocide, Forensics, and What Remains*. New York: Crown, 2023.

Hall, Tia, Kimber Heinz, Robert Korstad, Melissa Norton, and Tim Stallman. "Uneven Ground: Dismantling Hayti." Bull City 150. 2017. Accessed May 29, 2023. https://www.bullcity150.org/uneven_ground/dismantling_hayti/.

Hanley, Robert. "Tombstones Defaced with Pro-Nazi Slogans in North Jersey Jewish Cemetery." *The New York Times*, September 22, 1993. https://www.nytimes.com/1993/09/22/nyregion/tombstones-defaced-with-pro-nazi-slogans-in-north-jersey-jewish-cemetery.html.

Haraway, Donna J. *Staying with the Trouble: Making Kin in the Chthulucene*. Durham, NC: Duke University Press, 2016.

Harding, Vanessa. "Whose Body? A Study of Attitudes Towards the Dead Body in Early Modern Paris." In *The Place of the Dead: Death and Remembrance in Late Medieval and Early Modern Europe*, edited by Bruce Gordon and Peter Marshall, 170–87. Cambridge: Cambridge University Press, 2000.

Harmon, Louise. "Honoring Our Silent Neighbors to the South: The Problem of Abandoned or Forgotten Asylum Cemeteries." *Touro Law Review* 34, no. 4 (2018): 901–82.

Hartman, Saidiya. "Venus in Two Acts." *Small Axe* 12, no. 2 (2008): 1–14. https://doi.org/10.1215/-12-2-1.

————. *Wayward Lives, Beautiful Experiments: Intimate Histories of Social Upheaval*. New York: W. W. Norton, 2019.

Hauser, Christine, and Isabella Grullón Paz. "U.S. to Search Former Native American Schools for Children's Remains." *The New York Times*, June 23, 2021. https://www.nytimes.com/2021/06/23/us/indigenous-children-indian-civilization-act-1819.html.

Hauslohner, Abigail. "'Muslim Town': A Look Inside Philadelphia's Thriving Muslim Culture." *The Washington Post*, July 21, 2017. https://www.washingtonpost.com/news/post-nation/wp/2017/07/21/muslim-town-how-one-american-city-embraced-a-muslim-community-in-decline/.

"HB 1547—Virginia House (2017)." Open States. https://openstates.org/va/bills/2017/HB1547/.

Henderson, Lisa Y. "Lane Street Project: Cemetery Records Request Update, No. 5, the City's Response." *Black Wide-Awake*, February 23, 2020. https://afamwilsonnc.com/2020/02/23/cemetery-records-request-update-no-5-the-citys-response/.

———. "Lane Street Project: March 27 Mini-Projects." *Black Wide-Awake*, March 24, 2021. https://afamwilsonnc.com/2021/03/24/lane-street-project-march-27-mini-projects/.

———. "Lane Street Project: Seek and Ye Shall Find." *Black Wide-Awake*, July 8, 2022. https://afamwilsonnc.com/2022/07/08/lane-street-project-seek-and-ye-shall-find/.

Holloway, Karla FC. *Passed On: African American Mourning Stories, A Memorial.* Durham: Duke University Press, 2003.

Holtzclaw, Mike. "Rest in Peace? Ashe's Grave Sparks Controversy." *Daily Press*, June 13, 1993. https://www.dailypress.com/news/dp-xpm-19930613-1993-06-13-9306130080-story.html.

Inge, Leoneda. "Blacks on the Move, Back to the South." *News & Notes.* North Carolina Public Radio, April 20, 2006. Audio, 5:57. https://www.npr.org/templates/story/story.php?storyId=5353041.

"In Plain Sight—Geer Cemetery Exhibit Opening." Friends of Geer Cemetery. January 23, 2021. YouTube video. https://www.youtube.com/watch?v=6BZPlb92DlQ.

"In Plain Sight—Reclaiming Hidden Histories." Friends of Geer Cemetery. February 20, 2021. YouTube video. https://www.youtube.com/watch?v=9HW_6xQ76uA.

"Inquest Clears Mother in 'Pepper Death' of Son." *The Daily Intelligencer*, January 29, 1960. Newspapers.com.

"Investment Advisor Sentenced in Fraud That Added to NC Mutual's Troubles." *Insurance Journal*, October 31, 2022. https://www.insurancejournal.com/news/southeast/2022/10/31/692364.htm.

Jablow, Paul. "After Decades of Neglect, Volunteers Work to Save a Historic Main Line Jewish Cemetery." *The Inquirer*, December 28, 2022. https://www.inquirer.com/real-estate/gladwyne-jewish-memorial-cemetery-har-hasetim-beth-david-20221228.html.

Jackson, Antoinette T. *Speaking for the Enslaved: Heritage Interpretation at Antebellum Plantation Sites.* Heritage, Tourism, and Community. Walnut Creek, CA: Left Coast Press, 2012.

Jackson, Estelle. "Cemeteries Fight Losing Battle." *Richmond Times-Dispatch*, July 22, 1981, sec. C, 1–2. Courtesy of John Shuck.

Jackson, Steven J. "Rethinking Repair." In *Media Technologies: Essays on Communica-*

tion, Materiality, and Society, edited by Tarleton Gillespie, Pablo J. Boczkowski, and Kirsten A. Foot, 221–40. Cambridge, MA: MIT Press, 2014.

Jamieson, Ross W. "Material Culture and Social Death: African-American Burial Practices." *Historical Archaeology* 29, no. 4 (1995): 39–58. https://doi.org/10.1007/bf033 74216.

Jenkins, Erin. "Enrichmond Acquires Evergreen Cemetery." Enrichmond Foundation. May 24, 2017. Site inactive as of June 2022. Accessed via Internet Archive May 31, 2023. https://web.archive.org/web/20221002042632/https://enrichmond.org/2017/ 05/enrichmond-evergreen/.

Jerkins, Morgan. "Black Cemetery Loss Is a National Crisis." ZORA, July 15, 2020. https: //zora.medium.com/black-cemetery-loss-is-a-national-crisis-875adf6b7448.

Johnson, Charles. "Historic Fayetteville St.: The Fifth Avenue of Black Durham." Durham County Library/Digital NC. https://deegsnccu.maps.arcgis.com/apps/Cas cade/index.html?appid=75566fb038b24ebc90b2b51f72fb5c74.

Kaiser, Menachem. *Plunder: A Memoir of Family Property and Nazi Treasure.* Boston: Houghton Mifflin Harcourt, 2021.

Kastenbaum, Robert, and Christopher Moreman. *Death, Society, and Human Experience.* 12th ed. Routledge, 2018.

Kebeder, Laura. "Volunteers Rescue 4 Cemeteries." *Richmond Times-Dispatch*, February 16, 2014. NewsBank.

Keels, Thomas H. *Philadelphia Graveyards and Cemeteries.* Images of America: Pennsylvania. Mount Pleasant, SC: Arcadia Publishing, 2003.

Kendall, Jonathan. "Remembering When Americans Picnicked in Cemeteries." Atlas Obscura, October 18, 2021. https://www.atlasobscura.com/articles/picnic-in-ceme teries-america.

Kilgannon, Corey. "A Million Bodies Are Buried Here. Now It's Becoming a Park." *The New York Times*, March 24, 2023. https://www.nytimes.com/2023/03/24/nyregion/ hart-island-cemetery-park.html.

———. "Dead of AIDS and Forgotten in Potter's Field." *The New York Times*, July 3, 2018. https://www.nytimes.com/2018/07/03/nyregion/hart-island-aids-new-york.html.

Kim, Jaymelee, and Adam Richard Rosenblatt. "Whose Humanitarianism? Whose Forensic Anthropology?" In *Anthropology of Violent Death: Theoretical Foundations for Forensic Humanitarian Action*, edited by Roberto C. Parra and Douglas H. Ubelaker, 153–176. Hoboken, NJ: John Wiley & Sons, 2023.

Kirk, Robin. "Reflections on a Silent Soldier." *The American Scholar*, September 3, 2019. https://theamericanscholar.org/reflections-on-a-silent-soldier/.

Klinkenborg, Verlyn. *Several Short Sentences About Writing.* New York: Vintage Books, 2013.

Krasner, Jonathan. "The Place of Tikkun Olam in American Jewish Life." *Jewish Political Studies Review* 25, no. 3–4 (November 1, 2014). https://jcpa.org/article/place-tik kun-olam-american-jewish-life1/.

Kreuger, Sarah. "'Black Wall Street' Icon NC Mutual Life Insurance Company Begins Liquidation Process." WRAL, October 11, 2022. https://www.wral.com/story/black -wall-street-icon-nc-mutual-life-insurance-company-begins-liquidation-process/ 20517940/.

Kueber, Gary. "Geer Cemetery." Open Durham. Last modified August 20, 2011. https:// www.opendurham.org/buildings/geer-cemetery.

Laderman, Gary. *The Sacred Remains: American Attitudes Toward Death, 1799–1883.* New Haven, CT: Yale University Press, 1999.

LaMotte, Sandee. "Cremation Has Replaced Traditional Burials in Popularity in America and People Are Getting Creative with Those Ashes." CNN, January 23, 2020. https://www.cnn.com/2020/01/22/health/cremation-trends-wellness/index.html.

Laqueur, Thomas W. *The Work of the Dead: A Cultural History of Mortal Remains.* Princeton, NJ: Princeton University Press, 2015.

LaRoche, Cheryl J., and Michael L. Blakey. "Seizing Intellectual Power: The Dialogue at the New York African Burial Ground." *Historical Archaeology* 31, no. 3 (September 1, 1997): 84–106. https://doi.org/10.1007/BF03374233.

Lazarus, Jeremy M. "City Officials Debate How to Investigate Defunct Nonprofit." *Richmond Free Press*, July 28, 2022. http://richmondfreepress.com/news/2022/jul/28/ city-officials-debate-how-investigate-defunct-nonp/.

———. "Enrichmond Foundation's Status Is Unclear." *Richmond Free Press*, June 30, 2022. http://richmondfreepress.com/news/2022/jun/30/enrichmond-foundations -status-unclear/.

———. "Enrichmond Unveils $18.6M Master Plan for Evergreen Cemetery." *Richmond Free Press*, March 6, 2020. http://richmondfreepress.com/news/2020/mar/06/ enrichmond-unveils-186m-master-plan-evergreen-ceme/.

———. "History Marker to Be Placed at Shockoe Hill African Burying Ground." *Richmond Free Press*, June 24, 2021. http://richmondfreepress.com/news/2021/jun/24/ history-marker-be-placed-shockoe-hill-african-bury/.

———. "Woodland Cemetery Sale Completed to Nonprofit Evergreen Restoration Foundation." *Richmond Free Press*, August 6, 2020. http://richmondfreepress.com/ news/2020/aug/06/woodland-cemetery-sale-completed-nonprofit-evergre/.

"Lemon Project Committee on Memorialization." The Lemon Project, William & Mary. Accessed May 23, 2023. https://www.wm.edu/sites/lemonproject/memorialization %20/index.php.

Lepore, Jill. "When Black History Is Unearthed, Who Gets to Speak for the Dead?" *The New Yorker*, September 27, 2021. https://www.newyorker.com/magazine/2021/10/04 /when-black-history-is-unearthed-who-gets-to-speak-for-the-dead.

"Letter to the Honorable Ralph S. Northam," March 10, 2021. Accessed May 30, 2023. https://acrobat.adobe.com/link/track?uri=urn%3Aaaid%3Ascds%3AUS%3A592f a397-79df-4b02-b13f-e6ae5b0478b8#pageNum=1.

Levenson, Michael. "Protesters Topple Statue of Jefferson Davis on Richmond's Monument Avenue." *The New York Times*, June 11, 2020. https://www.nytimes.com/2020/06/11/us/Jefferson-Davis-Statue-Richmond.html.

Levinson, Amanda. "Reckoning with the Legacy of Jewish Enslavement of African Americans in the South." Medium, October 3, 2022. https://medium.com/@amanda_levinson/beyond-solidarity-reckoning-with-the-legacy-of-jewish-enslavement-of-african-americans-in-the-861da4860d44.

Linden-Ward, Blanche. *Silent City on a Hill: Landscapes of Memory and Boston's Mount Auburn Cemetery.* Columbus: Ohio State University Press, 1989.

"List of Unarmed African Americans Killed by Law Enforcement Officers in the United States." Wikipedia. September 4, 2021. Accessed May 31, 2023. https://en.wikipedia.org/wiki/List_of_unarmed_African_Americans_killed_by_law_enforcement_officers_in_the_United_States.

"Louis Farrakhan." Southern Poverty Law Center. Accessed October 24, 2022. https://www.splcenter.org/fighting-hate/extremist-files/individual/louis-farrakhan.

Low, Setha M., and Sally Engle Merry. "Engaged Anthropology: Diversity and Dilemmas." *Current Anthropology* 51, no. S2 (2010): S203–26. https://doi.org/10.1086/653837.

Mack, Kristen, and John Palfrey. "Capitalizing Black and White: Grammatical Justice and Equity." MacArthur Foundation, August 26, 2020. https://www.macfound.org/press/perspectives/capitalizing-black-and-white-grammatical-justice-and-equity.

Mack-Hardiman, David. *Of Grave Importance: The Restoration of Institutional Cemeteries.* Abandoned History Series. Buffalo, NY: Museum of disABILITY History and People Ink Press, 2014.

"Maggie L. Walker Historic Gravesite Spray-Painted." WWBT/NBC12, August 4, 2020. https://www.nbc12.com/2020/08/03/maggie-l-walker-historic-gravesite-spray-painted/.

Mason, Kyrie. "Things Which Don't Exist." *ROOM: A Sketchbook for Analytic Action*, March 9, 2021. https://analytic-room.com/essays/things-which-dont-exist-by-kyrie-mason/.

Massey, Doreen. "A Global Sense of Place." In *The Cultural Geography Reader*, edited by Timothy S. Oakes and Patricia L. Price, 269–275. London: Routledge, 2008.

McCrery, Anne, Erol Somay, and the Dictionary of Virginia Biography. "Mitchell, John Jr. (1863–1929)." Encyclopedia Virginia. Virginia Humanities, February 12, 2021. https://encyclopediavirginia.org/entries/mitchell-john-jr-1863-1929/.

McDonald, Thomasi. "Durham Residents Uncover Their Ancestral Legacies in the County's Old Black Cemeteries." *INDY Week*, September 1, 2021. http://indyweek.com/news/durham/durham-residents-are-uncovering-their-ancestral-legacies-in-countys-old-black-cemeteries/.

———. "Durham's Hayti District Receives $10 Million in Newly Adopted Budget for Rebuilding." *INDY Week*, June 28, 2023. http://indyweek.com/news/durham/durhams-newly-adopted-budget-includes-10-million-to-rebuild-hayti/.

"Meet Our Board." National Association of Park Foundations. Accessed September 21, 2023. https://www.the-napf.org/board.

Melville, Greg. *Over My Dead Body: Unearthing the Hidden History of America's Cemeteries*. New York: Abrams, 2022.

Miéville, China. *The City & The City*. New York: Del Rey Ballantine Books, 2009.

Mihesuah, Devon A. *Repatriation Reader: Who Owns American Indian Remains?* Lincoln: University of Nebraska Press, 2000.

Milbern, Stacey. "On the Ancestral Plane: Crip Hand Me Downs and the Legacy of Our Movements." Disability Visibility Project, March 10, 2019. https://disabilityvisibil ityproject.com/2019/03/10/on-the-ancestral-plane-crip-hand-me-downs-and-the -legacy-of-our-movements/.

"Millie Markham." Federal Writers' Project: Slave Narrative Project, Vol. 11, North Carolina, Part 2, Jackson-Yellerday. 1936. Manuscript/Mixed Material. https://www.loc .gov/item/mesn112/.

Mitford, Jessica. *The American Way of Death*. New York: Simon & Schuster, 1963.

Modest Mouse, "So Much Beauty in Dirt." Track 6 on *Everywhere and His Nasty Parlor Tricks*. Epic Records, 2001.

Modlin-Jackson, Cat. "A New Funding Stream for Historic African American Cemeteries." Radio IQ, August 18, 2020. https://www.wvtf.org/post/new-funding-stream -historic-african-american-cemeteries#stream/0.

Moodie, Ellen, and Leigh Binford. "Selling Affect, Seeing Blood: The Economy of Pain at El Mozote, El Salvador." In *Detours: Travel and the Ethics of Research in the Global South*, edited by M. Bianet Castellanos, 122–46. Tucson: University of Arizona Press, 2019.

Mortice, Zach. "Perpetual Neglect: The Preservation Crisis of African-American Cemeteries." *Places Journal*, May 30, 2017. https://doi.org/10.22269/170530.

Mount Moriah Cemetery Association of Philadelphia. "Mount Moriah Cemetery." Cooperative Printing Co., 1871. Courtesy of the Friends of Mount Moriah.

Muhammad, Michael Z. "Philadelphia Muslim Tends to Burial Ground for Believers." *The Final Call*, August 4, 2018.

Mulgan, Tim. "The Place of the Dead in Liberal Political Philosophy." *Journal of Political Philosophy* 7, no. 1 (1999): 52–70. https://doi.org/10.1111/1467-9760.00065.

Mullins, Paul R. *Revolting Things: An Archaeology of Shameful Histories and Repulsive Realities*. Gainesville: University Press of Florida, 2021.

Murray, Pauli. "Oral History Interview with Pauli Murray, February 13, 1976. Interview G-0044." Interview by Genna Rae McNeil. Southern Oral History Program Collection (#4007). Audio, 5:18:41. https://docsouth.unc.edu/sohp/playback.html?base_ file=G-0044&duration=05:18:41.

———. *Proud Shoes: The Story of an American Family*. Boston: Beacon Press, 1999.

Murrell, David. "What Happens When a Cemetery Dies?" *Philadelphia Magazine*, July

30, 2016. https://www.phillymag.com/news/2016/07/30/mount-moriah-cemetery-friends/.

"Naji Muhammad: The Passing of a Soldier's Soldier Who Was 'a Gift from God.'" *The Final Call*, June 7, 2022. https://new.finalcall.com/2022/06/07/naji-muhammad-the-passing-of-a-soldiers-soldier-who-was-a-gift-from-god/.

National Trust for Historic Preservation and African American Cultural Heritage Action Fund. *Engaging Descendant Communities in the Interpretation of Slavery at Museums and Historic Sites*. Version 1.0. Montpelier Station, VA: Montpelier Descendants Committee, 2018. https://montpelierdescendants.org/rubric/.

Nehusi, Kimani S. K. *Libation: An Afrikan Ritual of Heritage in the Circle of Life*. Lanham, MD: University Press of America, 2015.

Nelson, Maggie. "Let's Talk About the Anxiety Freedom Can Cause." Interview by Ezra Klein. *The Ezra Klein Show*. October 8, 2021. Transcript. https://www.nytimes.com/2021/10/08/podcasts/transcript-ezra-klein-interviews-maggie-nelson.html.

Nelson, Marilyn. "Communal Pondering in a Noisy World." Interview by Krista Tippet. *On Being*, February 23, 2017. Audio, 51:02. https://onbeing.org/programs/marilyn-nelson-communal-pondering-in-a-noisy-world/.

"Notice!!!" *The Richmond Planet*, page 8, February 8, 1902. Chronicling America: Historic American Newspapers. https://chroniclingamerica.loc.gov/lccn/sn84025841/1902-02-08/ed-1/seq-8/.

Odell, Jenny. *How to Do Nothing: Resisting the Attention Economy*. Brooklyn, NY: Melville House, 2019.

Page, Max. *Why Preservation Matters*. New Haven, CT: Yale University Press, 2016.

Palmer, Brian. "Confederate Monuments Topple in Richmond, Virginia." Reveal, August 17, 2020. http://revealnews.org/article/confederate-monuments-topple-in-richmond-virginia/.

———. "The Enrichmond Files." Medium, May 26, 2023. https://medium.com/@bxpnyc/the-enrichmond-files-948e0fbcd8af.

———. "Enwhatnow?" Medium, December 23, 2022. https://medium.com/@bxpnyc/enwhatnow-312157ef4ca7.

———. "For the Forgotten African-American Dead." *The New York Times*, January 7, 2017. https://www.nytimes.com/2017/01/07/opinion/sunday/for-the-forgotten-african-american-dead.html.

———. "Friends of East End Cemetery." Interview by Bret Payne. *Burning Bright*, July 2020. Audio, 41:29. https://open.spotify.com/episode/1wMTOoJW11ayBXDyzA6Jpk.

———. "Historic Black Cemeteries Need Substance from Lawmakers, Not Symbolism." Medium, July 15, 2022. https://medium.com/@bxpnyc/historic-black-cemeteries-need-substance-from-lawmakers-not-symbolism-aab2bfb93826.

———. "Into the Woods." Wok Docs, December 22, 2014. http://www.wokdocs.com/blog.

————. "It's the Looking That Matters: An Update on the Documentary." Wok Docs, September 13, 2016. http://www.wokdocs.com/blog.

————. "These Abandoned Black Cemeteries Were Long Forgotten—Until Now." Economic Hardship Reporting Project, June 9, 2016. http://economichardship.org/archive//these-abandoned-black-cemeteries-were-long-forgotten-until-now.

Palmer, Brian, and Seth Freed Wessler. "The Costs of the Confederacy." *Smithsonian Magazine*, December 2018. https://www.smithsonianmag.com/history/costs-con federacy-special-report-180970731/.

Palomba, Asia London and Szu Yu Chen. "Below the Surface: A Special Report." Accessed May 31, 2023. https://below-the-surface.github.io/main.html.

Palomba, Asia London. "The Quest to Honor Disabled Patients Buried in Anonymous Graves." Atlas Obscura, July 1, 2021. https://www.atlasobscura.com/articles/met fern-cemetery.

Parry, Tom. "Preserve Indigenous Residential Schools as Sites of Conscience, MPs Urged." CBC, September 26, 2017. https://www.cbc.ca/news/politics/indigenous -residential-schools-sites-ry-moran-1.4306944.

Pennsylvania Supreme Court. *Pennsylvania State Reports*. West Publishing Company, 1877. Google Books, 241.

Petrosino, Kiki, and Brian Palmer. "The Lives of East End: Recovering African American Burial Grounds." *The Virginia Quarterly Review* 96, no. 4 (Winter 2020): 60–83.

"Philadelphia Prison Population Report: July 2015-July 2023." Prison Policy Institute. Accessed October 2, 2023. https://www.phila.gov/media/20230811114011/July-2023 -Full-Public-Prison-Report.pdf.

Pradelli, Chad, Cheryl Mettendorf, and Maia Rosenfeld. "Data Investigation: Philadelphia Metro Area Among Most Racially Segregated in Country." 6abc Philadelphia, July 22, 2021. https://6abc.com/philadelphia-metro-housing-equality-segregation -census-bureau-data/10901948/.

"Protect Richmond's African American Cemeteries." Change.org. Accessed May 31, 2023. https://www.change.org/p/ralph-s-northam-protect-richmond-s-african -american-cemeteries.

Rabben, Keneth J. "Dead Tot's Mother Called Outstanding Parent by Pastor, Neighbors, Agency." *The Bristol Daily Courier*, January 13, 1960. Newspapers.com.

Rainville, Lynn. *Hidden History: African American Cemeteries in Central Virginia* Charlottesville: University of Virginia Press, 2016.

Rankine, Claudia. "'The Condition of Black Life Is One of Mourning.'" *The New York Times*, June 22, 2015. https://www.nytimes.com/2015/06/22/magazine/the-condi tion-of-black-life-is-one-of-mourning.html.

Raudon, Sally. "Huddled Masses: The Shock of Hart Island, New York." *Human Remains and Violence: An Interdisciplinary Journal* 8, no. 1 (2022): 84–101. https://doi.org/10 .7227/hrv.8.1.6.

"Reclamation East End: Resisting the Recreation Plantation (Feat. Brian Palmer)." Produced by Chelsea Higgs Wise, Naomi Isaac, Kalia Harris. *Race Capitol*, March 2021. Audio, 1:26:55. https://soundcloud.com/user-461048344/reclamation-east-end-re sisting-the-recreation-plantation-feat-brian-palmer.

"Recommendations." East Marshall Street Well Project. September 2021. https://emsw .vcu.edu/recommendations/.

"Red Hill." Red Hill Patrick Henry Memorial Foundation. Accessed May 31, 2023. https: //www.redhill.org/red-hill/.

Reineke, Robin C. "Forensic Citizenship Among Families of Missing Migrants Along the U.S.-Mexico Border." *Citizenship Studies* 26, no. 1 (January 2, 2022): 21–37. https: //doi.org/10.1080/13621025.2021.2018675.

Reineke, Robin, and Bruce E. Anderson. "Missing in the US-Mexico Borderlands." In *Missing Persons: Multidisciplinary Perspectives on the Disappeared*, 249–68. To- ronto: Canadian Scholars' Press, 2016.

Renshaw, Layla. *Exhuming Loss: Memory, Materiality and Mass Graves of the Spanish Civil War*. Walnut Creek, CA: Taylor & Francis Group, 2011.

"RE: Parity, LLC v. Trustees in Liquidation of East End Burial Association—Case No. CL17-5911-2." December 21, 2018. Courtesy of Erin Hollaway Palmer.

"Respect for Our Dead." *The Carolina Times*, August 2, 1941. Courtesy of Carissa Trotta.

"Ritta Geer (1860–1932)—Find a Grave Memorial." Find a Grave. Accessed May 30, 2023. https://www.findagrave.com/memorial/116784232/ritta-geer.

Robinson, Mark. "Battered by Demolition and Displacement, Jackson Ward Stands Strong at 150th Anniversary." *Richmond Times-Dispatch*, April 17, 2021. https://rich mond.com/news/local/battered-by-demolition-and-displacement-jackson-ward -stands-strong-at-150th-anniversary/article_4d064300-4d2c-56cf-b73d-4956b43b 26ea.html.

Romero, Simon. "Burial Ground Under the Alamo Stirs a Texas Feud." *The New York Times*, November 25, 2021. https://www.nytimes.com/2021/11/25/us/alamo-burial -native-americans.html.

Rosen, Jody. "How Covid-19 Has Forced Us to Look at the Unthinkable." *The New York Times*, April 29, 2020. https://www.nytimes.com/2020/04/29/magazine/covid-hart -island.html.

Rosenberg, Lauren. *The Desire for Literacy: Writing in the Lives of Adult Learners.* Urbana, Illinois: Conference on College Composition and Communication/Na- tional Council of Teachers of English, 2015.

Rosenblatt, Adam Richard. "Cemetery Credibility and What It Means to Be a Descen- dant." Radical Death Studies, June 14, 2021 (page no longer available), https://radi caldeathstudies.com/2021/06/14/cemetery-credibility/.

———. *Digging for the Disappeared: Forensic Science after Atrocity*. Stanford Studies in Human Rights. Stanford, CA: Stanford University Press, 2015.

———. "Engraved: A Family Forensics." *Fieldsights*. Society for Cultural Anthropology. February 9, 2023. https://culanth.org/fieldsights/engraved-a-family-forensics.

———. "Wider Concerns About Cemetery Reclamation Lacking in Article." *Richmond Free Press*, December 31, 2020. http://richmondfreepress.com/news/2020/dec/31/wider-concerns-about-cemetery-reclamation-lacking-/.

Rosenblatt, Adam Richard, Erin Hollaway Palmer, and Brian Palmer. "Permanent Reconstruction in Richmond's Black Cemeteries." In *Grave History: Death, Race, and Gender in Southern Cemeteries*. Athens, GA: University of Georgia, 2023, 253–282.

Rosenblatt, Adam Richard, and Ryan K. Smith. "Letter to the Editor: Enrichmond Took Credit for the Work of Others." *Richmond Times-Dispatch*, March 4, 2020. https://richmond.com/opinion/letters-to-editor/letter-to-the-editor-march-3-2020-enrichmond-took-credit-for-the-work-of-others/article_8428233b-a84c-5252-8d8d-809e965aea05.html.

Rotman, Genia [later Jean Bialer]. Record of Witness Testimony 194. Interview by Luba Melchior. March 2, 1946. The Polish Research Institute. http://www.alvin-portal.org/alvin/view.jsf?pid=alvin-record%3A102719&dswid=-8778.

Rowson, Denise and Durham Service Corps. *Reclaiming Yesterday: The Geer Cemetery Project*. Durham: Durham Service Corps, 1992. Courtesy of the Friends of Geer Cemetery.

Sander-Staudt, Maureen. "Care Ethics." Internet Encyclopedia of Philosophy. Accessed May 24, 2023. https://iep.utm.edu/care-ethics/.

Savoy, Lauret Edith. *Trace: Memory, History, Race, and the American Landscape*. Berkeley: Counterpoint Press, 2015.

Scheper-Hughes, Nancy. "The Primacy of the Ethical: Propositions for a Militant Anthropology." *Current Anthropology* 36, no. 3 (1995): 409–40.

Schneider, Gregory S. "Two Years after Protests, Some of Richmond's Confederate Statues Remain." *The Washington Post*, July 26, 2022. https://www.washingtonpost.com/dc-md-va/2022/07/23/richmond-confederate-statues-stonewall-hill/.

Seidemann, Ryan M., and Christine L. Halling. "Landscape Structural Violence: A View from New Orleans's Cemeteries." *American Antiquity* 84, no. 4 (2019): 669–683. https://doi.org/10.1017/aaq.2019.49.

"Several Cases Were Tried During the Day—Negro Preacher Was Tried for an Affray." *Durham Morning Herald*, September 1, 1922. Courtesy of the Friends of Geer Cemetery.

Sherman, David. "Grave Matters: Segregation and Racism in U.S. Cemeteries." The Order of the Good Death, April 20, 2020. https://www.orderofthegooddeath.com/article/grave-matters-segregation-and-racism-in-u-s-cemeteries/.

"Shockoe Bottom." Venture Richmond. Accessed May 16, 2023. https://venturerichmond.com/live-downtown/historic-neighborhoods/shockoe-bottom/.

Sisk, Drew. "Jackson Ward: Displacement and Buried History." GDES Workshop, September 12, 2016. https://drewsisk.com/workshop/jackson-ward-displacement-and-buried-history/.

Smith, Kim, and Stephanie Davis. "An Open Letter: The Fitzgerald Family Cemetery and Henderson Cemetery," November 4, 2021. Updated January 27, 2022. https://drive.google.com/file/d/149knrJL_lRDxyNsBv3KKdiuOulqeNTqQ/view.

Smith, Ryan K. *Death and Rebirth in a Southern City: Richmond's Historic Cemeteries.* Baltimore: Johns Hopkins University Press, 2020.

———. "Disappointing Preservation Plans." *Richmond Cemeteries*, July 6, 2021. https://www.richmondcemeteries.org/2021/07/06/disappointing-preservation-plans/.

———. "East End Goes the Way Things Go." *Richmond Cemeteries*, January 24, 2019. https://www.richmondcemeteries.org/2019/01/24/east-end-goes-the-way-things-go/.

———. "Enrichmond's Collapse." *Richmond Cemeteries*, July 6, 2022. https://www.richmondcemeteries.org/2022/07/06/enrichmonds-collapse/.

———. "Shockoe Hill African Burying Ground." *Richmond Cemeteries*. Accessed May 18, 2023. https://www.richmondcemeteries.org/potters-field/.

———. "Three Minutes Each at the Horror Show." *Richmond Cemeteries*, October 26, 2020. https://www.richmondcemeteries.org/2020/10/26/three-minutes-each-at-the-horror-show/.

Smith, Suzanne E. *To Serve the Living: Funeral Directors and the African American Way of Death.* Cambridge, MA: Harvard University Press, 2010.

Sostaita, Barbara. "Making Crosses, Crossing Borders: The Performance of Mourning, the Power of Ghosts, and the Politics of Countermemory in the U.S.-Mexico Borderlands." *Conversations: An Online Journal of the Center for the Study of Material and Visual Cultures of Religion*, August 18, 2016. https://doi.org/10.22332/con.med.2016.3.

Spade, Katrina. "Death Is Not an Emergency: How Recompose Is Redesigning the End of Life." Interview by Michael Zakaras. *Forbes*, October 18, 2019. https://www.forbes.com/sites/ashoka/2018/10/19/death-is-not-an-emergency-how-recompose-is-redesigning-the-end-of-life/.

Sprackland, Jean. *These Silent Mansions: A Life in Graveyards.* London: Jonathan Cape, 2020.

Stauffer, Jill. *Ethical Loneliness: The Injustice of Not Being Heard.* New York: Columbia University Press, 2015.

Steele, Linda. "Sites of Conscience Redressing Disability Institutional Violence." *Incarceration* 3, no. 2 (July 1, 2022): 1–19. https://doi.org/10.1177/26326663221103435.

Steele, Linda, Bonney Djuric, Lily Hibberd, and Fiona Yeh. "Parramatta Female Factory Precinct as a Site of Conscience: Using Institutional Pasts to Shape Just Legal Futures." *University of New South Wales Law Journal* 43, no. 2 (2020): 521–51. https://doi.org/10.53637/gcar4734.

Streever, David. "Keeping the Faith." *Style Weekly*, March 12, 2019. https://www.styleweekly.com/richmond/keeping-the-faith/Content?oid=14132112.

Sturkey, William. "The Geer Cemetery: A Lesson in Black History." *Durham Herald Sun*, February 5, 2019. https://www.heraldsun.com/opinion/article225427335.html.

Suarez, Chris. "Enrichmond Foundation Executive Director Gone after Years of Tumult over Stewardship of Historic Black Cemeteries." *Richmond Times-Dispatch*, May 20, 2022. https://richmond.com/news/local/enrichmond-foundation-executive -director-gone-after-years-of-tumult-over-stewardship-of-historic-black-ceme teries/article_3bf061e1-05f0-5e6f-a6c3-c5f387bdd0f4.html.

———. "Maggie L. Walker's Grave Site Among Those Vandalized at Historic Cemeter- ies." *Richmond Times-Dispatch*, August 3, 2020. https://richmond.com/news/local/ maggie-l-walkers-grave-site-among-those-vandalized-at-historic-cemeteries/arti cle_aef50403-bc87-5c77-b1db-7095db70c896.html.

———. "Richmond Withholding Money for Enrichmond Foundation after Concerns Raised about Management, Oversight of Historic Black Cemeteries." *Richmond Times-Dispatch*, May 16, 2021. https://richmond.com/news/local/govt-and-politics/ richmond-withholding-money-for-enrichmond-foundation-after-concerns-raised -about-management-oversight-of-historic-black/article_bc8e54bc-7ffc-5282-a20c -04317313428a.html.

———. "Still No Answers for Missing $3 Million the Enrichmond Foundation Was Managing for Local Groups." *Richmond Times-Dispatch*, September 17, 2022. https:/ /richmond.com/news/local/still-no-answers-for-missing-3-million-the-enrich mond-foundation-was-managing-for-local-groups/article_b8347d9c-d79a-5082 -a713-4eebc4f12e25.html.

"Support Preservation of African American Burial Grounds." National Trust for His- toric Preservation, June 16, 2023. https://savingplaces.org/african-american-cultur al-heritage/updates/support-preservation-of-african-american-burial-grounds. Accessed September 14, 2023.

Sussman, Charlotte, Grant Glass, Isabel Bradley, Kelsey Desir, Jane Harwell, Tye Landels, Anya Lewis-Meeks, Perry Sweitzer, and Daisy Zhan. "Small Boy." Remem- bering the Middle Passage: A Duke Bass Connections Project. 2022. Accessed May 31, 2023. http://rememberingthemiddlepassage.com/#small_boy.

Thorson, Alex, and Amelia Heymann. "Cemetery Worker Discovers Exposed Human Bones Spilling from Embankment in Henrico." ABC 8 News, July 20, 2020. https:// www.wric.com/news/local-news/henrico-county/bones-found-out-of-place-in -henrico-cemetery/.

"A Treasure Trove of Historical Data on the History of Mental Illness Among African Americans." *The Journal of Blacks in Higher Education*, February 6, 2014. https:// www.jbhe.com/2014/02/treasure-trove-of-historical-data-on-the-history-of-men tal-illness-among-african-americans/.

Tuck, Eve. "Suspending Damage: A Letter to Communities." *Harvard Educational Review* 79, no. 3 (October 6, 2009): 409–28. https://doi.org/10.17763/haer.79.3.n001 6675661t3n15.

"Unmarked." Reel South. Season 5, Episode 2. PBS, April 13, 2020. Video, 26:34. https:// www.pbs.org/video/unmarked-99cmss/.

Va. Code Ann. § 57-27.1 (2011). https://lis.virginia.gov/cgi-bin/legp604.exe?111+ful+CH AP0257&111+ful+CHAP0257.

Valenzuela, Angela. *Subtractive Schooling: U.S.-Mexican Youth and the Politics of Caring.* The Social Context of Education. Albany, NY: SUNY Press, 1999.

Valinsky, Jordan. "Walmart Apologizes for Selling Juneteenth Ice Cream." CNN Business, May 24, 2022. https://www.cnn.com/2022/05/24/business-food/walmart -juneteenth-ice-cream/index.html.

Vann, André D. "From a Dream to New Horizons." North Carolina Central University News, April 22, 2020. https://www.nccu.edu/news/dream-new-horizons.

Violet Park Cemetery Correspondence (NCC.0250). North Carolina Collection, Durham County Library, NC. Donated by R. Kelly Bryant. https://archive.durhamcountyli brary.org/repositories/2/resources/54.

"Virginia HB284," 2018. LegiScan. https://legiscan.com/VA/text/HB284/id/1786618.

vMLK Project Team. "'A Creative Protest ["Fill Up the Jails"].'" Virtual Martin Luther King, Jr. Project, November 27, 2018. https://vmlk.chass.ncsu.edu/experience/ historical/a-creative-protest/.

Walker, Alice. "Looking for Zora," *In Search of Our Mothers' Gardens: Womanist Prose.* New York: Harcourt Brace Jovanovich, 1983: 93–116.

Weare, Walter B. *Black Business in the New South: A Social History of the NC Mutual Life Insurance Company.* Durham, NC: Duke University Press, 1993.

Weekly Notes of Cases Argued and Determined in the Supreme Court of Pennsylvania, the County Courts of Philadelphia, and the United States District and Circuit Courts for the Eastern District of Pennsylvania. Vol. 2. Google Books. Philadelphia: Kay & Brother, 1876.

Weill, Kelly. "Gritty Is Antifa Now." The Daily Beast, October 3, 2018. https://www.the dailybeast.com/gritty-the-philadelphia-flyers-bizarre-new-mascot-is-antifa-now.

Wessler, Seth Freed. "Developers Found Graves in the Virginia Woods. Authorities Then Helped Erase the Historic Black Cemetery." ProPublica, December 16, 2022. https://www.propublica.org/article/how-authorities-erased-historic-black-ceme tery-virginia.

"When Remains Unclaimed, NC's Dead Scattered at Sea." WRAL News, August 8, 2014. https://www.wral.com/story/when-remains-unclaimed-nc-s-dead-scattered-at -sea/13876971/.

"Wilkins Cemetery." Wilkins Cemetery Committee. Accessed May 25, 2023 (page no longer available). https://wilkinscemetery.com/the-enslaved.

Williams, Michael Paul. "Uncovering Hidden Histories in Virginia's Black Cemeteries." *Richmond Times-Dispatch*, October 8, 2015. https://www.richmond.com/news/ local/michael-paul-williams/williams-uncovering-hidden-histories-in-virginia-s -black-cemeteries/article_2563311a-44a6-5b7e-88ff-fd9a8357d3e1.html.

Williamson, Elizabeth. "America's Black Cemeteries and Three Women Trying to Save

Them." *The New York Times*, September 27, 2023, https://www.nytimes.com/2023/09/27/us/black-cemeteries.html.

Winberg, Michaela. "Racism and Deadly Traffic on Cobbs Creek Parkway." WHYY, September 8, 2020. https://whyy.org/episodes/how-racism-fueled/.

Wise, Alana. "Montpelier Says It's Open to Parity with Slave Descendants. Descendants Call Foul." NPR, April 20, 2022. https://www.npr.org/2022/04/20/1093673939/montpeliers-fight-with-descendants-of-the-enslaved-brings-employee-firings.

"Woman's Death Called Accident, Due to Fall." *Richmond Times-Dispatch*, September 7, 1956. Newspapers.com.

Wysong, Lori. "Cemeteries, Segregation, and the Funerals of Henry Jones." Hidden City Philadelphia, October 9, 2020. https://hiddencityphila.org/2020/10/cemeteries-segregation-and-the-funerals-of-henry-jones/.

Yellow Bird, Pemina. "Wild Indians: Native Perspectives on the Hiawatha Asylum for Insane Indians." National Empowerment Center. https://power2u.org/wild-indians-native-perspectives-on-the-hiawatha-asylum-for-insane-indians-by-pemima-yellow-bird/.

Young, Steve. "S.D. Revisits Past at Native American Insane Asylum." *USA Today*, May 5, 2013. https://www.usatoday.com/story/news/nation/2013/05/05/sd-native-american-insane-asylum/2137011/.

INDEX

Page numbers in italics denote figures, and endnotes are indicated by "n" followed by the endnote number.

The authorized representative in the EU for product safety and compliance is:
Mare Nostrum Group
B.V Doelen 72
4831 GR Breda
The Netherlands

www.ingramcontent.com/pod-product-compliance
Lightning Source LLC
Chambersburg PA
CBHW020842270326
41928CB00006B/516

9 781503 639119